DATE DUE

NOV 2 6 2008	
NOV 2 4 2009 / JAN 3 1 2012	
JAN 3 1 2012	
Feb 14, 2012	
Feb. 28, 2012	
APR 1 9 2012	
JUN 1 9 2017	
Feb. 19, 2018	
MAR 2 1 2018	

Death Penalty USA 2005 - 2006

Death Penalty USA

2005 - 2006

Michelangelo Delfino
and
Mary E. Day

MoBeta Publishing
Publishers since 2002
105 West Adalee Street
Tampa, Florida 33603-5709
www.mobeta.com

SAN 254-9050

Library of Congress Cataloging-in-Publication Data

Delfino, Michelangelo.
  Death penalty USA : 2005 - 2006 / Michelangelo Delfino and Mary E. Day.
    p. cm.
Includes bibliographical references and index.
ISBN 978-0-9725141-2-5 (hardcover)
1. Capital punishment--United States--Cases. I. Day, Mary E. II. Title.
KF9227.C2D45 2007
345.73 '0773--dc22

                        2007049252

First Printing December 2007
Printed in the United States of America

Preface

The taking of a human life is in all circumstances reprehensible.

> The penalty of death differs from all other forms of criminal punishment, not in degrees but in kind. It is unique in its total irrevocability. It is unique in its rejection of rehabilitation of the convict as a basic purpose of criminal justice, and it is unique, finally, in its absolute renunciation of all that is embodied in our concept of humanity. (*Furman v. Georgia* (1972) 408 U.S. 238, 306)

This is the first book in a series of books providing a brief history of 21st century capital-punishment cases in the United States. Each volume in the series begins with an overview of capital punishment in the United States and follows with the case histories of a single year of executions.

These books are not intended to be easy reading. The crimes for which the death penalty was imposed are truly horrific and described in graphic detail based on public record. Compilations are taken from and referenced to case citations. Original names and places are retained. Some cases are necessarily more comprehensive than others. In general, high profile murders and those involving multiple victims, difficult conviction, and vigorous defenses have more extensive records than capital crimes involving the murder of a homeless person or a clerk during a convenience store robbery. Cases where the conviction is based on circumstantial evidence tend to be more detailed than those based on voluntary confessions.

Each case history is written in a nonsensationalized way that is respectful of all those touched by death. Supplemental information such as a condemned prisoner's last meal and last words are included when such material is insightful. The names of the executed prisoners are indexed chronologically in the Table of Contents. A reference list and an Index are provided.

Michelangelo Delfino and Mary E. Day
26 November 2007

Table of Contents

Table of Contents

Table of Contents

U.S. Law and the Death Penalty

In the United States of America "the death penalty is said to serve two principal social purposes: retribution and deterrence of capital crimes by prospective offenders" (*Gregg v. Georgia* (1976) 428 U.S. 153, 183). Does it?

The propensity of the people and the ability of the State to execute a condemned prisoner are not without their ups and downs. Luis Monge was executed in a Colorado gas chamber on June 2, 1967, at a time when the popularity of capital punishment was declining. Thereafter no executions were carried out for nearly a decade, in part because in 1972 the Supreme Court of the United States banned the practice altogether ruling that the death penalty was considered cruel and unusual punishment in violation of the Eighth Amendment (*Furman v. Georgia* (1972) 408 U.S. 238).

On July 2, 1976, the death penalty was reinstated after guidelines were put in place instructing the judge and jury as to what circumstances allowed for a death sentence; requiring separation of the guilty and penalty phases of a trial; and allowing for automatic appellate review of both of these phases (*Gregg v. Georgia* (1976) 428 U.S. 153; *Proffitt v. Florida* (1976) 428 U.S. 242; *Jurek v. Texas* (1976) 428 U.S. 262; *Woodson v. North Carolina* (1976) 428 U.S. 280; and *Roberts v. Louisiana* (1976) 428 U.S. 325). Utah was the first state to resume the death penalty after the moratorium when on January 17, 1977, it executed Gary M. Gilmore by firing squad.

Murder in and of itself (*Godfrey v. Georgia* (1980) 446 U.S. 420) and the rape of an adult woman (*Coker v. Georgia (*1977) 433 U.S. 584) are not capital crimes in the United States and are thus not subject to the death penalty. To date, the federal government, the U.S. military, and 37

1

of the 50 states officially sanction the death penalty imposing it for both homicide (the killing of a person by a person) and certain non-homicide-related crimes.[1] Since lifting the moratorium in 1976 the U.S. military and four states, New Hampshire, New Jersey, New York, and Kansas, have not exercised their right to execute.

Homicide-related crimes for which a death sentence may be imposed include: murder related to the smuggling of aliens; destruction of aircraft, motor vehicles, or related facilities resulting in death; murder committed during a drug-related drive-by shooting; murder committed at an airport serving international civil aviation; retaliatory murder of a member of the immediate family of a law enforcement official; civil rights offenses resulting in death; murder of a member of Congress, an important executive official, or a Supreme Court justice; death resulting from offenses involving transportation of explosives, destruction of government property, or destruction of property related to foreign or interstate commerce; murder committed by the use of a firearm during a crime of violence or a drug-trafficking crime; murder committed in a federal government facility; genocide (the deliberate and systematic killing of an entire people or ethnic group); first-degree murder (killing that is deliberate and intentional or done recklessly with extreme disregard for human life); murder of a federal judge or law enforcement official; murder of a foreign official; murder by a federal prisoner; murder of a U.S. national in a foreign country; murder by an escaped federal prisoner already sentenced to life imprisonment; murder of a state or local law enforcement official or other person

---

[1] The states: Alaska, Hawaii, Iowa, Maine, Massachusetts, Michigan, Minnesota, New York, North Dakota, Rhode Island, Vermont, West Virginia, and Wisconsin have no death penalty. The death penalty is also not sanctioned in the District of Columbia, American Samoa, Guam, the Northern Mariana Islands, Puerto Rico, or the U.S. Virgin Islands.

aiding in a federal investigation; murder of a state correctional officer; murder during a kidnapping; murder during a hostage taking; murder of a court officer or juror; murder with the intent of preventing testimony by a witness, victim, or informant; retaliatory murder of a witness, victim, or informant; mailing of injurious articles with intent to kill or resulting in death; assassination or kidnapping resulting in the death of the president or vice president; murder for hire; murder involved in a racketeering offense; willful wrecking of a train resulting in death; bank-robbery-related murder or kidnapping; murder related to a carjacking; murder related to rape or child molestation; murder related to sexual exploitation of children; murder committed during an offense against maritime navigation; murder committed during an offense against a maritime fixed platform; terrorist murder of a U.S. national in another country; murder by the use of a weapon of mass destruction; murder involving torture; murder related to a continuing criminal enterprise[2] or related murder of a federal, state, or local law enforcement officer; and death resulting from aircraft hijacking.

Non-homicide-related crimes for which a death sentence may be imposed include, espionage (spying); treason (attempting to overthrow the government); trafficking (distribution, sale, exchange, or giving away) in large quantities of drugs; attempting, authorizing, or advising the killing of any officer, juror, or witness in cases involving a continuing criminal enterprise, regardless of whether such killing actually occurs; perjury causing death

---

[2] *A continuing criminal enterprise* is defined by federal statute as a continuing series of felony violations by a person in concert with five or more other persons in which the offender occupies a position of organizer, a supervisory position, or any other management position, and from which the offender obtains substantial income or resources.

(only in California and Idaho); aggravated rape[3] (only in Louisiana); sexual battery[4] (only in Florida); and multiple rape[5] (only in Montana). No one has been executed in the United States for a non-homicide related crime since 1964.

Criminal guilt must be established before the death penalty can be imposed in the United States where the defendant is presumed innocent.

The law presumes that persons charged with crime are innocent until they are proven, by competent evidence,

---

[3] *Aggravated rape* is defined by statute as a rape committed upon a person 65 years of age or older; or where the anal, oral, or vaginal sexual intercourse is deemed to be without lawful consent because it is committed under any one or more of the following circumstances: when the victim resists the act to the utmost, but the victim's resistance is overcome by force; when the victim is prevented from resisting the act by threats of great and immediate bodily harm, accompanied by apparent power of execution; when the victim is prevented from resisting the act because the offender is armed with a dangerous weapon; when the victim is under the age of 13 years (lack of knowledge of the victim's age shall not be a defense); when two or more offenders participated in the act; when the victim is prevented from resisting the act because the victim suffers from a physical or mental infirmity preventing such resistance.

[4] *Sexual battery* is defined by statute as oral, anal, or vaginal penetration by, or union with, the sexual organ of a person under 12 years of age or the anal or vaginal penetration of a person under 12 years of age by any other object not done for a *bona fide* medical purpose.

[5] *Multiple rape* is defined by statute as rape committed by an offender who was previously convicted of rape, and who has inflicted serious bodily injury upon a person in the course of committing each offense.

4

to be guilty. To the benefit of this presumption the defendants are all entitled, and this presumption stands as their sufficient protection, unless it has been removed by evidence proving their guilt beyond a reasonable doubt. (*Coffin v. United States* (1895) 156 U.S. 432)

In order to preserve the presumption of innocence a person in custody—that is, not free to leave—must, in principle, and prior to interrogation be clearly informed of his or her right to remain silent and informed that anything said can be used against him or her in court (*Miranda v. Arizona* (1966) 384 U.S. 436). A typical *Miranda* warning reads as follows: "You have the right to remain silent. Anything you say can and will be used against you in a court of law. You have the right to an attorney. If you cannot afford an attorney, one will be provided for you at interrogation time and at court."

The suspect must be clearly informed of his or her right to consult with an attorney and to have that attorney present during interrogation. Arrests in California, Florida, North Carolina, and Texas often include the following query: "Do you understand the rights I have just read to you?" "With these rights in mind, do you wish to speak to me?" If the suspect is indigent he or she must be clearly informed that an attorney will be provided at no cost. Indiana, Nevada, and Oklahoma often add the following statement as part of the *Miranda* warning: "We have no way of giving you a lawyer, but one will be appointed for you, if you wish, if and when you go to court."

The typical process for determining a defendant's innocence or guilt is trial by a jury consisting of twelve persons. The oft referred to "peer jury" is misleading in that there is no requirement that a juror be of the same age, gender, race, religion, and social status as the accused.

A defendant can waive the right to trial by jury and seek a determination by a panel of judges, usually numbering three. If the defendant is found guilty a sentencing hearing is held wherein the mitigating and aggravating circumstances are introduced. Federal law requires that a jury of twelve, unless waived, must find the existence of at least one aggravating circumstance by unanimous decision in order for the defendant to be eligible for the death sentence (*Ring v. Arizona* (2002) 536 U.S. 584).

Aggravating circumstances are factors that increase the seriousness or outrageousness of the crime and pave the way for a death sentence. Aggravating factors for the killing of one person by another include: killing that person during the commission of another crime; previous conviction for a violent felony involving a firearm; previous conviction for an offense for which a sentence of death or life imprisonment was authorized; heinous, cruel, or depraved manner of committing murder; procurement of murder by payment; pecuniary gain; continuing criminal enterprise involving drug sales to minors; creating a great risk to many persons; committing the murder for the purpose of avoiding arrest or to effect escape; murdering a law enforcement agent engaged in performing his or her official duties; and murdering a youth, typically a person less than 12 years of age.

Mitigating circumstances are factors that do not excuse or justify the crime but are considered out of mercy or fairness and may justify a reduction of the penalty. Mitigating factors include: impaired capacity; duress; limited participation; equally culpable defendants; no prior criminal record; severe mental or emotional disturbance; and victim's consent as in assisting the terminally ill.

If the judge or jury determines the aggravating circumstances outweigh the mitigating circumstances, the person convicted of a capital crime can be sentenced to death or imprisonment for life without the possibility of parole. If the jury recommends life imprisonment the

6

Supreme Court of the United States has declared that the trial judge may override the jury's recommendation and impose a death sentence (*Spaziano v. Florida* (1984) 468 U.S. 447) since it is the trial judge's responsibility, as the thirteenth juror, to make findings that will support a death sentence. Of the 37 states that have a death penalty all but New Mexico allow for a penalty of life without parole. Of the 13 states that do not have a death penalty all but Alaska allow for life without parole.

The venue in which a capital crime is committed and where it is prosecuted can make all the difference between a life and death sentence. Some states, counties, and districts are more likely to impose the death penalty than others.

In Texas the legislature (Article 37.071 of the Texas Code of Criminal Procedure) dictates if the defendant is found guilty of a capital crime, the jury is required to answer three interrogatories—formal questions that must be answered either "yes" or "no", and under oath.

First, the jury must answer two interrogatories: "whether there is a probability that the defendant would commit criminal acts of violence that would constitute a continuing threat to society" and "whether the defendant actually caused the death of the deceased, or did not actually cause the death of the deceased but intended to kill the deceased or another, or anticipated that a human life would be taken."

If both interrogatories are answered "yes" by a unanimous vote the jury is asked a third interrogatory: "whether, taking into consideration all of the evidence, including the circumstances of the offense, the defendant's character and background, and the personal moral culpability of the defendant, there is a sufficient mitigating circumstance or circumstances to warrant that a sentence of life imprisonment rather than a death sentence be imposed."

7

The third interrogatory must be answered "no" unanimously in order to impose the death penalty.[6] Texas is the only state that uses this system. Oregon requires similar interrogatories to be submitted to the jury but does not limit evidence of aggravating circumstances to the issues contained in the interrogatories.

In Florida if a unanimous jury finds a defendant guilty of capital murder the same jury hears evidence as to whether statutory aggravating factors are proven without a reasonable doubt and whether the jury is "reasonably convinced" that mitigating circumstances exist. If the jury finds one or more aggravating circumstances it must consider whether the mitigating circumstances outweigh the aggravating circumstances. If the jury decides that this is not the case it can recommend the death penalty by a simple majority vote. Florida is unique in this respect. Alabama requires a vote of at least 10-2 and Georgia requires a unanimous vote to recommend the death penalty.

Not everyone who commits an aggravated murder in the United States can be executed even when guilt is proved beyond a reasonable doubt. If the judge or jury determines that the mitigating factors outweigh or are of equal weight

---

[6] For capital crimes committed prior to September 1, 1991, if the jury returns a unanimous "yes" to these first three interrogatories then the defendant can be put to death: "whether the conduct of the defendant caused the death of the deceased was committed deliberately and with the reasonable expectation that the death of the deceased or another would result; whether there is a probability that the defendant would commit criminal acts of violence that would constitute a continuing threat to society; and if raised by the evidence, whether the conduct of the defendant in killing the deceased was unreasonable in response to the provocation, if any, by the deceased."

to the aggravating factors or if any of automatic bars to the death penalty exist, a death sentence cannot be imposed.

There are three important Supreme Court of the United States cases limiting who can be executed. In *Roper v. Simmons* (2005) 543 U.S. 551, the Court concluded that both the Eighth and the Fourteenth Amendments to the Constitution prohibit the execution of a person who was under 18 years of age at the time of the offense.[7] In *Atkins v. Virginia* (2002) 536 U.S. 304, the Supreme Court, in a 6-3 ruling, determined that executing a person who is mentally retarded is a violation of the Eighth Amendment. And in *Ford v. Wainwright* (1986) 477 U.S. 399, the Court determined that it is illegal to execute a person who is insane—a legal term designating a person who is unable to appreciate the wrongfulness or criminality of his or her conduct. The philosophically divided *Ford* court ruled that it was abhorrent to take the life of persons who are so mentally ill as to be unable to comprehend the reason for their penalty. Most recently the Court in *Panetti v. Quarterman* (2007) 127 S.Ct. 2842, ruled that those who do not comprehend the meaning and the purpose of their death sentence may not be executed.

A person convicted of a capital crime and sentenced to death can appeal the sentence in both state and federal courts. While the appeal proceeds the condemned prisoner sits on death row—the cellblock in a prison where he or she awaits execution. The cellblock conditions vary with venue. In Arizona the cellblock is eleven feet seven inches long by seven feet nine inches wide; out-of-cell time is limited to outdoor exercise in a secured area, two hours a day, three times a week, and a shower, three times a

---

[7] Prior to March 2005 the Supreme Court of the United States concluded that both the Eighth and the Fourteenth Amendments to the Constitution prohibit the execution of a person who was under 16 years of age at the time of his or her offense (*Thompson v. Oklahoma* (1988) 487 U.S. 815).

week; inmates may place two 10-minute telephone calls per week; and personal property is limited to hygiene items, two appliances, two books and writing materials (Arizona Department of Corrections 2005).

There are 3350 death row prisoners in the United States as of January 1, 2007. Of that number 59 are female, 45 percent are white, 42 percent are black, 11 percent are Hispanic, and 1 percent is Asian. As a point of reference, the people of United States in the 15 to 44 year age group have a male/female ratio of 1.02 and classify themselves as 80 percent white, 14 percent Hispanic, 13 percent black, and 4 percent Asian.[8] California, the most populous state in the nation, leads with 660 death row prisoners; Texas and Florida, the second and fourth most populous states, follow with just under 400 inmates each.

The suicide rate for death row prisoners is approximately ten times the national average and six times that of the general U.S. prison population (Lester and Tartaro 2002). Some condemned inmates actually welcome their fate and accelerate the capital punishment process by limiting appellate review. Nine "volunteers" dropped their appeals in 2004 and "consented" to being executed.

Every defendant is entitled to an automatic no-waivable review by the state supreme court, which "must consider whether the sentence was influenced by passion, prejudice, or any other arbitrary factor; whether the evidence supports the finding of a statutory aggravating circumstance; and whether the death sentence 'is excessive or disproportionate to the penalty imposed in similar cases, considering both the crime and the defendant" (*Gregg v. Georgia* (1976) 428 U.S. 153).

---

[8] U.S. Census Bureau figures for 2005. Note: percentages do not add up to 100 percent due to rounding and because, for example, Hispanics may be of any race and therefore counted under more than one category.

After the state supreme court affirms the trial judgment each subsequent court is allowed discretion as to whether it will review the case. The first discretionary review begins when the defendant petitions the Supreme Court of the United States for a *writ of certiorari* (court order directing a lower court to transmit records for a case that it will hear on appeal) for the purposes of showing that the state court was wrong in deciding that the defendant's Constitutional rights were not violated.

If the Supreme Court of the United States denies review the defendant's direct-appeal process is complete and the defendant can then seek state *habeas corpus* (court order that determines whether or not a person is imprisoned lawfully and whether or not the person should be released from custody) review. During *habeas* review the defendant may include facts that were not part of the original trial or make an assertion such as the defense attorney improperly handled the trial—otherwise known as ineffective assistance of counsel.

If the defendant's *habeas* review is denied the defendant may once again appeal to the Supreme Court of the United States and although it is unlikely to grant review, it may be asked to intervene on behalf of the defendant. Counsel may ask the court to stay an execution pending a determination that the defendant has become insane. If it is later determined that the defendant is in fact sane the death penalty can be reinstated.

A claim of actual innocence that is based on newly discovered evidence is not a ground for federal *habeas* relief (*Herrera v. Collins* (1993) 506 U.S. 390) and thus while "the execution of a legally and factually innocent person would be a constitutionally intolerable event," it would not be unlawful.

Clemency and commutation are historic remedies for preventing miscarriages of justice after the judicial process has been exhausted. The clemency review process is subjectively based on humanitarian reasons with authority to pardon a function of jurisdiction.[9] In federal cases only the President of the United States can grant clemency, William J. Clinton being the last president to do so.

From 1976 to date,[10] 231 death row inmates were granted clemency: 172 in Illinois,[11] followed by 9 in Ohio, 7 in Virginia, and 6 or less in other states. In 2005 Indiana Governors' Joe Kernan and Mitch Daniels commuted the death sentence of Michael Daniels and Arthur P. Baird II respectively to life without parole, and Governor Mark R. Warner of Virginia commuted the death sentence of Robin Lovitt to life without parole. Clemency was not granted in 2006.

Executions in the United States are traditionally preceded by a so-called "last meal," a specially prepared dinner requested by the condemned prisoner given a day

---

[9] In thirteen states (Alabama, California, Colorado, Kansas, Kentucky, New Jersey, New Mexico, North Carolina, Oregon, South Carolina, Virginia, Washington, and Wyoming) the governor has sole authority to grant clemency; in eight states (Arizona, Delaware, Florida, Louisiana, Montana, Oklahoma, Pennsylvania, and Texas) the governor must have the recommendation for clemency from an advisory group; in ten states (Arkansas, Illinois, Indiana, Maryland, Mississippi, Missouri, New Hampshire, Ohio, South Dakota, and Tennessee) the governor decides if clemency is warranted after receiving a non-binding recommendation from an advisory group; and in six states (Connecticut, Georgia, Idaho, Nebraska, Nevada, and Utah) the advisory group alone determines clemency. In Florida, Nebraska, Nevada, and Utah, the governor is a member of the advisory board.

[10] On September 14, 2007, Tennessee Governor Phil Bredesen commuted the death sentence of Michael Joe Boyd.

[11] On January 11, 2003, Illinois Governor George Ryan commuted the sentences of all 167 death row inmates citing a flawed judicial process as reason for pardon.

or two before the execution. Restrictions in food and drink vary with state venue but in all cases, alcohol is not allowed and in some states even tobacco products are barred.

No one was executed for a capital crime in the United States in 1976, 1978, or 1980. There were 98 executions carried out in 1999 and 85 in 2000 making these years the

Table I

Executions in the United States

Jurisdiction	2005	2006	To date
Texas	19	24	405
Virginia	0	4	98
Oklahoma	4	4	86
Missouri	5	0	66
Florida	1	4	64
North Carolina	5	4	43
Georgia	3	0	40
Alabama	4	1	38
South Carolina	3	1	37
Arkansas	1	0	27
Ohio	4	5	26
Indiana	5	1	19
Delaware	1	0	14
California	2	1	13
Nevada	0	1	12
Mississippi	1	1	8
Maryland	1	0	5
Tennessee	0	1	4
Montana	0	1	3
Connecticut	1	0	1
Total	60	53	1099

To date executions are as of October 1, 2007 and include all executions since the 1976 death penalty moratorium was lifted.

first and second most active since 1976. Between January 2005 and December 2006 the federal government and the U.S. military carried out no executions. Table I lists by state the 60 and 53 executions for 2005 and 2006 respectively. Texas, the state that accounts for 7.7 percent of the U.S. population and most active death penalty state since 1976 accounted for 39 percent of the executions in 2005 and 45 percent of the executions in 2006. However, Oklahoma, the 27th most populous state and third most active death penalty state since 1976 executed the most prisoners per capita between January 2005 and December 2006—2.3 executions per million people compared to 1.8 executions per million people in Texas. In contrast, California, the state with the highest population and the largest number of death row inmates executed 0.08 inmates per million during the same time period.

Since the U.S. death penalty moratorium was lifted in 1976, a disproportionate 11 female inmates—less than 1 percent of the total put to death—were executed. Between January 2005 and December 2006, one female inmate was executed, and she, Frances E. Newton, was black. The sexual disparity is inexplicable in that females comprise slightly more than half of the U.S. population and males are no more than 10 times more likely than females to commit murder (U.S. Department of Justice 2006).

Between January 2005 and December 2006, 55 percent

Table II

Executions in the United States

Race/Ethnicity	2005	2006
White	37	25
Black	19	21
Hispanic	3	7
Asian	1	0
Total	60	53

of the 113 people executed in the United States were white, followed by 35 percent black, 9 percent Hispanic, and less than 1 percent Asian (*see* Table II). During this time period, one foreign national was executed, and he, Angel M. Reséndiz, was a Mexican citizen.The religious beliefs of the people executed in the United States are in most cases not available and the inmates beliefs often change from the time they commit the crime and the date they are executed. Nationally, some 77 percent of the people of the United States identify themselves as Christian, 14 percent claim no religion, 1.3 percent are Jewish, 0.5 percent are Muslim, and another 0.5 percent are Buddhist (U.S. Demographics. 2006).

The preferred method of execution in the United States is lethal injection authorized by 36 states, the U.S. military, and the federal government. In 20 states death row inmates may also be executed by electrocution, lethal gas, firing squad, and hanging, depending on the inmate's choice, the date of the execution or sentence, and if a method becomes unconstitutional.[12]

No one was executed in the United States by hanging since 1936, and in 1996 John A. Taylor was the last person executed by firing squad. Between January 2005 and December 2006 all but one of the condemned prisoners were executed by lethal injection—Brandon W. Hedrick:

---

[12] Ten states (Alabama, Arkansas, Florida, Illinois, Kentucky, Nebraska, Oklahoma, South Carolina, Tennessee, and Virginia) also allow for death by electrocution (electric chair), five states (Arizona, California, Maryland, Missouri, and Wyoming) for death by lethal gas (gas chamber), three states (Idaho, Oklahoma, and Utah) for death by firing squad, and two states (New Hampshire and Washington) for death by hanging.

When Hedrick entered the death chamber at 8:59 p.m., he appeared calm but alert. He did not struggle when guards strapped him into the chair with leather restraints and attached a metal clip to his leg and placed a metal helmet on his head ***.

At 9:02 p.m., a prison staffer pressed a button that delivered an 1800-volt [at 7.5 amperes for 30 seconds] burst of electricity to Hedrick's body. A coil of smoke rose from his leg as he jerked upward in the chair and clenched his fists. He briefly jerked again when a second current [240 volts at 1.5 amperes for 60 seconds] pulsed through his body (Rondeaux 2006).

The electric chair is a 19th century American invention, first adopted as`a method of execution in Ohio in 1896. Today, Nebraska is the only state that requires death by electrocution. Adopted in 1913, the electric chair has been used 15 times by the state, most recently in 1997.

Lethal injection was developed in Oklahoma and first used in Texas in 1982 to execute Charles Brooks Jr. The North Carolina lethal injection procedure is typical: the condemned prisoner is first secured to a gurney with lined ankle and wrist restraints. Cardiac monitor leads and a stethoscope are attached and two intravenous saline (aqueous sodium chloride) lines are started, one in each arm, with the prisoner covered with a sheet.

The condemned prisoner is then given opportunity to speak and pray with a spiritual advisor. The warden then gives the prisoner an opportunity to record a final statement that will be made public. After the witnesses are in place, correctional officers who draw a curtain and exit take the prisoner's gurney into the death chamber. Other personnel then enter behind the curtain and connect the cardiac monitor leads, the injection devices, and the stethoscope to the appropriate leads. Next the warden informs the witnesses that the execution is about to begin and returns to the chamber giving the order to proceed.

The lethal injection process involves the simultaneous slow pushing into two intravenous lines of chemicals contained in two separate sets of syringes. The syringes are prepared in advance and each contains only one drug. The first syringe contains sodium thiopental (Pentothal), an ultra short acting barbiturate that quickly puts the prisoner to sleep. The second syringe contains saline to flush the intravenous lines clean. The third syringe contains pancuronium bromide (Pavulon), a chemical paralytic agent. The fourth syringe contains a high dose of aqueous potassium chloride, a chemical that interrupts nerve impulses to the heart causing it to stop beating. The fifth syringe contains saline to flush the intravenous lines clean.

After a flat line displays on the electrocardiogram (EKG) monitor for five minutes the warden pronounces the prisoner dead and a physician certifies that death has occurred. The witnesses are escorted out to and the body is released to the medical examiner. There may or may not be an autopsy (North Carolina Department of Correction 1995-2007). The Supreme Court of the United States ruled unanimously that the lethal injection procedure may be challenged as a civil rights claim (*Hill v. McDonough* (2006) 126 S.Ct. 2096).

Indeed, one scientific analysis of empirical after-the-fact data suggests that the use of the chemicals prescribed creates a foreseeable risk of the gratuitous and unnecessary infliction of pain (Koniaris et al. 2005). This study reports that in almost half the cases examined by post-mortem autopsy, the Pentothal that is intended to prevent pain actually wears off before the onset of the massive heart attack that is brought on by the potassium chloride. Thus the initial anesthesia is too low and the prisoner actually experiences substantial pain from the state-induced heart attack. As the prisoner is prevented from communicating pain because the Pavulon will have paralyzed the face, arms, and entire body, the prisoner's suffering goes largely unnoticed.

In 2006 North Carolina began to use a bispectral index (BIS monitor) to measure brain waves for the purpose of ranking consciousness during the lethal injection process. Willie Brown Jr. and Samuel R. Flippen were so monitored but due to ethical issues, no medical professionals participated in their execution.

Chris Tisch, a reporter, who also witnessed the Florida executions of Arthur D. Rutherford and Danny H. Rolling provided these exact transcript notes during the 2006 execution of Angel N. Diaz:

> 6 p.m.: Diaz turns head and mumbles his last statement. Eyes slightly bloodshot and bleary. thatch of black and white hair. Turns head back up and is strapped.
>
> 6:02: Blinks. Swallows hard. Blinks slower. Looks up at guy. Grimaces. Says something. Looks at guy. Grimacing. Talking. Looks at man. Winces eyes.
>
> 6:06: Cheek bones pinch up. Talking still. As if in pain. Wrinkled eyes. Squints. Guards act like nothing wrong.
>
> 6:07: Still wincing.
>
> 6:08: Even juts up chin and stiffens his body. Talking and tensing his body.
>
> 6:09: Still talking. Looks at guy.
>
> 6:10: Still moving mouth. Eyes closed now. Pursed lips. Shakes his head. Guard has to re-apply strap.
>
> 6:11: Mouth still moves. Eyes closed.
>
> 6:12: His head faces to the right toward audience. He coughs several times. Shudders. Face reddening.
>
> 6:13: Still breathing. His body tenses and he coughs again.
>
> 6:14: Still breathing.
>
> 6:15: Still breathing. Mouth agape. Deep breaths.
>
> 6:16: Mouth moves when breathing.
>
> 6:17: Still breathing.
>
> 6:18: Still breathing.

6:19: Unusual. Guy talking on phone. Gives phone to guy.

6:20: Still breathing.

6:24: Mouth stops moving. Had gotten shallower and shallower. Mouth and eyes open. Face drains of color.

6:26: Body jolted slightly. No more motion. Eyes open more and more. Guy again on fone.

6:34: Dr comes out.

6:35: Comes out again.

6:36: Called. 23 minutes longer than Ruth and Rolling. (Tisch and Krueger 2007)

Since 1936 all U.S. executions have been done in an enclosure that prevents public viewing. Typically less than a few dozen or so adult witnesses including news media are allowed to view an execution (South Dakota Department of Corrections 2006). The federal sanctioned execution of mass murderer Timothy J. McVeigh by lethal injection in 2001 was a notable exception in that in addition to 10 on-site witnesses in Terre Haute, Indiana, 232 survivors and family members were allowed to watch McVeigh's death on closed-circuit television some 650 miles away.

References

Alabama Department of Corrections. <http://www.doc.state.al.us/>.

Arkansas Department of Correction. <http://www.arkansas.gov/doc/index.html>.

Arizona Department of Corrections. Copyright 2005. <http://www.azcorrections.gov/newindex.asp>.

Barron, P.T. Gender discrimination in the U.S. death penalty system. Radical Philosophy Rev. 3(1): 89-96 (2000).

Capital Punishment Statistics. Revised 11 January 2007. <http://www.ojp.usdoj.gov/bjs/cp.htm#top>.

Central Intelligence Agency. The world factbook. <https://www.cia.gov/library/publications/the-world-factbook/geos/us.html>.

Death Penalty Information Center. Copyright 2007. <http://www.deathpenaltyinfo.org/>.

Death Penalty News Bulletin – Amnesty International. <http://web.amnesty.org/pages/deathpenalty-developments-eng>.

Death Row U.S.A. Winter 2007. A quarterly report by the Criminal Justice Project of the NAACP Legal Defense and Educational Fund, Inc. <http://www.naacpldf.org/content/pdf/pubs/drusa/DRUSA_Winter_2007.pdf>.

Eaton Jr., O.H. Conducting the penalty phase of a capital case. 2006 Update. Florida College of Advanced Judicial Studies. <http://www.flcourts18.org/PDF/2006%20AJS%20Materials%20Dec%20Update.pdf>.

1.3.D.3 Execution of an inmate. August 2006. <http://www.ap.org/southdakota/Execution%20of%20an%20Inmate.htm>.

Florida Department of Corrections. Death row fact sheet. <http://www.dc.state.fl.us/oth/deathrow/index.html>.

Koniaris, L.G., T.A. Zimmers, Lubarsky, D.A., and Sheldon, J.P. Inadequate Anesthesia in Lethal Injection for Execution. *Lancet* 365:412-414 (2005).

Lester, D. and Tartaro, C. Suicide on death row. *J. Forensic. Sci.* 47:1108-1111 (2002).

National Coalition to Abolish the Death Penalty. Updated 24 May 2007. <http://ncadp.org/>.

North Carolina Department of Correction. The death penalty. Copyright 1995-2007. <http://www.doc.state.nc.us/DOP/deathpenalty/index.htm>.

Reinhart, C. 28 January 2005. Connecticut death penalty laws. <http://www.cga.ct.gov/2005/rpt/2005-R-0136.htm>.

Rondeaux, C. Washington Post. Murderer executed by electric chair. 21 July 2006. <http://www.washingtonpost.com/wp-dyn/content/article/2006/07/20/AR2006072001852.html?nav=emailpage>.

South Carolina Department of Corrections. Copyright 2007. <http://www.doc.sc.gov/news/deathrow.jsp>.

Tisch, C. and Krueger, C. Second dose needed to kill inmate. St. Petersburg Times. 14 December 2006. <http://www.sptimes.com/2006/12/14/Worldandnation/Second_dose_needed_to.shtml>.

U.S. Census Bureau, National population estimates. <http://www.census.gov/popest/estimates.php>.

U.S. Department of Justice. 29 June 2006. Homicide trends in the U.S. <http://www.ojp.usdoj.gov/bjs/homicide/gender.htm>.

Inmates Executed in 2005

James Scott Porter, a 33-year-old white male, was voluntarily executed by lethal injection at the Texas State Penitentiary in Huntsville, Texas on January 4, 2005. Porter was found guilty of the 2000 murder of Rudy Delgado, a 40-year-old Hispanic male. Porter, who was 28-years old when he committed the capital crime, was sentenced to death on March 14, 2001.

On May 28, 2000, Porter was serving prison time[13] at the Texas Department of Criminal Justice's Barry Telford Unit in Bowie County, Texas, when in the prison day room he attacked Rudy Delgado who was seated at at table. Porter struck Delgado from behind with a rock sheathed in a pillowcase. Delgado, an inmate serving a 15-year sentence for molesting a boy, fell to the floor and lay helpless on the ground as Porter continued to bludgeon his face and head with the rock. When the pillowcase finally ripped, Porter stabbed Delgado in the head and face with a shank (a makeshift knife). Porter then stomped on Delgado's head and face with steel-toed work boots before surrendering to a correctional officer. Prosecuting attorney James Elliot later noted that Delgado's face "could not be recognized as that of a human."

Porter confessed to the murder, and in his written statement admitted that he had been planning to kill someone for some time, and had decided to use the rock

---

[13] On April 21, 1995, Porter began serving a 45-year sentence for first-degree murder. Porter had shot a 40-year-old white male transient two times in the head with a .25-caliber pistol and dumped his body in a water-well. He expressed no remorse for the murder and thought he had done society a favor. Porter had also been convicted of burglary in 1990 and 1991.

and shank the week before the murder. He also admitted picking his victim at random and taking eleven Dilantin pills (antiepileptic drug) the night before the murder to help with the "rush of killing someone, no one in particular."

A Bowie County jury convicted Porter of capital murder and recommended the death penalty. Porter declined his federal appeals and did not request clemency (*Porter v. State* (2003) No. 74,095).

———

Donald Jay Beardslee, a 61-year-old white male, was executed by lethal injection at the San Quentin State Prison in Point Quentin, California on January 19, 2005. Beardslee was found guilty of the 1981 murder of Patty Geddling, a 23-year-old white female. Beardslee, who was 37-years old when he committed the capital crime, was sentenced to death on March 12, 1984.

Beardslee, a 1960's U.S. Air Force veteran, was living in his studio apartment in Redwood City, California with Ricarda Sue Soria, an 18-year-old female, whom he had met two months earlier while she was hitchhiking. Beardslee wanted to help Soria stop using drugs and to separate her from Ed Geddling—Patty Geddling's estranged husband—and Frank Rutherford, who were both drug dealers. Rutherford had a reputation for carrying guns and collecting drug debts, and had bragged that he would never go to jail because he or his brothers would take care of any witnesses.

On April 24, 1981, Beardslee returned home from work and discovered that Soria and a few of her friends had arranged to "get back at" Geddling, and her close friend and roommate, Stacy Benjamin, a 19-year-old white female. Benjamin sold drugs and had a reputation for "ripping people off." Geddling on occasion also sold drugs.

Benjamin had taken $185 in drug money from William Forrester, a 19-year-old white male, but had not delivered the drugs. Forrester, Soria, and Rutherford planned to lure

24

her to return the money. First, Rutherford cut a wire and twisted the ends around shotgun shells. At Beardslee's request, Soria went out and bought tape for gagging Benjamin and Geddling. It was agreed that when Benjamin and Geddling arrived, Soria would sit on the sofa, Beardslee would open the door, and Rutherford and Forrester would hide. Beardslee testified he expected Rutherford and Forrester to "rough [Benjamin and Geddling] up a little bit," tie and gag them, take their money and drugs, and leave. Beardslee claimed he was especially fearful of Rutherford, who brought a sawed-off shotgun to the apartment that evening.

Beardslee agreed to allow the plan to proceed in his apartment and participated in the preparations, although he claimed he did so reluctantly. After Benjamin and Geddling arrived, Beardslee closed the apartment door and heard the shotgun go off behind him. Rutherford had shot Geddling in the shoulder, apparently accidentally. After explaining away the noise to his landlords, Beardslee spent several hours in the bathroom with Geddling trying to stop the bleeding, although he also left to dispose of some evidence and clean Rutherford's clothing. Geddling's hands and feet were tied.

Eventually, Beardslee helped Geddling into a van driven by Forrester, and the three of them drove toward the coast, followed by Soria in Beardslee's car. Geddling was told she was being taken to a hospital. However, Beardslee knew she would be killed.

After driving some distance along the coast, Beardslee told Forrester to turn off the main road, and Forrester stopped the van where Geddling got out and began pleading for her life. Beardslee then loaded the shotgun and handed it to Forrester, who shot Geddling twice. After feeling Geddling's wrist, Beardslee returned to the car, reloaded the gun, and shot Geddling two more times. Beardslee initially admitted shooting Geddling to put her out of her misery later claiming he thought she was already dead and had merely pretended to shoot her in order to demonstrate his involvement and impress Rutherford.

When Geddling's body was found, about one-third of her head was missing. According to the doctor who performed an autopsy, there were multiple shotgun wounds. One, in her left shoulder, preceded the others by several hours. A wound in her chest and another in her back, which occurred about the same time, would not have been immediately fatal; she could have survived for several minutes. The head wound, however, was inflicted by a shot or shots fired at extremely close range and caused instant death.

After Geddling was killed, Beardslee and Soria dropped Forrestor off and returned to Beardslee's apartment where they received a telephone call from Rutherford, asking them to join him at the nearby apartment of his girlfriend, Dixie Davis. Arriving at Davis's apartment between 3 a.m. and 3:30 a.m. they found Benjamin watching television. They told Benjamin that Geddling had been taken to a hospital. Out of Benjamin's hearing, Beardslee told Rutherford that Forrester had "chickened out" and Beardslee had to finish the job. Rutherford said Beardslee should have killed Forrester, and Beardslee replied that Soria had refused to give him more shells for that purpose.

About 5 a.m. Beardslee, Rutherford, Soria, and Benjaimin left in Beardslee's car. They stopped at a service station where Benjamin collected money she was owed for drugs, stopped in the city of Pacifica, where Soria obtained cocaine, and made two more stops to consume the cocaine before crossing the Golden Gate Bridge. They stopped to see Rutherford's brother in Sebastopol, a town 52 miles north of San Francisco, where Beardslee heard Rutherford obtain advice from the brother on where to "drop off" Benjamin. Beardslee understood this to refer to killing Benjamin and leaving her body somewhere.

With Beardslee driving the foursome headed north on Highway 101 and turned onto a winding side road.

Rutherford told Benjamin they were going to obtain drugs. They stopped at a turnout. Benjamin was upset, but Rutherford coaxed her out of the car, and all four walked up the hill. Soria and Rutherford went back to the car, and Benjamin asked if Beardslee was supposed to strangle her then. He said, "No." When Soria returned with Rutherford, she told Beardslee in a low voice that Rutherford had "fixed up" the wire. Beardslee and Soria walked further, where they could not see Rutherford and Benjamin. Beardslee heard some commotion, and Soria urged him to go help Rutherford.

Beardslee found Rutherford sitting on Benjamin, strangling her with his left hand and heard Rutherford call Benjamin a "die hard bitch." A broken wire lay under Benjamin's neck as Benjamin gave Beardslee a pleading look. Beardslee then punched Benjamin in the left temple, attempting unsuccessfully to knock her out. Beardslee then held one end of a wire wrapped around Benjamin's throat while Rutherford pulled on the other end. Rutherford took both ends of the wire, pulled it tight, and twisted it. The two men dragged Benjamin to a more secluded area. Beardslee asked for Rutherford's knife and used it to slit Benjamin's throat twice. After she was dead, Beardslee, at Rutherford's suggestion, pulled down her pants to make it appear that she had been assaulted sexually. Late that afternoon, Rutherford, Soria, and Beardslee returned to Davis's apartment.

Early that morning, joggers found Benjamin's body. A pathologist who examined the body testified that the knife wound cut Benjamin's left jugular vein and exposed her air passage but did not cut the carotid artery. From the presence of blood in her lungs, he concluded that Benjamin must have been still alive when her throat was cut. He said the blood loss was relatively slow, "not the kind of blood loss you get from an artery." The forensic evidence strongly suggested that Benjamin died from the knife wound.

27

A shoe repair claim ticket, recovered from Benjamin's clothing, bore Beardslee's telephone number. Accordingly, Detective Sergeant Robert Morse of the San Mateo County California Sheriff's Office called on Beardslee, who agreed to come to the sheriff's office to give a statement. Morse began the interview by talking about the difference between a witness and a suspect, and then asked Beardslee if he were involved in the case. Beardslee replied: "Well, Frank [Rutherford] shot her but I guess I'm involved because I shot her in the head twice myself. I was afraid."

Beardslee was then advised of his *Miranda* rights and gave a detailed, taped statement about both killings. Beardslee initially claimed he wanted to end her suffering. He later claimed he thought she was already dead when he cut her throat and was only acting out of fear of Rutherford. From Beardslee's directions, officers found Benjamin's body as well as numerous items of physical evidence at scattered locations throughout the county.

On April 26 Beardslee made a formal statement to police, and on May 3 he was charged with both homicides. Beardslee had already told police he was on parole from a prior homicide in Missouri, and he was also charged with the special circumstance of a previous murder conviction.[14]

---

[14] On January 2, 1982, Beardslee submitted to a lengthy interrogation by investigators. According to Beardslee he met Laura Griffin in a Missouri bar in 1969 and accompanied her home. At some point in the evening he felt insulted. As a result he eventually held Griffin's head underwater and stabbed her in the throat. Beardslee claimed he could not remember much about that night because he had been drinking.

Shortly after murdering Griffin, Beardslee confessed his involvement to a girlfriend, who referred him to clergy and eventually to a lawyer. His attorney took him to a county hospital for psychiatric counseling, instructing police officers not to question him. After the attorney had departed, the detectives engaged Beardslee in conversation about the killing and used the information they acquired to gather sufficient evidence about

As had been informally arranged between Gray and Holm, Beardslee's codefendants were tried first. Soria pleaded guilty to second-degree murder and received 15 years. Forrester was acquitted of the Geddling killing. Rutherford was found guilty of first-degree murder for the Benjamin killing and received a sentence of life without parole. He died in prison in 2002 of natural causes.

On October 18, 1983, a jury convicted Beardslee of two counts of first-degree murder. The prosecutor argued that both women were killed because they had witnessed the shooting in Beardslee's apartment, and the jury found the special circumstances of multiple murders and witness killing to be true for each homicide. On January 23, 1984, a second jury sentenced Beardslee to death for the murder of Geddling, and to life in prison for the murder of Benjamin. Governor Arnold Schwarzenegger denied Beardslee clemency the day before he was executed (*Beardslee v. Woodford* (2004) 358 F.3d 560; *People v. Beardslee* (1991) 53 Cal.3d 68).

---

the crime. Beardslee's lawyer moved to suppress all evidence obtained as a result of this interrogation. The officer involved, Jack Patty, testified that he had obtained all relevant evidence from other sources and so Beardslee's motion was denied.

Carl Holm, the prosecutor, considered introducing this prior homicide as a special circumstance in the California case, and he sent two detectives to Missouri to gather additional evidence. When their report raised serious questions about constitutional violations by the Missouri officers, Holm called Patty and secretly recorded an extended conversation about the case. Patty admitted he had talked to Beardslee despite his lawyer's instructions, had obtained evidence as a direct result of the conversation, and had lied about these facts at Beardslee's 1970 suppression hearing. Holm disclosed this information to defense counsel and did not introduce the conviction as evidence. However, he did introduce forensic evidence from the Missouri crime scene, and Beardslee's confession of the Griffin killing.

Troy Albert Kunkle, a 38-year-old white male, was executed by lethal injection at the Texas State Penitentiary in Huntsville, Texas on January 25, 2005. Kunkle was found guilty of the 1984 murder of Steven Wayne Horton, a 31-year-old white male. Kunkle, who was 18-years old when he committed the capital crime, was sentenced to death on February 26, 1985.

On the night of August 11, 1984, Kunkle, a six foot one inch native of Nuremburg, Germany, and his 18-year-old girlfriend Lora Lee Zaiontz, accompanied by three white males, Jerry Russell Stanley, 17, Aaron Allen Adkins, 19, and Tom Sauls, left San Antonio, Texas for a two hour drive to Corpus Christi. All five were then under the influence of alcohol and LSD.

While en route to the coast, Stanley removed a .22-caliber pistol from the glove compartment of the vehicle, fired it into the air, and asked Adkins if he wanted to make some money. Sauls told Stanley that "guns and acid don't mix," and Stanley returned the gun to the glove compartment. During the course of the 140-mile trip, Stanley took out the gun several more times. Stanley and Adkins discussed committing a robbery and slowed the vehicle several times to assess potential victims.

When the group arrived in Corpus Christi they drove to the beach where Kunkle and Zaiontz kept to themselves. Stanley, Adkins, and Sauls went for a walk, and Stanley and Adkins again discussed robbing someone. The group left the beach and went to a convenience store to buy beer. In the store Stanley and Adkins robbed a man in a phone booth at gunpoint while Kunkle, Zaiontz, and Sauls remained in the car and did not participate in the robbery or share in its proceeds. Stanley and Adkins got only $7, so they left the store to search for another victim. They spotted Steven Horton walking along the road, pulled up next to him, and Zaiontz asked if he needed a ride. Though he resisted at first, Horton was eventually

30

persuaded to get into the car. He sat in the front seat, next to Zaiontz.

Once inside the car Stanley put the .22-caliber pistol to the back of Horton's head and told him to give them his wallet. Horton turned to look at Stanley but Zaiontz scratched his face and told him to look forward. Kunkle told Stanley to kill him but Stanley refused. Kunkle then took the gun from Stanley, put it to Horton's head, and said, "We're going to take you back here and blow your brains out." Adkins drove the car behind a skating rink and Kunkle shot Horton in the back of the head. They pushed his body out of the car, and Zaiontz took his wallet. After the shooting Kunkle quoted the following line from Metallica's No Remorse: "another day, another death, another sorrow, another breath," and told the group that the murder was "beautiful."

On October 17, 1984, a Nueces County grand jury indicted Kunkle, who had no prior criminal record, of capital murder. On February 22, 1985, Kunkle was convicted and seven days later he was sentenced to death. On June 18, 1986, the Texas Court of Criminal Appeals affirmed his conviction and sentence. Zaiontz was convicted of capital murder and given a life sentence. Stanley and Adkins were convicted of murder and given a 30-year sentence. Sauls was never arrested or charged with any offense (*Kunkle v. Dretke* (2003) 352 F.3d 980; *Kunkle v. State* (1986) 771 S.W.2d 435).

———

Timothy Don Carr, a 34-year-old white male, was executed by lethal injection at the Georgia Diagnostic and Classification Prison in Jackson, Georgia on January 25, 2005. Carr was found guilty of the 1992 murder of Keith Patrick Young, a 17-year-old white male. Carr, who was 22-years old when he committed the capital crime, was sentenced to death on April 28, 1994.

31

On October 7, 1992, Carr was at a party in Macon, Georgia with his girlfriend, Melissa Leslie Burgeson, a 22-year-old white female, and Keith Young. The people at the party consumed alcohol and the juice from boiled hallucinogenic mushrooms and some also smoked marijuana. Carr and Burgeson discussed robbing Young at the party.

In the early hours of the following day Burgeson took Young's car keys and talked him into letting her drive him home. Burgeson obtained Young's car keys claiming that he was too intoxicated to drive. She and Carr discussed robbing Young of his gold 1986 Pontiac Grand Prix. They also knew that Young had just cashed his paycheck.

That morning Burgeson, Carr, Young, and a 16-year-old boy and girl left the party in Young's Grand Prix. Burgeson was driving, Young was in the front passenger seat, and the others were in the back seat. During the drive Carr displayed a knife to one of the juveniles and whispered to her that he was going to kill Young. There was also a baseball bat in the back seat of the car.

Burgeson later stopped the car on a dirt road some 15 miles northwest of Macon under the pretense that they were going to look for mushrooms and everyone exited except for the female juvenile. When Young was looking in the trunk Burgeson whispered to Carr to "do it now" whereupon Carr grabbed Young from behind and cut his throat twice. Burgeson said, "that ain't enough," and Carr stabbed Young several times in the chest. Young pleaded for his life but Carr laughed and said, "I'm going to kill you, boy."

After Young had fallen to the ground Carr rolled him over on his stomach and stabbed him several times in the lower back. The male juvenile then handed Carr the baseball bat and Carr beat Young in the head, fracturing his skull. Burgeson took $125 from Young's pockets and they returned to Macon where they dropped off the male juvenile and then drove to Tennessee where Carr,

Burgeson, and the female juvenile were arrested after they crashed following a high-speed chase.

After receiving medical treatment at a local hospital Carr and Burgeson were placed in the back of a police car in which police had activated a hidden tape recorder. Their recorded conversation, in which Carr admitted killing Young, was introduced into evidence at Carr's trial. The knife used to stab Young was also discovered in Burgeson's purse and presented as evidence.

Following a jury trial in Monroe County Carr was sentenced to death for the Young murder and to 20 years' imprisonment for the theft of Young's car. The day before his execution the state Board of Pardons and Paroles denied clemency. Accomplice Burgeson was convicted of malice murder and sentenced to life in prison (*Carr v. State* (1997) 480 S.E.2d 583; *Head v. Carr* (2001) 544 S.E.2d 409).

———

Dennis Wayne Bagwell, a 41-year-old white male, was executed by lethal injection at the Texas State Penitentiary in Huntsville, Texas on February 17, 2005. Bagwell was found guilty of the 1995 murder of four white females: Libby Best, 24, Reba Best, 4, Tassy Boone, 14, and Leona McBee, 47. Bagwell, who was 31-years old when he committed the capital crime, was sentenced to death on November 7, 1996.

On September 20, 1995, Ronald Boone returned from work to his rural Wilson County, Texas home to find the bodies of his wife Leona McBee, her daughter Libby Best, his granddaughter Reba Best, and his granddaughter Tassy Boone. McBee and Tassy had been beaten and strangled such that their necks were broken, and Tassy had been sexually assaulted. Libby had been shot twice in the head, and Reba's skull had been crushed with a hammer and a metal exercise bar.

McBee's son, Bagwell, and his girlfriend Victoria Wolford, had been living in a small travel trailer on her property. Earlier in the month McBee had asked Bagwell and Wolford to leave her trailer and on the 20th they were living some 35 miles away in a San Antonio apartment.

On the 20th Wolford testified that she and Bagwell drove to his mother's house to borrow money. When they arrived Wolford retired to the trailer because she had a headache. A short time later Bagwell walked over to the trailer and told Wolford that his mother would only give him $20. Bagwell then went back into his mother's house, while Wolford stood outside the trailer. Through the window Wolford saw Bagwell strike McBee, then heard screams and two popping noises. She heard Tassy yell, "No, no," and heard Reba scream. Everything was quiet for a while when she heard McBee yell at the dogs and gasp for air. Through the window she saw Bagwell hit his mother with a long-handled gun. Later Bagwell took some towels and wetted them with a water hose. He wiped off a hammer and told Wolford he was going to go inside and wipe off fingerprints he might have left in the house, adding that he was trying to make the crime look like a robbery and rape of Tassy.

Wolford led police to various locations along the getaway route where Bagwell had discarded incriminating evidence, and police officers recovered numerous items taken from the Boone residence including a pair of tennis shoes and a pair of shorts. An expert witness testified that one of the tennis shoes matched a bloody shoe print found at the crime scene under the body of Tassy and other witnesses testified that those tennis shoes belonged to Bagwell. A firearms expert testified that the bullet fragments removed from Libby's cranium matched the shattered rifle the law enforcement officers recovered.

On November 21 Bagwell was indicted by a Wilson County grand jury for capital murder. Transferred to Atascosa County because of a change in venue, it took a jury three hours of deliberation to return a guilty verdict and another four hours to sentence Bagwell to death. On March 31, 1999, the Texas Court of Criminal Appeals affirmed his conviction and sentence.

On September 5, 1995, in Seguin, 40 miles east of San Antonio, a delivery person found the body of 63-year-old George Barry in the supply room of a local bar, Jim's Place, where Barry had worked as a night stocker. Police arrived on the scene shortly after the discovery, took photographs of the body and the supply store, and dusted for fingerprints. As the investigation progressed Bagwell became a suspect, and Wolford, after being promised immunity from prosecution by the state, once again testified against Bagwell.

Wolford testified that on the evening of September 4 she and Bagwell met Donnie Halm, the owner of Jim's Place, at a rest stop on Highway 123. There, Bagwell sold Halm a television, stereo, and VCR, all of which belonged to a local rent-to-own store. Halm paid $200 for the equipment and Bagwell and Wolford took the money from this sale and went to the home of Anthony Jackson where they bought some rock cocaine for $150. The pair took the cocaine to the trailer they shared where they smoked it, and Wolford prepared for bed. Wolford further testified that Bagwell then wanted to return to Jim's Place for more drugs, this time, marijuana. Wolford dressed and they drove to Jim's Place. Bagwell drove around the bar a couple of times telling Wolford he was looking for an employee, Robin Whitman, who Bagwell thought would sell him some marijuana.

Bagwell had been to Jim's Place several times, had sold or tried to sell items to employees there, and knew all the employees by name. When Bagwell didn't see Whitman he stopped the car and went into the bar. He came back shortly and asked Wolford for a quarter as he had not found Whitman and wanted to call him at his home. At that point he told Wolford he planned to rob and kill

Barry, who was in the restaurant, stocking beer for the next day. It was also Barry's job to make the night deposit for the bar.

Bagwell returned to the restaurant and Wolford remained in the car. According to Wolford, while Bagwell was in the bar, she could hear pounding and thumping noises after which Bagwell returned 20 to 25-minutes later with three moneybags and an injured finger. Bagwell and Wolford then left Seguin stopping to move the money from the bags to Bagwell's pockets. They went to Jackson's where they purchased more rock cocaine, and on the drive from Jackson's to their trailer, Bagwell told Wolford that he had killed Barry by smashing his throat in with his foot. Wolford testified that Bagwell was wearing black, heavy boots the night of the murder. The next morning Bagwell and Wolford left Seguin for San Antonio.

Already sentenced to death for the murder of his mother and three other people, Bagwell was tried in Guadalupe County for the Barry murder. In the November 1997 trial a fingerprints expert testified that one of Bagwell's fingerprints and one of his palm prints were found on the file cabinet near Barry's body where the deposit money was kept. A "pattern injuries" expert testified that he could not rule out the possibility that Bagwell's shoes had caused the injuries to Barry's face and neck, and a San Antonio police officer testified to finding one cloth bank bag with the words "First Commercial" on it in the room Wolford and Bagwell shared in San Antonio. Bar employees testified that this bag was "similar" to those used by Jim's Place.

Finally, several witnesses testified that Bagwell had given inconsistent stories about how he had hurt his hand, saying at times that he had hit a black man, that he had hit a black man and robbed him, or that he had smashed his hand down on the roof of an automobile. The defense presented no witnesses, and the jury sentenced Bagwell to life imprisonment in a case where the State waived the death penalty (*Bagwell v. Dretke* (2004) 372 F.3d 748; *Bagwell v. State* (1997) 956 S.W.2d 709).

———

Stephen Anthony Mobley, a 39-year-old white male, was executed by lethal injection at the Georgia Diagnostic and Classification Prison in Jackson, Georgia on March 1, 2005. Mobley was found guilty of the 1991 murder of John C. Collins, a 24-year-old white male. Mobley, who was 25-years old when he committed the capital crime, was sentenced to death on February 28, 1994.

Shortly after midnight on February 17, 1991, Mobley robbed a Domino's pizza store in Hall County, Georgia where he shot John Collins, the store manager, in the back of the head with a Walther .38-caliber semiautomatic pistol that he had stolen previously. The physical evidence from the scene was consistent with a statement Mobley later made to a cellblock inmate that Collins, who was the only one in Domino's at the time, was on his knees when Mobley shot him.

Approximately three weeks afterwhich Mobley had committed six additional armed robberies of restaurants and dry-cleaning shops, Mobley used the same pistol while robbing a dry cleaning store and tried to dispose of it by tossing it out his car window onto the side of a road when he realized that an unmarked police car was following him. The pistol was later recovered and Mobley was arrested after a high-speed chase.

Mobley made statements to police confessing to the murder of Collins and the robbery of the Domino's pizza store. In response to Mobley's statement to police that on the night of the crimes he was en route from his residence to a family member's home where he was not expected, and that he robbed the pizza store because it was the only open establishment he passed, the State introduced testimony establishing that out of the three routes available to Mobley, only one passed the pizza store, and that this route exceeded by over 10 miles the next shortest route to the family member's house.

On March 19, 1991, Mobley was indicted in Hall County. On February 20, 1994, he was found guilty of malice murder and felony murder based upon the aggravating factors of armed robbery, three counts of aggravated assault, and possession of a firearm in the commission of a crime.[15] On February 25, 2005, the State Board of Pardons and Paroles denied a clemency appeal in which six of his trial jurors asked that Mobley not be executed (*Mobley v. State* (1995) 265 Ga. 292; *Mobley v. State* (1995) 455 S.E.2d 61; *Turpin v. Mobley* (1988) 502 S.E.2d 458).

William Henry Smith, a 47-year-old black male, was executed by lethal injection at the Southern Ohio Correctional Facility in Lucasville, Ohio on March 8, 2005. Smith had been found guilty of the 1987 murder of Mary Virginia Bradford, a 47-year-old black female. Smith, who was 29-years-old when he committed the capital crime, was sentenced to death on April 15, 1988.

---

[15] Following his incarceration, Mobley had the word "Domino" tattooed on his back, placed a Domino's pizza box in his cell on the wall, carried a domino piece in his pocket with the same dot configuration as that used by Domino's Pizza, told a guard that he wished the guard had been up at Domino's instead of that other boy, in referring to Collins stated that "If that fat son-of-a-bitch had not started crying, I would never have shot him," told another guard that he was "going to apply for the night manager's job at Domino's because he knew they needed one," told another guard that the guard was "beginning to look more and more like a Domino's pizza boy everyday," told another guard that "anywhere Mobley was put [in jail] he'd kill anybody he came in contact with," and forcibly sodomized his cellmate on two separate occasions.

On Saturday afternoon, September 26, 1987, Mary Bradford visited the Race Inn, a neighborhood bar, in Cincinnati, Ohio. While at the bar she had several beers and met, talked, and danced with Smith, a regular bar patron. Bradford left the Race Inn around 11:45 p.m.

At around 4:00 p.m. on the 27th Marvin Rhodes, Bradford's boyfriend, stopped by her apartment because he had not seen her since Friday, the 25th. No one answered the doorbell, and Rhodes finding the door unlocked, went in. Rhodes saw blood near the front door and found Bradford in the bedroom. Feeling her face he found no life in her body and called police.

Responding police officers found Bradford lying stabbed to death on her bed, nude from the waist down. On the floor near her bed, police found a woman's pants and panties, bloodstained and turned inside out, and on the bed, an oxygen machine used by asthmatics. Forensic examination disclosed a 0.13 percent blood-alcohol level and revealed sperm in her vagina and on her abdomen.

Near the front door of the apartment police found a chair with a pool of blood in it, and on the floor, blood smears including a bare bloody footprint leading to the bedroom. The apartment was otherwise exceptionally neat and clean with no signs of disorder, disarray, or a struggle, and police found no murder weapon in the apartment. One color television, one black and white television, and a stack stereo with two speakers were missing from Bradford's apartment.

Dr. Harry J. Bonnell, Chief Deputy Coroner, testified that Bradford died as a result of ten stab wounds to her upper body and consequent loss of blood. She was five feet three inches tall, weighed 116 pounds, and a portion of her lungs were missing, which explained her asthmatic condition. Bonnell numbered the wounds one to ten for descriptive purposes and not to indicate the order in which they were inflicted. The most lethal wounds, causing incapacitation within five minutes, were wound eight, a four-inch wound into Bradford's right lung and heart, and wound nine, a four-inch wound into the sternum and the heart's right ventricle. Wound seven, a five-inch puncture into the rib and liver, and wounds eight and nine all fractured bony structures. Wound two, four-inches in depth, crossed her neck from left to right. Wound ten punctured the liver and was no more than four-inches in depth. Two wounds, one and five, showed no signs of hemorrhage and thus were inflicted after death or when the heart was not pumping sufficient blood. Wounds one, three, four, and six were superficial. Bradford's body exhibited no other evidence of injury or trauma such as bruises or defense wounds, and Bonnell observed no twisting motion in the stab wounds that would indicate a violent struggle. All of the wounds could have been inflicted by one single edged knife.

On September 28 homicide detectives went to where Smith lived at the home of Bertha Reid, Smith's mother, a residence that was about four blocks from Bradford's house. When police arrived Smith was not at home and Reid let the officers in. While at Reid's home police noticed a television set matching the description of one of the two sets missing from Bradford's home. Thereafter police secured a warrant, found the missing two televisions in Reid's home, and seized them.

Reid testified that when her son came home around 2:00 a.m. on the 27th he did not act unusual nor did he appear to be drunk, high, or upset. Smith did carry into Reid's home the two televisions in question along with a large stereo system and two speakers. Reid asked where he got the televisions and stereo and Smith replied that his girlfriend Carolyn gave them to him. Reid did not accept her son's explanation telling him he would "have to explain to me a little more about what's going on." Later that morning Smith and his cousin, Greg, took the stereo and two speakers away but left the televisions. Reid also showed police clothing that her son had worn on the 26th and 27th of September, which police seized. Subsequent forensic analysis revealed that Smith's shirt and shoes bore traces of human blood.

At 1:30 p.m. on the 28th police apprehended and took Smith to police headquarters for questioning. After being advised of his *Miranda* rights Smith agreed to talk to police. Smith initially asserted that he had driven Bradford home that night but had just dropped her off. He later admitted that he had been in her apartment but had left when her boyfriend arrived. Smith told police that he met Bradford at the Race Inn, later drove her and her girlfriend, Janice Echols, to the Queen Anne Café bar, and then drove Bradford home. While at her house Smith claimed that someone he thought to be Bradford's boyfriend arrived, and Smith decided to leave quickly. After Smith left he realized that he had left a packet of cocaine worth $2500 at Bradford's house. Bradford's boyfriend and the cocaine were both gone after he returned. Smith then talked with Bradford.

"She said she'd give me some of that body. I said okay, it's good enough for me, you know, but then after I got that it wasn't good enough, you know, so I asked her like you got any money and stuff, you know. She said she ain't have no money. So we start arguing and stuff and next thing you know she slid over to the kitchen and got little blade." Bradford was stabbed in the stomach during the ensuing struggle and fell onto a chair. He removed the knife from her stomach, and she dragged or walked by herself to the bedroom.

Smith recalled stabbing Bradford in the neck in the bedroom after she called him a motherfucker, but he did not admit inflicting the other stab wounds. When she was lying on the bed he took her clothes off and got back on top of her and had sex again. Police asked, "After you had sex with her the second time, after she was stabbed, then what'd you do?" Smith answered, "I gathered up my things together and started taking her stuff downstairs." Police

41

asked, "What'd you take out of there?" And Smith answered, "Her two TVs and her stereo."

Smith said he made four trips carrying her things down to his car and that he took her things in order to sell them. Although Smith initially claimed that he did not know whether Bradford had stopped breathing, he later admitted he decided to have sex with her again because "she was still breathing then." He said that he pulled his penis out as he started to climax and finished ejaculating on her stomach because he was thinking about getting out of the apartment.

Smith claimed he threw the knife into the Ohio River and sold Bradford's stereo in Dayton although police recovered her stereo in Cincinnati. When police interviewed Smith they also seized a pair of undershorts from him stained with blood of the same type as Bradford's.

On October 21, 1987, Smith was indicted on two counts of felony-murder: one alleging murder during rape, and the second alleging murder in the course of aggravated robbery, with each count containing two death penalty specifications. Smith pleaded not guilty and not guilty by reason of insanity, but later withdrew the insanity plea.

The following year a panel of three judges convicted Smith as charged and afterwards sentenced him to death on each murder count. In 2005 the Ohio Parole Board acknowledged that "Smith suffered an abysmal childhood of deprivation and abuse," and that he had "demonstrated exemplary conduct and adjustment within a structured prison setting." The Board recommended against both commutation and a reprieve by a vote of 8-0, and on March 7, 2005 Governor Bob Taft denied Smith clemency (*State v. Smith* (1991) 61 Ohio St.3d 284).

———

George Anderson Hopper, a 49-year-old white male, was executed by lethal injection at the Texas State Penitentiary in Huntsville, Texas on March 8, 2005. Hopper was found guilty of the 1983 murder of Rozanne Gailiunas, a 33-year-old white female. Hopper, who was 27-years-old when he committed the capital crime, was sentenced to death on March 16, 1992.

On October 4, 1983, 4-year-old Peter Gailiunas Jr. found his mother, Rozanne Gailiunas, naked and unconscious in her Richardson, Texas bedroom. The boy's mother had been brutally assaulted and shot twice in the head. She never regained consciousness and died at the hospital two days later after which Peter Gailiunas put up a $25,000 reward for information leading to an arrest for his wife's murder. At the time of her death Rozanne had been having an affair with Larry Aylor.

Several years later, Carol Garland, in pursuit of the reward, told police that her sister, Joy Davis Aylor, a 34-year-old white female, had arranged to have Rozanne murdered. Police confirmed that Joy, Larry's wife, had paid $5000 to Carol's husband, William Westley Garland, to have Rozanne killed, and they were able to trace the money as it then passed to Brian Lee Kreafle who in turn hired Hopper. Each individual had skimmed a little of the money and passed the remainder along. Hopper apparently received $1500 of the original $5000.

Police began looking for Hopper in the summer of 1988 to discuss Rozanne's murder. At that time police did not know whether Hopper was Rozanne's killer—all police knew then was that Hopper was the most recent person to receive the money.

On December 20, 1988, Hopper was arrested and arraigned the following day even though counsel was not appointed and Hopper made no request for counsel at that arraignment. On December 22 and despite his lack of counsel Hopper contacted Detective McGowan offering to cooperate. Hopper admitted that he had received the money to kill Rozanne and that he had passed $1000 of that money on to a drug dealer named "Chip." Hopper also gave McGowan a description of Chip as well as information regarding Chip's usual haunts.

Hopper was not appointed counsel until December 27, six days after his arraignment and five days after he first willingly spoke with McGowan and gave the detective the "Chip story." Jan Hemphill, the court appointed counsel, met with Hopper several times over the next few weeks as well as with the prosecution. The prosecution informed Hemphill of its intent to seek the death penalty for Joy Aylor as well as the shooter. The prosecution also told Hemphill that it was willing to work with all of the middlemen in the chain to get those two death penalty convictions. Hemphill repeatedly advised Hopper of the prosecution's plans and discussed with him the risks of cooperation. She also advised Hopper that her advice was based on the information that Hopper had given her.

On February 21, 1989, Hopper again contacted McGowan and informed the detective of his intent to cooperate. He told McGowan that he had spoken with Hemphill and that Hemphill had given Hopper permission to contact police. McGowan then called the prosecution who verified with Hemphill that Hopper had her permission to talk with police. The prosecution also secured Hemphill's consent to give Hopper a polygraph examination, and a blanket consent to talk to Hopper in the future without having to contact her first.

The following day Hopper met with McGowan. Hopper was read his *Miranda* rights, and after waiving those rights, completed a six page written statement detailing and supplementing the story he had previously given to McGowan that inculpated the drug dealer Chip. After this interview Hopper was told that the story would be verified by a polygraph examination to be scheduled in the upcoming few days.

On Februrary 27 Hopper was given a polygraph examination. Prior to this examination he was again read his *Miranda* rights. After being told that the polygraph examination indicated falsity and after receiving a fresh *Miranda* recitation Hopper was questioned by McGowan who asked Hopper to tell his story once again, starting at the beginning. After Hopper recounted the "Chip story," McGowan told Hopper that McGowan believed Hopper was not telling police the entire story. McGowan then showed Hopper a picture of Chip and told Hopper that the police were close to locating Chip. The detective asked Hopper what would happen if police questioned Chip and Chip passed a polygraph. Hopper said that the investigation would "lead back to me [Hopper]" and asked "Can I go back and think about it?" The detective responded, "Andy, I want the truth now." After a brief pause Hopper admitted that he killed Rozanne and gave a factually detailed confession that was both audio and videotaped.

Hopper's confession and the gun used to shoot Rozanne were admitted into evidence at his trial. Also admitted into evidence was testimony regarding an independent confession Hopper made to a jailhouse informant, and an admission of guilt in a letter Hopper wrote to a close friend. The testimony of the jailhouse informant closely tracked the confession that Hopper gave to police. The letter admission of guilt was not detailed, but in that letter Hopper wrote: "I am the one who killed this person."

Joy Aylor was convicted of capital murder and sentenced to life in prison.[16] Garland and Kreafle were

---

[16] Arrested in September 1988 and released on $140,000 bail the night before her 1990 murder trial was to begin, Aylor emptied her bank accounts and fled to Canada with her attorney, who was also reportedly her lover. After the lawyer was arrested in Canada on a drug charge, Aylor fled to Mexico and then Europe. She settled around Nice, France living under the alias Elizabeth Sharp. Her identity was exposed after she became involved in a minor traffic accident while driving a rental car. She
(continued)

each sentenced to 30 years' imprisonment (*Hopper v. Dretke* (5th Cir. 2004) No. 02-11337).

Donald Ray Wallace Jr., a 47-year-old white male, was executed by lethal injection at the Indiana State Prison in Michigan City, Indiana on March 10, 2005. Wallace was found guilty of the 1980 murder of Patrick Gilligan, a 30-year-old white male, Teresa Gilligan, a 30-year-old white female, Gregory Gilligan, a 5-year-old white male, and Lisa Gilligan, a 4-year-old white female. Wallace, who was 22-years old when he committed the capital crime, was sentenced to death on October 21, 1982.

On January 14, 1980, Indiana State Trooper Thomas Snyder was called to the Evansville home of Ralph Hendricks as it had been reportedly burglarized. Snyder went to the home of Patrick and Teresa Gilligan, which was next door to Hendricks's house, to inquire whether the Gilligans might have seen or heard anything unusual. Synder, discovering that the window to the Gilligans' back door was broken, checked inside the house and discovered four dead bodies in the family room—Patrick and Teresa and their two children, Gregory and Lisa. Teresa had her hands tied behind her, and the two children were tied together. Dr. David Wilson, the coroner, testified that the cause of all four deaths was brain damage from gunshot wounds.

The evidence also showed that on the 14th Wallace was seen driving a blue Plymouth automobile that belonged to Richard Milligan. And while Milligan and Milligan's girlfriend, Debbie Durham, were known to have

---

(*continued*)
was arrested in March 1991 but the French government refused to extradite her because of its opposition to capital punishment. In December 1993 Aylor was returned to Texas after the State pledged that she would not face the death penalty.

committed several prior burglaries using this same automobile, Milligan was in jail on burglary charges this particular night. Witnesses recalled seeing the Plymouth in the Evansville neighborhood about the time the murders occurred.

Donna Madison was at the home of her sister, Debbie Durham, the night of the 14th when earlier that evening she witnessed Wallace driving the blue Plymouth. Between 7:00 p.m. and 9:00 p.m. Wallace returned to Durham's home, and Madison heard him ask for matches. He found a cigarette lighter, and Madison saw him in the backyard burning the jacket he had been carrying over his shoulder upon arrival.

Neighbor Sherry Grayson saw a fire at the same time and saw a man with shoulder length hair that was characteristic of Wallace, standing by it. Officer John Crosser recovered the remains of the jacket and other items found on the ground. Among these items was a set of wedding rings without stones in them and some fragments of glass. State Police Specialist Oliver examined the glass and found the pieces fit into a pattern matching the hole in Gilligans' window.

On the evening of the 14th Wallace and Durham had a Carl Durham take pictures of them with many of the items taken from the Gilligan and Hendrick residences. The pictures also showed money and pistols connected with these burglaries, and were later admitted into evidence.

Durham gave William Kune, a serologist, the blue jeans worn by Wallace the night of the crime, upon which Kune found type AB blood. Wallace had blood type O, but Teresa Gilligan and one of the children had blood type AB. Kune also found type B blood on a brown cotton glove, identified as one of a set Wallace wore while burglarizing homes. Patrick Gilligan had type B blood.

William Madison, the brother of Durham and Madison, came to the Durham's home the evening of the 14th and saw Wallace come in wearing a gun in a holster to show

47

William a briefcase with a couple of guns in it. Wallace also had in his possession a CB, a police scanner, and some rings. That same night Wallace attempted to sell to Randy Rhinehart some guns, a CB, and a scanner. Several witnesses testified that Durham displayed to them pieces of jewelry that were later traced to the Gilligans. Durham gave one of the rings to Officer O'Risky that was identified by Dorothy Sahm, Teresa's mother, as belonging to Teresa. A jeweler that had sized the ring and kept pictures of it also identified it as belonging to Teresa.

Friends of Wallace, Mark Boyles and Anita Hoeche, testified they received a phone call on January 15 from Wallace who said he was in trouble and in need of a ride. While riding in the car, Wallace told them he had gotten too greedy the night before. He said he had broken into one house and never should have gone to the next house because he got caught there and that after he got caught a man in the house was giving him trouble, and he had to tie up the entire family. He said the little girl was crying and screaming, and it was bothering him. He felt he could not let the children grow up with the trauma of not having parents, and he did not "want to see the kids went through the tragedy of seeing their parents being killed," so he killed them also. He said the woman was screaming, and he had to shut her up. Later that night Wallace, while hiding in the attic of Hoeche's house, was arrested.

Durham testified that when Wallace visited her around 9:30 p.m on January 14 he immediately took his clothes off and gave them to her so he could change. On his blue jeans there was a piece of fleshy-whitish-red matter. Durham asked what it was, and Wallace stated it had to be a piece of brain because he had shot the residents, who had caught him, in the head. He told her a man had come in from the garage and surprised him. They struggled, and Wallace made him bring in the rest of the family. He said he tied up the man, made the woman tie up the children, and then Wallace tied her up. He shot the man in the head

48

after possibly breaking the man's neck in the struggle. He said he then shot the woman twice and because the children were crying for the mother, he shot each one of them once. Wallace, who was out on parole for a prior felony, said he shot the adults because they could identify him.

Wallace raised several issues concerning his mental competency to stand trial and four hearings were held before the trial judge found Wallace was competent to understand the proceedings and assist his counsel in his defense.[17] Following trial the jury recommended the death penalty (*Wallace v. State* (1985) 486 N.E.2d 445).

---

[17] A first hearing was instituted by the trial judge who detected reasonable grounds that Wallace lacked competency to proceed. The court then appointed two psychiatrists, Dr. Larry Davis and Dr. John Kooiker, to examine Wallace. In their reports they opined that Wallace was incompetent to proceed with trial because he was suffering from acute paranoid schizophrenia.

At a hearing held in May 1980 Davis and Kooiker described elaborate delusions expressed by Wallace of plots against him. He had told the doctors about his belief that the CIA and Masons were attempting to place him before a firing squad to prevent his release of secret matters including information on the Iranian hostage situation. He expressed concern about others plotting against him including his attorney and court personnel, he imagined radio-listening devices were planted in his cell and in the room where the psychiatrists interviewed him, and he expressed suspicion of the psychiatrists and of all those with whom he came in contact.

Davis and Kooiker concluded Wallace was unable to assist counsel at the time or to participate in and understand the trial proceedings. Each stated Wallace's apparent condition would be very difficult to feign. The State's two witnesses, Wallace's cellmate and a member of the Sheriff's department, testified Wallace displayed these mannerisms only at selective times, the implication being Wallace was feigning the psychosis. After taking the matter under advisement the judge found in May 1980

(continued)

(*continued*)
that Wallace was incompetent to stand trial, stating that despite evidence to the contrary, his decision was based on an overwhelming evidence of incompetency given by the doctors.

The Superintendent of Logansport State Hospital later certified to the court that Wallace had now attained competency to stand trial based upon a Dr. Matheu's opinion. However, the hearing scheduled pursuant to this certification was continued when Davis and Kooiker opined that Wallace needed further evaluation and treatment. After that Wallace had become oriented with time, place, and person, and now both psychiatrists considered Wallace competent to stand trial.

At the second hearing Wallace appeared too heavily sedated from the medication. The psychiatrists testified that Wallace's dosage of psychotic medication could be modified such that he would maintain competency but not experience the sedative side effects. Over Wallace's objection the court ruled that his competency depended upon an adjustment in his medication and ordered him back to Wishard Hospital for further treatment.

At the next and third hearing on January 16, 1981, Kooiker, Davis, and Moore opined that Wallace was incompetent to proceed with trial. All three psychiatrists testified that he was again suffering from symptoms of schizophrenia and that the suggested modified treatment from the previous hearing had failed. The general consensus was that Wallace was not feigning the psychosis. Moore testified that if Wallace was faking, he was "one of the best damn actors he had ever seen." Once again the court found Wallace incompetent to stand trial and ordered him committed.

In February 1982 the State moved for another competency hearing informing the court it could produce evidence that Wallace had been faking his psychosis to which the court so ordered. At the June 16 hearing the State introduced letters Wallace had written to Durham, during the time between his arrest and the first pretrial court appearance, at which his competency was put at issue. These letters indicated a full understanding of what he was doing and were intended to show he purposefully feigned incompetency to delay his trial and frustrate the State's attempt to have him sentenced to death. In the letters he discussed Durham's loyalty to him, their sex lives, and his feelings toward his attorney. He wrote he had a higher I.Q. than his attorney and so was planning to hire an attorney from San Francisco with the assistance of his uncle. His uncle would furnish the money for an attorney with the reputation for gaining acquittals for persons charged with murder. He said he was studying from materials furnished to him by a friend who was a professor from a local law school. His studies concentrated on suppression of evidence and the art of cross-examination. He indicated he was becoming very well informed on these subjects so that he would be in a position to attack the State in court and frustrate their case. Wallace also told Durham, who was in jail on a burglary charge herself, that she would not have to worry if she went to the Women's Prison because he had connections in the prison that would get her special consideration.

A former jailmate of Wallace testified that sometime in February or March 1980 Wallace told him he was using the Masons' story to get out of going to trial and stated that he would act psychotic only when non-prisoners were present. Two jailmates from Vigo County, Lofston and St. John, testified that during 1980 Wallace would act perfectly normal unless the doctors were around. Wallace told them he was fooling the psychiatrist by telling them he was collaborating with the Germans. Lofston testified that sometimes Wallace would give his medication to him and other inmates and that it would make them drowsy. St. John testified that Wallace told him he was pretending to be crazy to evade trial. Wallace told St. John he saved up his medication for a hearing so he would be extremely drowsy in the courtroom.

Several of the staff members from Logansport State Hospital, where Wallace had been for most of the preceding two years, testified in the same manner. Robert Cosgray testified that when Wallace first came to the hospital he acted psychotic but shortly thereafter admitted to Cosgray that he was feigning his mental illness. Wallace later denied this statement and told Cosgray that it was Cosgray's word against his. He said he

(continued)

William Dillard Powell, a 58-year-old white male, was executed by lethal injection at the Central Prison in Raleigh, North Carolina on March 11, 2005. Powell was found guilty of the 1991 murder of Mary Gladden, a 54-year-old white female. Powell, who was 45-years old when he committed the capital crime, was sentenced to death on April 29, 1993.

Mary Gladden was an employee of The Pantry on Charles Road in Shelby, North Carolina. She was killed on October 31, 1991, while on duty at The Pantry. On that day between 3:15 a.m. and 3:30 a.m. Scott Truelove bought $5 worth of gasoline at The Pantry. While paying at the counter he stood near a rough-looking man with

---

(*continued*)
would rather spend his life in the hospital than go to the electric chair. William Hardesty testified Wallace exhibited his psychosis early in 1980, but later Wallace told Hardesty that he liked to "beat people at their own game." Further, Wallace told Hardesty that the longer he drags this out the less chance the state had of convicting him.

Others at Logansport, James Campbell, Deborah Illes, Wilma McLaughlin, Richard Younce, and William Conn, each testified that during the two years of Wallace's hospitalization they saw his alleged psychotic delusions manifested very rarely. He appeared to have psychotic delusions perhaps once or twice, and then only when Dr. Keating was present or about to enter the room. Several of the staff members stated that Wallace gave them a contrasting impression and he was a sharp pool and card player.

After hearing all of this evidence the trial court concluded that Wallace was faking his psychosis and that he was in fact competent to stand trial. Wallace later asked the trial court to order that all of his medication be withdrawn from him but the trial court found this to be a medical matter and denied the motion.

unkempt, shoulder-length hair, facial hair, and a tattoo on his left forearm.

The next morning, November 1, Truelove read about the murder and gave a description of the man to Captain Ledbetter of the Shelby Police Department. On November 16 Truelove identified Powell as the man by picking him out of a photographic lineup.

At approximately 4:15 a.m. on October 31 Clarissa Epps stopped at The Pantry to buy gasoline. She went in to pay for her purchase and after waiting in vain for a clerk to appear called out but received no answer. Epps, after seeing Gladden lying in blood behind the counter, drove home and called police.

On the 31st, in response to a radio dispatch, Officer Mark Lee of the Shelby Police Department arrived at The Pantry at 4:26 a.m. Lee first ensured that all customers had left the store and then found Gladden behind the counter. She was lying on her back in a pool of blood with her head toward the cash register and her hands at her sides. Lee noticed injuries to her left eye and ear as well as other injuries to her head. He also saw a one-dollar bill on the floor near her left foot and another on the counter.

Dr. Stephen Tracey, who performed the autopsy, testified that Gladden had numerous lacerations on her head and that her skull was fractured in several places. Gladden's nose was broken and her left eye had been displaced by a fracture to the bone behind it. Her brain had hemorrhaged, was bruised and lacerated in several places, and contained skull fragments. Tracey determined that blunt trauma to the head caused Gladden's death and that she died from the trauma before she lost a fatal amount of blood. He also concluded that human hands had not inflicted the wounds, surmising from their size and shape that the perpetrator had used a lug-nut wrench, a tire wrench, or possibly a pipe.

Mark Stewart, an employee of The Pantry, testified that he worked on both October 27 and November 1. On the

27th Stewart saw a tire tool behind the counter to the side of the cash register. The tool had lain there for approximately one year. It was curved on one end with a round hole for a lug nut and was split on the other end for hubcap removal. Stewart noticed that the tool was missing when he worked on the 1st of November.

Thomas Tucker, a district manager of The Pantry, testified that he arrived at The Pantry sometime after 6:00 a.m. on October 31. He examined the cash register tape for that morning and it showed, among other transactions, a gasoline sale of $5 at 3:29 a.m. and a no-sale at 3:35 a.m. The cash register enters a no-sale when it is opened but no purchase is made. According to the tape no transaction occurred between the $5 purchase and the no-sale. Tucker opened the register at 6:22 a.m. at the direction of Captain Ledbetter to determine whether any money had been taken during the homicide. He concluded that approximately $48 was missing.

On November 16 Lieutenant Mark Cherka and Officer David Lail drove to Anthony's Trailer Park to find Powell and bring him to the police station for questioning. Powell came out of a trailer and allowed Cherka to take four photographs of him. He agreed to accompany Cherka and Lail to the police station for questioning as a possible suspect in a murder. Powell was told that he did not have to leave with them, as he was not under arrest at that time.

Powell and the officers arrived at the police station at approximately 4:00 p.m. whereupon Cherka began questioning Powell. Powell refused to allow Cherka to tape record the interview so Cherka made notes of what transpired shortly after the interview ended. Powell stated that he had gone to sleep at around 4:00 a.m. on the 31st of October after drinking with Don Weathers and Powell's girlfriend, Lori Yelton. Later that morning Yelton and Powell took Weathers to the hospital because he had cut himself at some point during the previous night.

Cherka left the interview room and related Powell's statement to Ledbetter. While Cherka had been questioning Powell Truelove had identified Powell from a lineup containing thirty-two photographs as the man he saw in The Pantry on October 31. Ledbetter informed Cherka of the identification and then accompanied Cherka back into the interview room.

Powell again indicated he did not want to be tape-recorded and Ledbetter complied. Ledbetter told Powell about Truelove's identification and asked him if he wanted an attorney. Powell stated that he had not killed anyone and did not want an attorney. Ledbetter advised Powell of his *Miranda* rights and Powell signed a waiver of those rights thereafter continuing to deny involvement in the murder.

Ledbetter then told him he knew Powell had killed Gladden and asked, "Why did you kill her?" Powell hung his head and answered, "She slapped me and I went off on her." Powell then asked to speak to Ledbetter alone and Cherka left the room. Ledbetter again asked Powell why he had killed Gladden. Powell stated that she had slapped him, he had panicked, he had not intended to harm her, and he merely wanted the money from the cash register.

Powell indicated that he wanted to speak to Ledbetter off the record. He asked him to tear up the *Miranda* waiver form, which Ledbetter ripped into four pieces. Powell then related additional details about the crime including information about the weapon he had used. At about 6:00 p.m. Powell asked for a lawyer and one was contacted for him. Powell was then arrested and taken into custody after he conferred with his lawyer.

Powell testified that he did not read the *Miranda* waiver form but signed it because he felt "agreeable" from cocaine he had ingested. He further testified that Ledbetter suggested they talk off the record. Powell further admitted he had given *Miranda* warnings during his tenure as a jailer in law enforcement and recited the warnings on the witness

55

stand. He also admitted he had not mentioned in his pretrial affidavit that Ledbetter proposed that they talk off the record.

Billy Joe Sparks testified that sometime after the Gladden murder he had a conversation with Paul Barnard, who called himself Rambo. During the conversation Rambo sniffed glue and both men drank beer. Rambo told Sparks he had killed a woman at a supermarket by beating her to death. Rambo died before Powell's trial and Sparks did not tell police about Rambo's statement until after his death.

Johnny Smith, the operator of a local entertainment center, testified that he had spoken to Truelove about the murder. Smith stated that Truelove told him he had seen a man with red hair in The Pantry on the day of the murder.

Truelove testified that he knew Rambo and that the lineup from which he identified Powell contained a photograph of Rambo. Truelove never picked Rambo as the person he saw at The Pantry on October 31 adding that he remembered having a conversation with Smith about becoming an uncle, and not about the murder. Truelove and his sister both have red hair, and his sister had recently given birth to a baby with red hair.

The State also called Officer James Glover of the Shelby Police Department in rebuttal. Glover testified that Rambo claimed to be a Vietnam veteran and to have a black belt in karate—neither claim was true. Before his death Rambo had telephoned Glover and told him he had lied to Sparks about committing the murder. He said he told Sparks he had killed a woman only to maintain his street image.

A Cleveland County jury found Powell guilty of first-degree murder under the felony murder rule, with robbery with a dangerous weapon as the underlying felony. At sentencing the same jury found that the murder was committed for pecuniary gain and no mitigating circumstance, and unanimously recommended the death sentence. On March 10, 2005, Governor Michael F. Easley denied clemency (*State v. Powell* (1995) 459 S.E.2d 219).

———

Jimmie Ray Slaughter, a 57-year-old white male, was executed by lethal injection at the Oklahoma State Penitentiary in McAlester, Oklahoma on March 15, 2005. Slaughter was found guilty of the 1991 murder of Melody Sue Wuertz, a 29-year-old white female, and Jessica Rae Wuertz, an 11-month-old white female. Slaughter, who was 44-years old when he committed the capital crime, was sentenced to death on December 9, 1994.

Around noon on July 2, 1991, Ginger Neal noticed that her pitbull, Ozie, was barking and acting strangely in her back yard in Edmond, Oklahoma. Ozie was somewhat skittish, more so around adults than with children. The dog was in such a hurry to get into the house that he practically ran over a child on his way to his place of refuge in the house. Neal was sufficiently concerned to glance out in the back yard to see if an intruder were present but saw nothing.

A few minutes later she heard a noise as if a car was backfiring or a firecracker had exploded. As Independence Day was only two days away she thought nothing of the noise. Rhonda Moss, who lived with Neal, also heard the noise and at least one other neighbor also heard a backfiring sound. Neither Moss nor Neal thought much about it until the bodies of Melody Wuertz and her baby daughter Jessica were found early that same evening in the house next door.

Melody was found on the floor in her bedroom. She had been shot once in the cervical spine and once in the head. In addition, he had been stabbed in the chest and in her genitalia, and there were carvings on her abdomen and breasts which authorities interpreted as symbols of some kind. A comb filled with Negroid hairs, some underwear

57

containing Negroid head hairs,[18] some unused condoms,

---

[18] Cecilia Johnson was a nurse who worked with Slaughter at the VA Hospital in Oklahoma City. After Melody became pregnant Slaughter started having sexual relations with Johnson who began openly expressing to coworkers her hostility to Melody whenever Melody sought money from Slaughter to support her child. Evidence showed that Johnson began helping Slaughter prepare for the murders by keeping him abreast of what Melody did and said while he was stationed at Fort Riley, by obtaining Negroid hairs and clothing from a patient at the hospital, and by mailing those items to Slaughter so he could plant them at the murder scene. The hairs were later determined to have come from a patient who was in the VA hospital in the ward where Johnson worked while Slaughter was at Fort Riley. Johnson mailed a package to Slaughter a short time before the murders were committed. Johnson and the prosecutors later reached an agreement that she would be immune from prosecution for assisting Slaughter if she agreed to cooperate with authorities in their investigation.

On January 11, 1992, Johnson received a call at work from a friend who told her there was an article on the Slaughter case in the early edition of the Sunday newspaper, and that Johnson's name was in it. When Johnson read the article she became very agitated, waving her arms around and saying "how could they do, how could this happen." Johnson then telephoned someone and, while on the telephone, yelled: "how could this happen, you were supposed to protect me." She repeated the remarks to the witness when she ended the telephone conversation, adding that "they used my words, they didn't have to be so explicit, they could have been more vague. How could they have let this happen." She then said: "I'm a goner, he's going to kill me. I'm going to get killed."

When the witness pointed out that Slaughter was in jail, Johnson looked at her as if she were completely ignorant, and told her Slaughter knew people who could have her killed, and he would have an alibi since he was in jail. Johnson then related how she had gone into a black patient's room, got hair off a brush, got a pair of underwear the patient had left behind, and

and some gloves were found near Melody's body. No seminal fluid was found in or on Melody. In the bathroom, Melody's curling iron was still plugged in. The baby, Jessica, was found in the hallway; she had been shot twice in the head. Medical examiners estimated the time of death to be approximately between 9:30 a.m. and 12:15 p.m. on July 2.

The prosecution's theory was that Melody, surprised in the bathroom as she was preparing to work the evening shift at the Oklahoma City VA Hospital, was paralyzed but not rendered unconscious by the shot to the cervical spine. Forced to lie paralyzed and conscious as her child was killed, Melody was subsequently dragged to the bedroom where she was killed by the shot to her head. The killer then planted the evidence in an attempt to throw investigators off the trail.

The killer likely entered the Wuertz home using a key and perpetrated a "blitz-style attack." There was no sign of forced entry, yet Melody was very security conscious and always kept her house locked even when she was inside. The confrontation between Melody and the killer appeared to have occurred in the hallway rather than near the front door, and although Slaughter denied having a key to

---

sent the items to Slaughter so he could plant them at the scene to mislead authorities.

The defense argued that Johnson was the murderer. When Johnson learned that both Melody and Jessica had been murdered, one witness said that Johnson immediately turned pale and white as if the blood had drained out of her face. Another witness testified that Johnson appeared "shocked" and grabbed a nearby pole as if she were fainting. Dr. Fred Jordan, the Oklahoma Medical Examiner, testifying for the prosecution, said that Johnson's response was genuine, and that Johnson either did not know the deaths were pending, or did not know that Jessica was also going to die. After an earlier failed attempt, Johnson committed suicide in February 1992.

Melody's house, investigators found those keys in Slaughter's car the day after the murders.

Melody and Jessica had been shot twice with Eley brand .22-caliber long-rifle, subsonic, hollow-point bullets that had not been copper washed. This imported ammunition was quite rare representing only 0.1 percent of the total .22-caliber ammunition sold in the United States during 1990 and 1991 and had to be special ordered.

Police found this same rare ammunition in Slaughter's gun safe in his Oklahoma home. Metallurgical tests indicated that the Eley ammunition in Slaughter's safe was elementally identical to the bullets used to kill Melody and Jessica and therefore had come from the very same box of Eley ammunition found in Slaughter's gun safe.

In addition to the shooting, the killer stabbed Melody once in the heart; deeply slashed both her breasts multiple times; scratched and cut her abdomen, including apparently inscribing a variation on the letter R; and inflicted a deep, nine inch cut running from her vagina through her anal canal and lower back. The medical examiner testified that the killer had used a single-edged knife, at least six inches long and one inch wide, and Slaughter had a large collection of knives.

Slaughter, a nurse at the VA Hospital, was immediately a suspect. He and Melody had had a sexual relationship the result of which she became pregnant. Slaughter signed an affidavit acknowledging paternity on July 17, 1990, ten days after Jessica was born. Despite this acknowledgment Slaughter's support of the child was meager—a fact Melody mentioned more than once.

Melody's insistence on getting Slaughter to provide monetary support for her child irritated him. He once remarked to a coworker at the hospital that Melody was getting "pushy" and if she continued to act that way he would have to kill her. To another he said Melody was causing him problems at work and one day he would have to kill both Melody and Jessica. Slaughter was concerned a paternity action by Melody could jeopardize his status as a reserve officer in the Army. Slaughter was also married and his wife did not know about the affairs with Melody and other women.

In the fall of 1990 Slaughter was called to active duty during the Desert Storm military operation and was stationed at Fort Riley, Kansas, where he remained on active duty until mid-July 1991. During this period what scant payments Slaughter had made to Melody stopped causing Melody to seek child support through the Department of Human Services, which enraged Slaughter. Before her death Melody expressed to several people her fear that Slaughter would take action against her because she had initiated child support proceedings against him.

Slaughter presented an *alibi* defense in a jury trial that lasted five months. Nicki Bonner, Slaughter's ex-wife, testified that he was with them all day on July 2. According to Bonner, Slaughter slept until 10:00 a.m. or 10:30 a.m. and ate a late breakfast at approximately 12:30 p.m. at the Country Kitchen.

The waitress at theCountry Kitchen testied that she did recall Bonner, adding that a man was with her and the girls, but she was unable to identify Slaughter as that man. When shown a photographic lineup that included Slaughter the waitress was unable to pick out Slaughter as the man who was present in her restaurant that day. The waitress stated Bonner ordered for all present at the table; Slaughter in his statement to authorities said each person ordered his or her own meal. The waitress also did not recall the man sitting with the family as having a receding hairline and Slaughter had a receding hairline.

Bonner testified that following the meal, somewhere between 1:15 p.m and 1:30 p.m., the family drove by a nearby lake, and went to Topeka, Kansas where they stopped at a Walmart department store. Inside Walmart Slaughter bought his daughter, Amanda, a watch at the jewelry counter at approximately 3:30 p.m. The family bought other items checking out at the main register. A receipt for these other items showed they checked out at 4:16 p.m.

The Walmart saleswoman recalled that Slaughter had purchased a watch for his daughter but was unable to recall the date and there was no receipt for the purchase. The Walmart checker recalled seeing Bonner and two girls come through her checkout line and not seeing a man with them. If Slaughter had left the murder scene soon after 12:30 p.m. he would have been able to drive from there to the mall by 5:00 p.m.

At 12:37 p.m. on the day of the murders several young teenage boys walking down a street near the Wuertz home noticed a man fairly matching Slaughter's description in a car parked away from the other houses next to an open field. The boy walking closest to that car positively identified Slaughter as the man he saw, both in the same photo lineup seen by the Country Kitchen waitress and conducted soon after the murders, and at Slaughter's trial, three years later. A second boy also positively identified Slaughter at trial as the man he saw in the car. Both boys described the car they had seen as a bluish-gray, four-door vehicle that also generally matched Slaughter's car's description, and although the second boy specifically identified the car he had seen as a Nissan, Slaughter's car was a Dodge.

Donald Stoltz, who had spent time with Slaughter in jail, corroborated the boys' identification testifying Slaughter had told him that the kids, who saw him the day the murders occurred, mistakenly identified his car as a Japanese-made vehicle. According to Stoltz Slaughter said he did not know why he had left his car window down, and that, if he had kept his tinted window raised, no one would have ever seen him.

Slaughter was convicted of shooting, stabbing and mutilating his former girlfriend, and shooting to death their daughter. He was also convicted of five counts of perjury.

During the penalty phase evidence showed that Slaughter enjoyed killing in Vietnam; that he did not know what the "big deal" was about a baby being killed, when thousands died in Vietnam; that while watching television with a coworker, Slaughter said of a character on television that he could "mutilate a sleazeball like that and he wouldn't be recognized"; that he referred to an uncooperative patient as "the type of sleazeball I could mutilate." Another witness testified that Slaughter once told him he had been in a special forces unit that would go into villages in Vietnam, seek out individuals identified as Vietcong sympathizers, and kill them, adding that when he cut their throats, it gave him an "erection." His last words were: "I've been accused of murder and it's not true. It was a lie from the beginning. God knows it's true, my children who were with me know it's true and you people will know it's true someday. May God have mercy on your souls" (*Slaughter v. Mullin* (2003) D.C. No. CIV-99-76-L; *Slaughter v. State* (1997) 950 P.2d 839).

———

Stanley L. Hall, a 37-year-old black male, was executed by lethal injection at the Eastern Reception Diagnostic and Correctional Center in Bonne Terre, Missouri on March 16, 2005. Hall was found guilty of the 1994 murder of Barbara Jo Wood, a 44-year-old black female. Hall, who was 26-years old when he committed the capital crime, was sentenced to death on June 21, 1996.

On the evening of January 15, 1994, Hall and Rance Burton, a 20-year-old male, borrowed a car and drove to the South County Shopping Center in St. Louis, Missouri searching for a vehicle to steal. Once there Hall and Burton got out of their car and approached Barbara Wood's car as she pulled into the parking lot. The two men forced her at gunpoint to the passenger side and then drove her in her car to the McKinley Bridge.

Wood was forced out of the car. There was a struggle on the bridge and at some point Burton shot Wood four or five times in the chest. Witnesses in a passing car saw her bleeding. Burton got back into Wood's car and drove away, leaving Hall and Wood struggling on the bridge.

Wood, pleading for her life, held onto Hall as he tried to lift her over the bridge railing. He eventually succeeded and Wood fell 90 feet to the river. Meanwhile, the two witnesses in the car had notified the Venice, Illinois police department. Police arrived and captured Hall moments after he pushed Wood off the bridge. Unable to begin a search and rescue attempt because of the icey river condition, seven and one-half months later, the lower portion of a torso matching Wood's physical description was found in the Mississippi River.

Both witnesses identified Hall as the man they had seen struggling with Wood and so Burton was not charged. After waiving his *Miranda* rights Hall identified Wood from a picture as the woman he had forced over the guardrail.

On March 7 Hall gave the St. Louis County police a complete confession that included a detailed account of his trip to the mall, the kidnapping of Wood, and the theft of her car. He recounted how Wood was pleading for her life as he struggled with her on the bridge and he described how first she grabbed on to the car door, and then she was shot. He said that she next grabbed hold of him and finally, clung to the bridge itself as he struggled to lift her over the guardrail. Hall confessed that he was the one who pushed her until she finally went over the railing.

On May 10 Hall entered a plea of not guilty to first-degree murder, kidnapping, first-degree robbery, and three counts of armed criminal action. On March 15, 1996, just three days before Hall's trial was set to begin, Hall, who had an I.Q. of 57 when tested at age seven, filed a motion seeking to enter a plea of guilty in exchange for a life sentence. The State rejected the plea and a jury found him guilty and awarded the death penalty. Governor Matt Blunt later denied clemency (*Hall v. State* (2000) 16 S.W.3d 582; *State v. Hall* (1997) 955 S.W.2d 198).

———

Glen James Ocha, a 47-year-old white male, was voluntarily executed by lethal injection at the Florida State Prison in Starke, Florida on April 5, 2005. Ocha was found guilty of the 1999 murder of Carol Skjerva, a 28-year-old white female. Ocha, who was 41–years old when he committed the capital crime, was sentenced to death on November 1, 2000.

On October 5, 1999, Ocha, who called himself "Raven Raven," met Carol Skjerva, at Rosie's Pub in Kissimmee, Florida. They left the bar together and Skjerva drove Ocha to his home in Buenaventura Lakes where they had consensual sexual intercourse. Afterwards Skjerva made disparaging comments about Ocha and threatened to tell her boyfriend about their affair. Ocha, high on alcohol and ecstasy, became angry and forcefully told Skjerva to sit in a chair as he paced back and forth deciding what to do.

Ocha entered the garage where he found a length of rope that he used to strangle Skjerva, lifting her off of the floor several times to ensure that she was dead. Believing that Skjerva's heart was still beating, Ocha again tightened the rope around her neck, hung the cord over an interior door to the garage, and closed the door on the rope catching it between the door and its frame leaving Skjerva hanging from the door.

Ocha then consumed a beer, cleaned the kitchen area removing bottles and ash from the kitchen table. He changed his clothing and after several minutes returned to the garage to lower Skjerva's body from the door and force it into an entertainment center cabinet located in the garage. Ocha then left his house and drove Skjerva's car some 74 miles to Daytona Beach where he was arrested on October 6 for disorderly intoxication. While in jail Ocha confessed to detectives of the Daytona Beach Police Department that he had murdered Skjerva. The detectives promptly notified the Osceola County Sheriff's Office of his statements. He was transferred to incarceration in Osceola County where he gave a detailed description of the murder to detectives.

On November 1 Ocha was indicted for first-degree murder. Based upon the testimony of three mental health professionals the trial judge concluded that Ocha was competent to enter a guilty plea. Ocha acknowledged to the trial court that he had, in fact, signed the plea form, waiver of jury trial, waiver of presentation of mitigation of evidence, and the acknowledgment that the State was seeking the death penalty, voluntarily and without coercion after reading and understanding the documents. Ocha further stated that he was not currently suffering from, nor had he been treated in the past for, mental or emotional disorders and was not under the influence of drugs or alcohol.

The State then related the facts of Ocha's crime and presented evidence of three aggravating factors: Ocha's prior commission of a violent felony conviction of attempted premeditated murder and robbery, that the Skjerva murder was especially heinous, atrocious, or cruel, and that it was cold, calculated and premeditated. After sentencing Ocha waived all further appeals and dismissed his attorneys (*Ocha v. State* (2002) 826 So.2d 956).

————

Richard Longworth, a 36-year-old white male, was executed by lethal injection at the Broad River Correctional Institution in Columbia, South Carolina on April 15, 2004. Longworth was found guilty of the 1991 murder of two white males: James Todd Green, 24, and Alex Hopps, 19. Longworth, who was 22-years old when he committed the capital crime, was sentenced to death on September 10, 1991.

On the night of January 7, 1991, an off-duty employee, David Hopkins, returned to the Westgate Mall Cinema in Spartanburg, South Carolina and found no employees present although films were still being shown. The body of Alex Hopps was discovered behind the theatre outside an exit door—he had been shot at close range in the left temple.

When Hopkins arrived at the theatre he had seen and recognized David Rocheville, a 22-year-old white male, rummaging through James Green's car in the parking lot. Rocheville and Longworth were former employees of the theatre owner. Green was the other employee on duty with Hopps and he was missing from the theatre.

At 5:00 a.m. the next morning police arrested Rocheville. A few hours later Rocheville led police to Green's body, which they found in a shallow ditch on the side of a rural road several miles from the cinema. Longworth was arrested later that day.

Longworth consented to be interviewed by police officers after waiving his *Miranda* rights. At the end of the interview Chief Murray prepared the following statement from his notes: "Longworth] stated that on January 7, 1991, he left his home at approximately four o'clock p.m. in route to meet his friend, David Rocheville, at a television repair shop where Rocheville worked. After meeting him, they both traveled to Rocheville's home in Duncan, South Carolina where Rocheville cleaned up.

"They left there in Longworth's mini van that is actually owned by his father in route to the Continental Cafe located in the Hillcrest Mall in Spartanburg. They arrived there at approximately 7:30 p.m. where he, Longworth, drank approximately six beers and three kamikazes [Vodka, Triple Sec, and lime juice cocktail]. While there, they spoke to a bartender by the name of Larry, last name unknown, who works there and knows them.

"After leaving the cafe, he and Rocheville drove around town in the mini van for a short time, and eventually stopped at an unknown place between Hillcrest and West Gate where they purchased a twelve pack of beer. They continued driving around all the while drinking beer, and decided to rob the West Gate Cinema.

"They arrived at the West Gate Theatre at an unknown time. But he knows it was before twelve o'clock midnight. Upon entering the theatre, Longworth remembered seeing James Greene, an employee, and, in fact, waved to him. Longworth and Rocheville walked around inside the theater for a short time, and believed the two of them went inside where the movie *Dances with Wolves* was playing. Longworth remembers that when they entered the theater through the front door, there was no one in the ticket booth. And accordingly, they walked in without having to pay.

"After being seated in the theater for a short time, they decided it was time to rob the place. As they walked out toward the lobby of the theater, Longworth saw the usher, Alex Hopps, standing near the end of a counter. He went over to him, and they started walking down a hallway talking. His plan was to take the usher outside and knock him unconscious.

"As they walked down the hallway, he knocked the usher to the floor by sweeping his feet out from under him. He then immediately jumped on him, and placed his hands over the usher's mouth. Rocheville, who had been given the gun that Longworth had carried into the theater in a shoulder holster hidden under his coat, was watching the activity. As Longworth and the usher walked outside using a side exit near where he and Rocheville had been seated in the theater, they were followed by Rocheville.

"Once outside, Longworth stated that he grabbed the usher by the right arm and twisted it up behind his back. He then forced the usher to lean over a waist high bar that was in place to, to protect the building or a cooling unit, and then took his left hand pushing the usher or pinning him on the bar. Rocheville then shot the usher in the left side of the head while Longworth was holding him. The weapon used and the one which Longworth earlier had given to him is [a] .44 magnum Ruger, and it was loaded with semi wod cutters.

"After the shooting, Rocheville returned the weapon to Longworth, and he placed it in the aforementioned shoulder holster. Longworth stated that he did not know the usher although it was pointed out to him that the usher had at one time worked for him at the Converse Theaters when Longworth was an assistant manager. After the shooting, Longworth advised that he and Rocheville walked around to the front of the theater to proceed with the robbery. However, when they arrived at the front, the doors were locked.

"Longworth stated that he again saw James Greene, and motioned to him to open the doors. Greene complied. Once inside, Longworth stated that he drew this same gun on Greene, and stated something to the effect that he was sorry. But he was going to rob the theater. And requested that Greene open the safe. Greene, upon seeing the gun, became so nervous that it took him three tries to successfully open the safe.

"Longworth took several money bags from the safe, and then asked Greene if he had made the deposits. Greene responded yes, and Longworth stated don't lie to me. Greene stated that the deposits were in his personal car. The three of them, Longworth, Greene, and Rocheville then walked to Greene's vehicle parked at the side of the cinema, obtained the remaining money bags, and gave them all to Rocheville. They then all got into the aforementioned mini van, which was parked next to Greene's vehicle. Longworth was driving. Rocheville was in the back. And Greene was seated in the passenger side.

"Longworth stated that he then gave the .44 magnum Ruger to Rocheville, and stated if he moves shoot him referring to Greene. The three of them then proceed to drive up highway number 176 toward Inman, and then turned right off number 176 onto an unknown road. They drove a short distance and stopped the van. Longworth then told Greene to get out of the van, walk five paces, get down on your knees, and stare straight ahead. He did as instructed. And at this point, Rocheville got partially out of the van perhaps with one foot on the ground and the other in the van, and shot Greene in the back of the head. Greene then rolled over into the ditch near where he had been kneeling ***. [Longworth] did mention that he initially told James Greene that he would not hurt him, and that he was going to let him out in a field unharmed. He stated that Greene apparently did not believe him as he pleaded for them not to hurt him, and assured them that he would not identify them. He just wanted to live so that he could see his girlfriend.

"At one point during the interview, Longworth slammed his fist on the table, and exclaimed my god we killed those kids for fifteen hundred dollars." When asked to sign the statement, Longworth declined saying he wanted an attorney to read it first. The statement was admitted at trial during Murray's testimony.

Longworth was found guilty of murdering Green and Hopps. He was sentenced to death for the murders and kidnapping, and 25-years for the armed robbery. Accomplice Rocheville was tried separately, also found guilty of the capital murder of Green, and on December 3, 1999, he was executed by lethal injection (*Longworth v. Ozmint* (2003) 302 F.Supp.2d 535; *State v. Longworth* (1993) 438 S.E.2d 219; *State v. Rocheville* (1993) 425 S.E.2d 32).

———

Douglas Alan Roberts, a 42-year-old white male, was executed by lethal injection at the Texas State Penitentiary in Huntsville, Texas on April 20, 2005. Roberts was found guilty of the 1996 murder of Jerry Lewis Velez, a 40-year-old Hispanic male. Roberts, who was 33-years old when he committed the capital crime, was sentenced to death on January 9, 1997.

On May 18, 1996, Roberts, while high on crack cocaine, abducted Jerry Velez at knifepoint outside his San Antonio, Texas apartment complex and forced Velez to drive out of the city on Interstate 10. In Kendall County Roberts instructed Velez to turn off on a desolate and rural road near the intersection of Highway 46 and stop the car. When Roberts demanded Velez's shirt Velez allegedly lunged at Roberts purportedly causing Roberts to stab him with a large bowie-like knife. In fleeing the scene Roberts ran over Velez's body with Velez's car. Within a few hours of the murder Roberts sobered up, called 9-1-1 in Austin, and confessed to the kidnapping and killing. Roberts waited for police who then charged him with the murder of Velez.

An autopsy determined that Velez was stabbed five times and that his ribs were fractured or broken, and his right lung was punctured. Velez also suffered "blunt trauma" to his brain. The Bexar County medical examiner stated the cause of Velez's death was a combination of the stab wounds and trauma.

The State appointed Roberts counsel to represent him in his capital trial. Roberts immediately instructed his trial counsel, Steven Pickell, to steer the trial towards the imposition of the death penalty. Although Pickell tried to discourage Roberts from this course of action, consistent with Roberts's instructions, Pickell chose jury members who favored the death penalty, did not interview family members before trial, called no witnesses during the guilt/innocence phase of the trial, called no witnesses during the punishment phase, did not request a jury instruction on parole laws, and made no argument in favor of a life sentence.

Pickell spent a total of 50 hours preparing for Roberts's trial, and so neither the conviction nor the punishment was contested in any meaningful way. Concerned that Roberts may not have been right of mind, Pickell requested, and Texas granted, $1000 funding for a psychiatrist, Dr. Michael Arambula, to analyze Roberts's mental state.

A short time prior to trial Arambula interviewed Roberts for two hours, and based on that interview, police reports about Roberts, and Velez's autopsy report, Arambula produced a psychiatric evaluation. In making this evaluation Arambula did not review any of Roberts's medical records including records relating to Roberts's psychiatric hospitalization that occurred after a recent "suicide ideation." Pickell did not collect these records and Arambula did not request them. Pickell also did not inform Arambula about a head injury that Roberts suffered as a child. Neither Pickell nor Arambula spoke to any of Roberts's family members or former treating physicians about his medical and psychiatric history.

Arambula's report noted that Roberts admitted he had previously "wanted to commit suicide," but that when asked, "Mr. Roberts denied any past psychiatric history, other than his addiction to crack cocaine," and denied that he currently had suicidal thoughts. It also noted that Roberts showed no signs of "anxiety, hallucinations, or delusions" and that "he denied that he felt sad." And finally it noted that Roberts explained that he "didn't want to be locked up the rest of his life" and that Roberts blamed his "crack cocaine addiction" for his "taking the life of an innocent bystander."

Based on these observations Arambula's stated in his report that "I cannot conclude that Mr. Roberts suffers from any significant degree of depression *** or for that matter any other psychiatric disturbance." He further stated, "the most salient issue in Douglas Roberts's history is his addiction to crack cocaine." And after first acknowledging that "depression can sometimes affect a person's judgment and decision-making so severely that [he] wish[es] for premature death," he concluded that "I cannot find that depression exists to such a degree that its presence would coerce Mr. Roberts into seeking the death penalty."

Based on Arambula's report and his own observations Pickell concluded that Roberts was competent to stand trial and to make decisions regarding trial strategy including decisions explicitly designed to ensure the imposition of the death penalty. He also concluded that it was unnecessary to request a competency hearing. The trial judge never saw Arambula's report but based on his own observations of Roberts decided that there was no reason to hold a competency hearing. Roberts was subsequently convicted and sentenced to death.

When the Supreme Court of the United States rejected Roberts's appeal, he asked his lawyers not to file last-minute actions to keep him alive. "Why go through the trouble for nothing?" he told *The Associated Press* a week before his execution. "The appeals have run their course through the system." He insisted he had no desire to die but saw his execution as a way to end the loneliness and isolation of death row, which he described as "23 hours a day in a cement box." "So if you've got to spend the rest of your life like this, and if you're like me and know the Lord, then today's a good day to go," he said (*Roberts v. Dretke* (2004) 356 F.3d 632; *Roberts v. Dretke* (2004) 381 F.3d 491).

———

Bill J. Benefiel, a 48-year-old white male, was executed by lethal injection at the Indiana State Prison in Michigan City, Indiana on April 21, 2005. Benefiel was found guilty of the 1987 murder of Delores Wells, a 19-year-old white female. Benefiel, who was 30-years old when he committed the capital crime, was sentenced to death on November 3, 1988.

At approximately 7:30 p.m. on October 10, 1986, Alicia Elmore, a 17-year-old white female, walked to a gas station two blocks from her home in Terre Haute, Indiana to purchase soft drinks for her mother and brother. Her family did not hear from her again for four months.

During those months Benefiel, a married man and father of three, tortured and raped Elmore repeatedly, 64 times, before she stopped counting. At various times Benefiel stuffed clothing or toilet paper in her mouth and put duct tape over her eyes and mouth. For the first two months Elmore's eyes were glued shut. He fastened her to a bed, naked, with a chain around her neck. At times he handcuffed her to the side railing of the bed and tied her feet together with a rope. When Elmore screamed he slapped her and cut her with a knife. Benefiel cut off one of her fingernails. He also cut off some of her hair and told her he was putting it in a scrapbook with hair samples from other women he had raped.

For the first months Elmore was fed only baked potatoes and water and was not allowed to use the bathroom without his permission. At one point he stuck a gun in her vagina and forced her to have anal intercourse.

Elmore was convinced escape was impossible because of his dogs, which she could hear from inside the house. All the while she was terrorized Benefiel asked her whether she wanted to die quickly or slowly. When Elmore said quickly he said her death would be long and painful.

Two months after being abducted Elmore began bleeding vaginally, and so Benefiel took off his mask, pried her eyes open, and took her to a distant hospital where they would not be recognized. Benefiel did not give Elmore a chance to tell doctors that she was his captive. Doctors advised her that she was pregnant and told her to refrain from intercourse. When Benefiel and Elmore returned he moved her to another house where he again chained her to the bed and left her eyes open so that she could see him.

About ten weeks into her captivity Elmore saw, for the first time, the house in which she was imprisoned. A few weeks later she was moved to another house across the street from the first one. In the second house Benefiel again chained Elmore to the bed and had sexual intercourse and oral sex with her. In this house she could hear the police scanner, which Benefiel used to determine which houses he could burglarize.

In January 1987 Elmore heard noises that indicated to her that someone else was in the house; it turned out to be Delores Wells. Elmore first saw Wells lying naked and handcuffed on a bed. She had tape over her eyes and paper towels stuffed in her mouth, which was then taped over.

On February 4 Benefiel began beating Wells while Elmore watched, first with his fist and then with an electrical cord. Another time he cut Wells's hair and cut off her finger. He also told her she would die slowly.

On February 7 Benefiel left the house, and when he returned he was muddy from the waist down. He told Elmore that he had been digging a grave that was big enough for two people—she assumed for Wells and her. That day Benefiel also made Elmore watch as he put super glue in Wells's nose and pinched it together. He then put toilet paper in her mouth and taped it shut. Wells began squirming trying to breathe. A little later Benefiel chained Elmore to her bed and left the house. When he returned about two hours later he told Elmore that he had killed Wells by tying her arms and legs to two separate trees and wrapping duct tape around her head until she died. To make sure she was dead he "popped" her neck. And then he buried her.

On February 11 based on information from an informant who communicated with Marilyn Benefiel, Benefiel's wife of 13 years, police went to Benefiel's house. Benefiel told Elmore police were coming, pushed her into a crawl space above the ceiling, and warned her not to make a sound. Police arrived with a search warrant. Benefiel first told them he did not know the person they were looking for but a few minutes later he told them where to find Elmore. When she was found, out of fear, she told police in Benefiel's presence that she was in the house voluntarily. Police took Elmore to the hospital afterwhich they arrested Benefiel.

Police found in Benefiel's van and in the four different houses he owned in the 300 block of South 13 1/2 Street in Terre Haute: a mask, a post-hole digger, a rake, a shovel, a knife, .22-caliber rifle shells, rope, and Wells's eyelash, eyebrow, and head hairs stuck to some duct tape.

Several days after his arrest Benefiel contacted a local police detective and offered to help him find Wells. A February 22 search of the woods surrounding Terre Haute revealed Wells's gravesite and her body. An autopsy of the body revealed internal and external injuries to the anus and injuries to the vagina indicating a violent rape. The cause of Wells's death was asphyxia. In the trash at Benefiel's home police found duct tape, which had hairs on it similar to the head, eyebrow, and eyelash hairs of Wells.

At trial the judge heard from Elmore, Wells's parents, and Wells's husband. All four testified that they did not want Benefiel to be sentenced to death. They wanted him to remain alive in prison and to have to confront daily what he had done. Death, in the words of Elmore, was the "easy way out" (*Benefiel v. Davis* (2004) 357 F.3d 655; *Benefiel v. State* (1991) 578 N.E.2d 338).

———

Donald Jones, a 38-year-old black male, was executed by lethal injection at the Eastern Reception Diagnostic and Correctional Center in Bonne Terre, Missouri on April 27, 2005. Jones was found guilty of the 1993 murder of Dorothy Knuckles, a 68-year-old black female. Jones, who was 26-years old when he committed the capital crime, was sentenced to death on June 18, 1994.

Around midnight on March 6, 1993, Jones went to his grandmother's house in St. Louis, Missouri to get some money to buy crack cocaine. When Jones arrived at the house, Dorothy Knuckles, his grandmother, let him in, and they went to her bedroom on the second floor where Jones asked her for money. Knuckles refused and then began lecturing Jones about his drinking and use of cocaine.

Jones went downstairs to the kitchen, picked up a butcher block that contained knives, hid it behind him, and went upstairs. His grandmother started lecturing him again and Jones hit her several times with the butcher block while she screamed. Jones apparently became afraid that the neighbors might hear her screaming, picked up a knife that had fallen out of the butcher block and stabbed her until she stopped screaming and fell back onto her bed. Jones took his grandmother's car keys, money, and VCR, and drove off in her car. Jones purchased some drugs, sold the VCR, and rented out the car to get money to buy drugs.

On March 8 Knuckles's son discovered her body. The next day police went to Jones's place of work to question him. Jones was not under arrest at that time and he agreed to follow police to the homicide office. After some conversations at the office Jones became a suspect and was informed of his *Miranda* rights. Jones then said, "It's the monster inside of me." He explained that the monster inside him was the crack cocaine that had caused him to kill his grandmother. He gave an audiotape statement on how he killed his grandmother.

Jones was charged by indictment with first-degree murder, first-degree robbery, and two counts of armed criminal action. The case went to trial on charges of first-degree murder and one count of armed criminal action. The jury returned guilty verdicts on both counts and recommended death for murder and life in prison for armed criminal action, which the court imposed. Governor Matt Blunt ignored a recommendation by the state's Board of Probation and Parole and denied Jones clemency, noting: "We have the death penalty because we believe as a society, we believe as a state and we believe as a people that some crimes are so horrific that the only appropriate punishment is the death penalty" (*State v. Jones* (1998) 979 S.W. 2d 171).

———

Mario Giovanni Centobie, a 39-year-old white male, was voluntarily executed by lethal injection at the Holman Prison in Atmore, Alabama on April 28, 2005. Centobie was found guilty of the 1998 murder of Keith Turner, a 29-year-old white male. Centobie, who was 32-years old when he committed the capital crime, was sentenced to death on May 14, 1999.

On June 25, 1998, Sheriff Maurice Hooks and retired Deputy Ray Butler of Jones County Mississippi were transporting Centobie and Jeremy Granberry, a 19-year-old white male, in a marked sheriff's car from Parchman Prison to court hearings in Laurel, some 250 miles away.[19]

On the trip Hooks stopped to allow the inmates to use a restroom in the small town of Richland where Centobie pulled Hooks's .45-caliber Ruger automatic pistol from his holster and forced Hooks and Butler at gunpoint to an isolated area where they were left unharmed, tied to poles, and found the next day. Centobie kept the Ruger as he and Granberry fled in the marked sheriff's car.

Several hours later in the evening hours of June 25 Captain Cecil Lancaster of the Tuscaloosa, Alabama Police Department was returning home after attending a meeting after work. Lancaster noticed Hooks's marked sheriff's car being driven by two individuals proceeding on I-359. The vehicle caught Lancaster's attention because it had no bumper or tag and as it passed neither occupant acknowledged him.

---

[19] Centobie began serving a 40-year sentence in 1996 for kidnapping his estranged wife, Cheryl, and 6-year-old son, Dominic. Granberry was serving a 6-year sentence for escape and burglary.

Lancaster pulled the vehicle over and as he approached it shots were fired by one of the occupants through the back driver's side window striking Lancaster twice. The bullets fired into Lancaster were consistent with having been fired from the .45-caliber Ruger belonging to Hooks. While Lancaster lay on the ground after being shot, the vehicle began to back up as if to run over him. Lancaster, however, managed to fire shots into the rear window of the vehicle, which then immediately fled the scene. After shooting Lancaster, Centobie and Granberry then abandoned the sheriff's patrol vehicle and stole a 1981 Mercury belonging to Brandon Blake from Marguerite's Lounge in Tuscaloosa.

At about 10:30 p.m. on June 27 Lori Mullins working Central Dispatch in Moody and 9-1-1 received a radio transmission from Officer Keith Turner who was on duty in a marked Moody patrol car that Turner had stopped Blake's Mercury.

Centobie told Granberry "I ain't going back to Parchman." As Centobie exited the Mercury he placed the Ruger against the back of the front seat and left the door open. Centobie then approached Turner, who asked Centobie, "Hey, what are y'all doing?" Centobie returned to the front seat of the Mercury under the guise of getting his license and registration.

Turner continued to approach the Mercury and when he was next to Centobie and the vehicle Granberry jumped out of the car. Centobie pulled the .45-caliber Ruger and shot Turner three times: one shot lodged in Turner's vest, one shot hit Turner in the hip area, and a third and fatal shot was fired directly into the back of Turner's head killing him instantly.

After fleeing the crime scene Centobie avoided an extensive manhunt for several days. On July 4 he kidnapped Daniel Alexander in the parking lot of a small store at about 9:30 p.m. while escaping the Moody area. After kidnapping Alexander Centobie forced him to drive to

Mobile, Alabama. Near the Alabama-Mississippi state line west of Mobile, Alexander escaped from Centobie and alerted law enforcement to Centobie's presence in the area. The next day Lieutenant Obie Wells found Centobie riding in a van on I-10 near Biloxi and arrested him. When arrested Centobie was still armed with Hooks's Ruger.

Centobie testified in his own behalf at trial and admitted to having committed all of the elements of the charged offense for which he was found guilty and sentenced to death by electrocution.[20] Centobie dropped his appeals, did not seek clemency, and did not choose how to be executed. Granberry pleaded guilty to Turner's murder and in July 2000 he was sentenced to life without parole (*Centobie v. State* (2001) 861 So.2d 1111).

———

Lonnie Wayne Pursley, a 43-year-old white male, was executed by lethal injection at the Texas State Penitentiary in Huntsville, Texas on May 3, 2005. Pursley was found guilty of the 1997 murder of Robert Earl Cook, a 47-year-old white male. Pursley, who was 35-years old when he committed the capital crime, was sentenced to death on January 20, 1999.

On the night of March 28, 1997, Robert Cook left work and drove down Highway 59 towards his trailer home near Livingston, Texas. Cook was on Highway 59 probably at about the same time that Pursley was walking down that highway having left his in-law's house in Shepherd on foot following an argument with his wife. Cook's niece and next-door neighbor, Sheila Dupree, testified that later that night she observed a large man smoking a cigarette in the doorway of Cook's trailer home. Dupree stated that Cook sat inside with an emotionless expression on his face and

---

[20] On July 1, 2002, the State of Alabama enacted law that allowed death row inmates to be executed by lethal injection unless they chose electrocution.

that she could tell from looking at him that something was wrong.

The following day Dupree noticed that the gate on Cook's property was not shut properly and that Cook's car was gone, and although Cook had plans to spend time with his mother that day, he never showed up. When Cook still had not returned home by the evening of the 30th his mother contacted police who began searching for Cook the next day. Upon learning that Cook was missing Dupree told police about the man that she had seen standing in Cook's doorway.

On the morning of the 29th and the following day several of Pursley's friends and relatives saw Pursley driving a turquoise car matching the description of Cook's vehicle. At least three of these witnesses noticed that the vehicle had blood on the inside and outside of it, and that Pursley had blood on his clothes. At least two witnesses later testified that Pursley had admitted to them that he had beaten someone and had left the victim to choke on his own blood.

Pursley's cousin, Richard Winfrey, testified that on the 30th Pursley told him that he was pretty sure he had beaten someone to death in his car. Pursley told Winfrey that he had hidden the victim's car in some woods located off of a dirt road and asked him for fake identification so that he could leave the country.

On April 6 a passer-by discovered Cook's decomposing body lying face down in a wooded area at the end of a dead-end dirt road approximately two and one-half miles from Cook's home. Trauma to the body indicated that Cook had been pummeled brutally in the chest and abdomen with the assailant's hands, feet, or with some other unknown object.

On April 15 police discovered Cook's car abandoned in a wooded area. There was a large amount of blood spattered throughout the vehicle, but the only DNA evidence that linked Pursley to the crime was found on a

81

cigarette butt in the ashtray of Cook's vehicle and which was discovered 18 months after the car was originally located by police

On August 7 Pursley was arrested and charged by indictment for the murder and robbery of Cook. Two years later a Polk County jury found him guilty for which he was sentenced to death. Pursley had prior convictions for burglary of a habitation, theft by appropriation, and unauthorized use of a motor vehicle and he was out on parole when he committed the capital crime. On January 31, 2001, the Texas Court of Criminal Appeals affirmed his conviction and sentence (*Pursley v. Dretke* (5th Cir. 2004) No. 03-41487).

———

Earl J. Richmond Jr., a 38-year-old black male, was executed by lethal injection at the Central Prison in Raleigh, North Carolina on May 6, 2005. Richmond was found guilty of the 1991 murder of Helisa Stewart Hayes, a 27-year-old black female, Philip Hayes, an 8-year-old black male, and Darien Hayes, a 7-year-old black female. Richmond, who was 29-years old when he committed the capital crime, was sentenced to death on June 1, 1995.

Richmond was a close friend of Helisa Hayes's ex-husband, Wayne Hayes. In the early morning hours of November 2, 1991, Richmond went to the Sunshine Mobile Home Park in Fayetteville, North Carolina, where Helisa and her children, Philip and Darien, resided. While there, Richmond and Helisa allegedly engaged in consensual intercourse afterwhich an argument ensued.

During the argument, after supposedly being struck with an object by Helisa, Richmond grabbed and carried Helisa into her bedroom. Richmond then struck Helisa in the face with his fist and proceeded to engage in "forceful" intercourse with her. After having "forceful" intercourse Richmond strangled Helisa to death with his hands and poured rubbing alcohol over her vaginal area.

Richmond then grabbed Phillip, who was laying down in the hallway outside of his mother's bedroom, carried him into the bathroom, stabbed him approximately 40 times with scissors, and wrapped an electrical cord five times around his neck. After killing Phillip, Richmond went into Darien's bedroom where she was sleeping, and strangled her to death with the cord from a curling iron.

On November 4 Helisa's father, William Stewart, discovered the bodies of his daughter and two grandchildren after having not heard from Helisa for two days. Having become concerned about Helisa's safety he broke into her home.

The medical examiner performed an autopsy and determined Helisa died as a result of strangulation. She had numerous blunt-force injuries—tears, scrapes, and bruises. There was abrading of the skin in the entrance to her vagina and blood over a portion of her brain beneath a bruise on her scalp. DNA evidence showed Richmond's semen in Helisa.

Richmond was convicted of murdering the three members of the Hayes family. Prior to the commencement of trial the court ruled that the State would be allowed to introduce evidence about Richmond's prior murder conviction[21] as an aggravating factor during the penalty phase. The jury also learned that Richmond had attended the funeral of his victims and had served as a pallbearer for one of the children, one witness testitifying that Richmond had said that carrying the body of a victim he had killed "never gave [him] a bad feeling." On May 5, 2005, the Supreme Court of the United States unanimously denied a

---

[21] While awaiting trial for the Hayes family murders Richmond was charged in the United States District Court for the District of New Jersey with the April 4, 1991, first-degree murder of Lisa Ann Nadeau, 24, an army dispersing clerk at the Fort Dix military base. On May 28, 1993, Richmond was convicted and subsequently sentenced to life imprisonment.

stay of execution, and Governor Michael F. Easley denied clemency (*Richmond v. North Carolina* (2005) 544 U.S. 1028; *Richmond v. Polk* (2004) 375 F.3d 309; *State v. Richmond* (1998) 347 N.C. 412).

————

George James Miller Jr., a 37-year-old black male, was executed by lethal injection at the Oklahoma State Penitentiary in McAlester, Oklahoma on May 12, 2005. Miller was found guilty of the 1994 murder of Kent Dodd, a 25-year-old white male. Miller, who was 27-years old when he committed the capital crime, was sentenced to death on October 31, 1996.

Kent Dodd worked as the night auditor for the Central Plaza Hotel located at the intersection of I-40 and Martin Luther King Drive in Oklahoma City, Oklahoma. At approximately 3:15 a.m. on September 17, 1994, Dodd registered a guest, and shortly thereafter an assailant attacked Dodd, stabbing him repeatedly, beating him with hedge shears and a paint can, and pouring muriatic acid (hydrochloric acid) on him and down his throat.

Two and one-half hours later a housekeeper arrived for the morning shift, called for Dodd, and when she saw he was not at the front desk heard "animal moans" coming from the unused restaurant area of the hotel. She ran to a nearby restaurant and summoned police. Dodd was still alive when police found him.

Dodd was able to respond to police questioning but most of his responses were unintelligible because of the acid burns in his mouth and throat. Police were able to understand him say his attacker was a black man who wore gray pants. Dodd died later that day at the hospital from blunt force trauma to his head.

Miller had worked as a maintenance man at the Central Plaza Hotel for two weeks about a month before the murder. Dodd knew Miller, but knew him as Jay Elkins. Photographs of the crime scene revealed what appears to be finger writing in the blood on the floor and wall that could be the letter "J" and the word, "Jay." Shortly after the murder Miller and his wife split up and he went to stay with his mother in Sherman, Texas. When charges were filed against him Miller was serving a federal sentence at Leavenworth, Kansas and so he was returned to Oklahoma pursuant to the Interstate Agreement on Detainers Act (IADA).[22]

The evidence against Miller was circumstantial. Miller's sandals could have left the bloody footprints found at the scene,[23] and a microscopic drop of blood found on Miller's

---

[22] The *IADA* provides that "whenever during the continuance of the term of imprisonment there is pending in any other party State any untried indictment, information, or complaint on the basis of which a detainer has been lodged against the prisoner, he shall be brought to trial within one hundred and eighty days after he shall have caused to be delivered to the prosecuting officer and the appropriate court of the prosecuting officer's jurisdiction written notice of the place of his imprisonment and his request for a final disposition to be made of the indictment, information, or complaint."

[23] FBI criminalist Sarah Wiersema explained that while the size and "interlocking dog bone" pattern of the sole was "consistent" with the footprints found at the scene, Miller's sandal could not be identified conclusively as the source of the print for no unique flaws in the sole of the sandal were present in the footprint. Wiersema explained that blood is an imperfect medium for the forensic identification of footprints as it fills in the very flaws used for exclusive identification. Wiersema also created an acetate overlay of a lifesize imprint of the sole of Miller's sandal that matched in size and shape when placed over a life size photograph of a bloody shoe print found at the scene of the crime.

sandal was consistent with Dodd's blood although it could not be exclusively identified as coming from Dodd.[24]

Miller told police he was home with his wife at the time of the murder, but she testified that he was not home and had taken her car keys from the place where she hid them under the mattress and had left. The next day she found sand in the car. She also testified she did the family laundry and after the murder a pair of Miller's khaki shorts and a silk shirt disappeared. She identified two buttons found at the crime scene as consistent with buttons on the missing shirt.

The night before the murder Miller was broke and tried unsuccessfully to borrow money from several different friends. According to Miller at approximately 10:00 p.m. on September 16 Miller, Chris Carriger, and Jeremy Collman, went to the Central Plaza Hotel to cash a check written by Carriger to Miller; the visit lasted about five minutes. Miller claimed that he was then taken back to his apartment where he remained until mid-morning the following day. After trying to cash the check at other locations Carriger returned home and asked his wife, Stephanie, to write a check to Miller for $75, and she complied.

The next day Miller cashed the check from Carriger during the bank's business hours, and on the morning after the murder, Miller gave his wife $120. When police questioned him he claimed he had cashed a paycheck, and when reminded that he was not working at the time, Miller denied he gave his wife any money.

The hotel cash drawer was open and empty when police investigated the crime scene. Hotel policy requires each shift to begin with $250 in the drawer. At the end of the shift the desk clerk places any excess money in a

---

[24] Dr. Moses Schanfield testified that DNA could not be used to exclusively identify Dodd as the donor since it could have come from 1 in 19 Caucasians, 1 in 16 African-Americans, or 1 in 55 Hispanics.

deposit envelope and drops it into the hotel safe and only desk clerks knew the amount of cash in the drawer.

Dodd was an exemplary employee who followed accounting procedures carefully and whose money count was always correct. After the murder the hotel manager discovered a deposit envelope containing $100 hidden behind registration forms in a separate drawer. The next day Miller told a friend that robbery could not have been the motive for the killing because only $150 was kept in the cash drawer. Evidence at trial showed that Dodd's wallet as well as $10 given to him by the manager was missing along with $122.01 from the motel cash drawer. Before he died Dodd told police, and two officers heard him say three or four times, "He robbed me."

A jury found Miller guilty of first-degree murder. At the capital sentencing proceeding the jury found four aggravating factors: Miller had a prior violent felony conviction for first-degree burglary in 1988, and pointing a firearm in 1992; Dodd's murder was especially heinous, atrocious, or cruel; Miller had killed Dodd to avoid arrest or prosecution for the robbery; and Miller was a continuing threat to society (*Miller v. State* (1998) 977 P.2d 1099; *Miller v. Mullin* (2004) 354 F.3d 1288).

———

Michael Bruce Ross, a 45-year-old white male, was voluntarily executed by lethal injection at the Osborn Correctional Institution in Somers, Connecticut on May 12, 2005. Ross was found guilty of the 1983 murder of Robyn Dawn Stavinsky, a 19-year-old white female, and the 1984 murder of three white females: April Brunais, 14, Leslie Shelley, 14, and Wendy Baribeault, 17. Ross, who was 24-years old when he committed the 1983 capital crime, was sentenced to death on July 1, 1987, and again on May 15, 2000.

On Thanksgiving Day 1983 Ross, a graduate of New York's Cornell University, accosted Robyn Stavinsky on the grounds of Uncas on Thames State Hospital in Norwich, Connecticut. He forcefully pulled Stavinsky into a wooded area and ordered her to remove her clothing. He then sexually assaulted her and, after ordering her to turn over on her stomach, strangled her. Before leaving he covered her body with leaves.

On Easter Sunday 1984 Ross picked up two hitchhikers—April Brunais and Leslie Shelley en route from Griswold, Connecticut. Once the girls had entered his car Ross drove them easterly on Route 165 and, over their protests, past their intended destination. When Brunais tried to force Ross to stop the car by threatening him with a knife he disarmed her and continued to transport the girls against their will through eastern Connecticut to the 430-acre Beach Pond State Park in Rhode Island.

At Beach Pond, Ross parked his car and bound both girls' hands and feet. He then untied Brunais's feet and forced her to walk a short distance from his car where he assaulted her sexually, turned her over on her stomach, and strangled her. Returning to the car Ross killed Shelley without sexually assaulting her. He then placed the bodies of both girls in his car and drove back to Preston, Connecticut where he deposited their bodies in a culvert.

On June 13, 1984, Ross accosted Wendy Baribeault as she was walking along Route 12 in Lisbon, Connecticut. After a short conversation he pulled her over a stone wall forcing her to go with him into a wooded area that led to an open field. There he sexually assaulted her, forced her to turn over on her stomach, and then strangled her.

In 1985 Ross was captured, and during his interrogation confessed to eight murders.[25] In 1987 Ross

---

[25] In addition to the Stavinsky, Brunais, Shelley, and Baribeault murders, Ross also admitted to murdering Dzung Ngoc Tu, 25, a Cornell University student, on May 12, 1981; Tammy Williams, 17, of Brooklyn, Connecticut (Ross's hometown) on Jan. 5, 1982; Paula Perrera, 16, of Wallkill, New

was tried for the 1983 murder and the three 1984 murders. He was convicted and sentenced to death in the Superior Court, Judicial District of New London. At trial the State's psychiatric expert, Dr. Robert Miller, testified that a serial killer like Ross was a sexual sadist but not legally insane. Miller further testified that sexual sadists, and by implication Ross, are capable of controlling their behavior, but later recanted in a letter.[26]

Because the trial judge did not allow Miller's letter into evidence, a new jury was reconvened for the penalty phase and 13 years later Ross was resentenced to death. Ross then dismissed his public defender and began representing himself with the explicit goal of being put to death. Ross waived his final appeals and because Ross did not request clemency, the Connecticut Board of Pardons and Paroles was unable to grant clemency (*State v. Ross* (2004) 849 A.2d 648).

York in March 1, 1982; and Debra Smith Taylor, 23, of Griswold, Connecticut on June 15, 1982.

On August 17, 2001, Ross was arraigned in New York for the Perrera murder, on September 21 he pleaded guilty to first-degree manslaughter, and on October 23 he was sentenced to 81/3 to 25 years.

[26] It was later discovered Miller had previously written a letter to the prosecutor in which he expressed his doubts about "how [he] could testify against psychopathology playing a sufficient role in [the] defendant's behavior to mitigate the type of penalty" and that "if it had been only one or two incidents I could have held up, but the repetitive nature of the acts as well as past history of assaultive behavior make my (our) position untenable."

Miller ultimately had concluded that he could not testify that Ross did not suffer from some psychopathology that impaired his ability to control his conduct, he continued to believe that sexual sadists—and by implication Ross—are not incapable of controlling their conduct.

Vernon Brown, a 51-year-old black male, was executed by lethal injection at the Eastern Reception Diagnostic and Correctional Center in Bonne Terre, Missouri on May 17, 2005. Brown was found guilty of the 1985 murder of Synetta Ford, a 19-year-old black female, and the 1986 murder of Janet Perkins, a 9-year-old black female. Brown, who was 33-years old when he committed the Perkins murder, was sentenced to death on December 12, 1988. In 1991 he was sentenced to death for the Ford murder.

Around 3:00 p.m. on October 24, 1986, Janet Perkins left the Cole School in north St. Louis, Missouri and walked toward her home three and a half blocks away. She generally took the same route each day walking west on Enright Avenue. Under normal circumstances the trip took less than 15 minutes.

Brown, who was then using the name Thomas Turner, had picked up his stepsons, Tommy Johnson and Jason Moore, from Cole School and returned to their home on Enright Avenue in time to see Perkins walking past. Brown called to her and ultimately enticed her to enter the house.

Brown's two stepsons saw Perkins enter the house. A neighbor's relative saw Brown on the front porch and Perkins walking up the steps to the house. Brown ordered his stepsons to their bedroom and locked the door from the outside. Brown claimed that he then began suffering PCP-induced blackouts.

Brown's own statements, the testimony of his stepsons, and the physical evidence showed that he took Perkins to the basement of the house, and bound her feet and one hand with a wire coat hanger, forcing her into a crouched position that permitted her head to reach the height of Brown's genitalia. Brown then strangled Perkins to death with a rope.

The next day law enforcement authorities found Perkins's body in two trash bags near a dumpster in an alley behind Brown's house. On October 27 police arrested

Brown and confronted him with their evidence including testimony of a neighbor who had seen Perkins enter Brown's house. Police asked Brown to tell them where to find Perkins' missing shoe, raincoat, and school papers. Brown led police to a different dumpster in which they found a bag containing the girl's missing property.

On October 29 Brown made a videotaped statement implicating himself as Perkins's killer after which he also admitted killing Synetta Ford who had been murdered on March 7, 1985. An autopsy indicated that Ford died from strangulation and had been stabbed twice, once in the chest and once in the neck.

In 1985 Brown and his wife, Kathy Moore, lived in an apartment at 3435 Washington in the City of St. Louis. Brown worked in that apartment complex as a maintenance worker, and he also worked next door at the Grand Cafe on Washington as a dishwasher. After February 13 Brown and his wife moved to 4028 Enright. A few days later Ford, moved into a basement apartment of the building at 3435 Washington.

On February 23 or February 24, Brown, Ford, her roommate, Alesia Brown, and Earl Bedford played cards together in Ford's apartment. Bedford testified that Brown flirted with Ford but she appeared not to be interested.

On February 28 Alesia checked into a hospital for about 10 days because she was pregnant. Prior to her admission into the hospital Alesia had discussed with Brown the possibility of him working on their apartment rug and vent. Brown went to the apartment twice to take up the rug but Ford told him to wait until Alesia came back from the hospital.

On March 5 Ford called her friend, Vickie Noland, and speaking very fast, asked Noland to "come get me now." Ford told Noland that she was afraid because she came home and found Brown on the stairway near the entrance of her apartment. Noland picked Ford up at about 2:35 p.m. and she spent the night with Noland. The last time that Noland saw Ford was when she left for work on the morning shift at Victor Foods at about 4:30 a.m. the next morning.

Anthony Brown, Alesia's brother, worked with Ford at Victor Foods. Anthony testified that he last saw Ford on Wednesday, March 6 between 3:30 p.m. and 3:45 p.m. at Victor Foods adding that he had spent the night with Ford on Tuesday night at her apartment, and she had told him about her encounter with the maintenance person.

At about 4:00 p.m. on March 8 Bedford picked up Alesia from the hospital. When they arrived at Alesia and Ford's apartment, she unlocked the front door. When they arrived at the door that led to the apartment they found out that the door was shattered from the frame. Upon entering the apartment they observed Ford's body on the floor with a cord around her neck and a knife in her throat. They ran out and called police.

After they returned to the front of the apartment building, people, including Brown, began to gather. Brown asked Alesia what happened and she replied that she found her roommate dead. Brown appeared surprised and was interviewed by police at the crime scene. Brown told police that he moved out of the apartment building where Ford lived three weeks earlier but that he still received mail there. Brown alleged that he stopped by to pick up some mail at about 10:15 a.m. on March 7 and he heard Ford arguing with a Cuban man.

Brown gave police a description of the purported Cuban man, and when he arrived home he told his wife that Ford had been found dead. Initially his wife was in disbelief. Brown later told her that he killed Ford. Brown's wife testified that Brown told her that he and Ford got into a fight over money and that Ford threatened to tell that they were having an affair. After Ford left the apartment Brown went inside and hid in the bathroom. Ford returned and changed into her nightclothes whereupon Brown came up behind her and wrapped a cord around her neck.

92

According to Brown they got into a scuffle over a knife, and he took the knife away from Ford and stabbed her in the neck with it. Brown then kicked in the door to make it look like someone broke into the apartment.

Police interviewed Brown on March 9, 22, and 26, afterwhich he told his wife that he was tired of police bothering him about Ford's murder. On the 28th Brown packed his clothes and left town. He told his wife to tell police that three men dressed in black and carrying guns in a red Pinto had abducted him. On April 1 Brown's wife told police the story when they came looking for Brown. The following day Brown's wife told them that the story about the abduction was not true and that she wanted to be a secret witness because she was afraid of Brown. She told police that Brown told her that he killed Ford and described how he had killed her.

On April 24 Brown was arrested pursuant to a warrant and taken to the police station where he was given his *Miranda* rights. Brown told them the abduction story. Police told him that they did not believe him because his wife had told them the truth.

On October 29, 1986, Brown finally confessed to the murder of Ford stating that around 10:00 a.m. on March 7, 1985, he left home and headed for his place of work at the Grand Cafe. According to Brown he arrived at work and told the cook that he was not feeling well. The cook told him that he could go home but instead Brown went to the basement apartment at 3534 Washington and saw Ford standing in the door way to her apartment. Ford asked him what he was doing there to which he replied, "I'm getting a pair of gloves." As he walked up the stairs Ford attacked him with a butcher knife.

They began to tussle and ended up in the apartment. As Ford swung the knife at him she accidentally stabbed herself in the chest. As he tried to leave she removed the knife from her chest and attacked him the second time at which point he grabbed an electric curling iron, wrapped its

93

cord around her neck several times, and tied a knot in the cord. They wrestled falling to the ground and in their struggle Ford stabbed herself in the throat with the knife. He got up and left Ford's apartment. When he reached the top of the steps he realized that he had left his keys inside her apartment. Brown kicked in the door, went back inside the apartment, got his keys, and left.

On November 18 Brown was indicted on two counts of first-degree murder for the deaths of Perkins and Ford. Brown's counsel successfully moved to sever the trials on the two murders. In 1988 Brown was convicted of Perkins's murder and sentenced to death, and in 1991 Brown was convicted of Ford's murder and again sentenced to death. The Missouri Board of Probation and Parole recommended against clemency, as did Governor Matt Blunt (*State v. Brown* (1995) 902 S.W.2d 278; *State v. Brown* (1999) 998 S.W.2d 531).

———

Bryan Eric Wolfe, a 44-year-old black male, was executed by lethal injection at the Texas State Penitentiary in Huntsville, Texas on May 18, 2005. Wolfe was found guilty of the 1992 murder of Bertha Lemell, an 84-year-old black female. Wolfe, who was 31-years old when he committed the capital crime, was sentenced to death on October 25, 1993.

On February 15, 1992, Bertha Lemell's friend, Brenda Vallian, had taken Lemell shopping and recalled seeing a little over $40 in cash in Lemell's wallet after she had made a purchase. Later that same day Lemell was found stabbed to death in her Beaumont, Texas home. According to the medical examiner Lemell had 26 stab wounds to the head, trunk, and abdomen. A change purse and some scattered coins amidst a few black-eyed peas that Lemell kept in her purse for good luck were near the body.

Wolfe, who had served prison time for armed robbery, once in Kansas in 1985 and once in Louisiana in 1990, lived in the same neighborhood as Lemell. She and Wolfe's wife were close friends and Lemell had babysat for Wolfe's children. Shortly before and after the murder Wolfe was seen within a few blocks of the crime scene and on February 17 he was arrested. In custody Wolfe had deep cuts on his right hand fingers that he said he had gotten from a broken beer bottle.

DNA tests using the so-called RFLP testing method were made on a bloody towel found in Lemell's home and on scrapings found outside Lemell's front door and compared those test results found in DNA samples from Wolfe. First, the banding patterns from the bloody towel matched Wolfe's DNA and showed that the odds of another African-American having the same banding patterns were 1 in 1,170,000. Second, the banding patterns from the scrapings on the door also matched Wolfe's DNA and showed that the odds of another African-American having the same banding patterns were 1 in 16,000,000.

On March 12 a Jefferson County grand jury indicted Wolfe for capital murder. On October 21, 1993, the jury found Wolfe guilty and four days later he was sentenced to death. After his conviction Wolfe requested additional DNA testing. The results of the newer PCR/STR tests also matched Wolfe's DNA. The tests on samples from the bathroom floor, bathtub, and a bedroom towel indicated that the odds of another African-American matching the DNA pattern were 1 in 1,200,000,000,000,000,000. The samples from the doorknob scrapings, the bathroom counter, and a bathroom towel, resulted in odds of another match at 1 in 415,000,000,000,000 African-Americans. And the DNA samples from a black coin purse found on Lemell resulted in odds of 1 in 1,200,000,000,000,000,000. On March 6, 1996, the Texas Court of Criminal Appeals affirmed Wolfe's conviction and sentence (*Wolfe v. State*

(5th Cir. 2003) No. 03-41626; *Wolfe v. State* (1996) 917 S.W.2d 270).

———

Richard Cartwright, a 31-year-old white male, was executed by lethal injection at the Texas State Penitentiary in Huntsville, Texas on May 19, 2005. Cartwright was found guilty of the 1996 murder of Nick Moraida, a 37-year-old Hispanic male. Cartwright, who was 22-years old when he committed the capital crime, was sentenced to death on March 21, 1997.

Cartwright, and two other white males, Dennis Hagood, 19, and Kelly Overstreet, 18, made plans to rob a gay man in the waterfront area of Corpus Christi, Texas by posing as homosexuals. Hagood and Overstreet knew each other for several years when in July 1996, Cartwright, who was six foot two inches tall and born and raised in Chicago, Illinois, met up with them.

On the night of August 1, 1996, Nick Moraida drove up to a remote gulfside park where he was lured away by Cartwright, Hagood, and Overstreet to go drink some beer. When the trio tried to rob Moraida, he resisted and Overstreet cut his throat with a knife. Cartwright then shot Moraida in the back with a .38-caliber pistol as Hagood searched Moraida's car. The three assailants then left with Moraida's wallet, watch, and money, estimated at between $60 and $200, to go buy marijuana. The following day Moraida's body washed up on the beach in the 100 block of Ocean Way.

Cartwright blamed Overstreet for the murder. A year later at trial the medical examiner testified the knife wound was not fatal and the gunshot wound was the cause of Moraida's death. The gun, owned by Hagood and Overstreet, was never found, and Cartwright, who had been sentenced in 1990 to two years probation for the felony offense of unlawful possession of a controlled substance, was convicted of the Moraida murder. The

Texas Board of Pardons and Paroles voted 7-0 against Cartwright's clemency plea. Hagood and Overstreet testified against Cartwright as part of a plea agreement in which Hagood was sentenced to 20 years for robbery and Overstreet was sentenced to 50 years for murder (*Cartwright v. Dretke* (5th Cir. 2004) No. 03-41626; *Cartwright v. State* (1999) No. 72,786).

———

Gregory Scott Johnson, a 40-year-old white male, was executed by lethal injection at the Indiana State Prison in Michigan City, Indiana on May 25, 2005. Johnson was found guilty of the 1985 murder of Ruby Hutslar, an 82-year-old white female. Johnson, who was 20-years old when he committed the capital crime, was sentenced to death on June 19, 1986.

At around 6 a.m. on June 23, 1985, a boy delivering morning papers in Anderson, Indiana passed Ruby Hutslar's house and saw smoke coming out from under the eaves of the roof. Alarmed, he roused a neighbor and reported the smoke. The boy and two passersby attempted to enter the house but found the main front door locked. They then broke open a front window of the house but were unable to enter. Going to the back of the house they found the back door open but were still unable to enter because of the heat and smoke. They observed that a basement window was unscrewed, broken, and removed.

At 6:30 a.m. firefighters arrived and observed one pane of glass in the front door broken but because of the intense heat they were unable to reach in to attempt to unlock the door. A fully equipped firefighter finally broke open the front door and entered the living room. He crawled in and found Hutslar on the floor, six feet from the front door. She was carried out of the house, but efforts to resuscitate her at the scene and later at the hospital were not successful. An autopsy revealed the cause of death as blunt force injuries to the head, neck and chest, and not smoke inhalation or burning.

The fire, which had started in the center of the house and had climbed a stairway and concentrated in the attic, was put out in about one-half hour. A closet and the stairway on the first floor burned but the rest of the first floor and its contents suffered mostly smoke and heat damage. The house was in disarray. It was observed that the drawers in the furniture had been pulled out and some dumped out. Some small boxes and containers had also been opened and their contents dumped out. The contents of a clothes closet were scattered about and the mattress had been removed from a bed. An investigation into the cause of the fire resulted in the opinion that the fire had been intentionally set.

At approximately 6:40 a.m. a police radio broadcast instructed officers to be on the lookout for Johnson because he was already suspected of setting several fires in the general area of the Hutslar residence. Within minutes Johnson was seen by Detective Miller to be standing on the street along with others watching the fighting of the Hutslar fire.

Miller knew Johnson, who appeared to be dirty and in disarray. Miller approached Johnson, spoke to him, and observed that his eyes were bloodshot, his breath smelled of alcohol, and he was unsteady on his feet, nervous, and anxious. Another onlooker testified that Johnson was sweaty and had approached and stood very close behind him. When the onlooker moved sideways, Johnson did also, so as to stand close behind him again. Miller placed Johnson under arrest for public intoxication.

Johnson made statements at the scene. Miller testified that after being arrested, Johnson was searched, placed in a squad car and read his *Miranda* rights for the first time. Johnson became agitated and cursed and said he understood his rights. Miller testified that in his opinion Johnson was then intoxicated from a slight to moderate extent. Johnson and his girlfriend testified at a hearing on suppression of statements that Johnson was an alcoholic who drank heavily each day, and that during the 12-hour period preceding his arrest he ingested huge quantities of alcohol and a variety of drugs.[27]

Within 10 minutes of the arrest Officer Adams arrived on the scene. Adams testified that Johnson was then in the squad car, in cuffs, and was kicking hard on the inside. Adams went over and asked what was wrong, and saw that Johnson appeared "somewhat" impaired by alcohol or drugs. He said "something about him not having a chance and about his upbringing," and "Wisehart did not kill the bitch, I did." Adams then asked, "Did you Scott?", whereupon Johnson replied, "No, but if that's the way you fuckers want to play." The statement referred to unrelated prior events in which Johnson had provided testimony for the prosecution at the trial of his friend Mark Allen Wisehart, for the murder of another woman.

Johnson was transported to the stationhouse where at 8:20 a.m. he was read his *Miranda* rights for the second time—this time by Captain Hanlon. Before questioning, Johnson signed a written acknowledgement and waiver of his rights. He then denied involvement in the Hutslar fire, but gave four written statements, confessing to having set or having attempted to set four fires in the area in recent times. At the time of the written rights waiver Johnson smelled strongly of alcohol, his eyes were a little bloodshot, and he manifested anger. Periodically Johnson was left

---

[27] A pharmacologist testified for Johnson that it was not possible to accurately predict the effect of the ingestion of the substances as described by Johnson, but that a person who had done so would suffer loss of muscle coordination and that Johnson would have had a blood-alcohol level of 0.15 percent (legally intoxicated for all bodyweights) at the time of his arrest and 0.10 percent (impaired reasoning, reflexes, and depth perception) at 8:20 a.m. when he signed a waiver of rights form.

alone during the interrogation and would sleep for a while. During the morning he was told that Hutslar had died. At noon he vomited. He received food, drinks, and cigarettes. He did not appear exhausted, and continued sobering up as the day went on.

At 3:30 p.m. Hanlon commenced an interrogation regarding the Hutslar fire by asking if that fire was not an attempt on Johnson's part to join Wisehart, who was then in prison and awaiting execution as the result of a conviction based upon Johnson's testimony.[28] Johnson responded by first placing his head in his hands and becoming emotional and then admitting breaking into the Hutslar house.

A fully incriminating statement was completed at 5:45 p.m. wherein Johnson stated that he broke the glass in the pane on the front door, entered, and immediately encountered Hutslar who collapsed on the floor breathing heavily. He then searched out and took a watch and silver dollars, and in checking out some noises outside, stepped on her cheek and neck twice. He then found some matches, started the fire, and ran out the back door. He threw away the watch and coins and then joined those watching the firefighters at the house, at which point he was arrested.

Johnson's death sentence was supported by the aggravating circumstance that the Hutslar murder was done intentionally while committing burglary and arson. The Indiana Parole Board recommended against clemency by a vote of 4-0, afterwhich Governor Mitch Daniels denied

---

[28] Mark Allen Wisehart has been on Indiana's death row since sentenced on September 26, 1983. On May 10, 2005, the Seventh Circuit Court of Appeals ruled that Wisehart should be released, retried, or given a further post conviction hearing addressing the issue of jury bias based upon a juror affidavit that the juror had been made aware outside the courtroom that Wisehart had been given a polygraph test.

clemency (*Johnson v. State* (1992) 584 N.E.2d 1092; *Johnson v. State* (1998) 693 N.E.2d 941).

———

Jerry Paul Henderson, a 58-year-old white male, was executed by lethal injection at the Holman Prison in Atmore, Alabama on June 2, 2005. Henderson was found guilty of 1984 murder of Jerry Wayne Haney, a 33-year-old white male. Henderson, who was 37-years old when he committed the capital crime, was sentenced to death in 1988.

Late in December 1983 Judy M. Haney, a 31-year-old white female, and her children fled their home in Talladega County, Alabama allegedly to escape the abusive environment that Judy's husband, Jerry Haney, had created. Judy and her children went to stay at the home of Jerry and Martha Henderson in Calhoun, Georgia. Martha and Judy were sisters.

Shortly after Judy's arrival in Georgia she and Henderson began discussing a plan pursuant to which Judy would pay Henderson $3000 in exchange for the murder of her husband. Henderson agreed to the proposed scheme in which it was decided that Jerry would be murdered on New Year's Day.

On January 1, 1984, Henderson went to the home of Michael Wayne Wright, an old friend and hunting partner, to ask Wright if he had any shotgun shells he could give him. Wright replied that he did not, but that his friend Robert Lewis probably did and so they went to Lewis's home where his wife Wanda gave them a number of shotgun shells.

Later that night Henderson and his wife were entertaining friends when Henderson complained of having the flu and retired to his bedroom. Once there he turned out the light and let himself out of the window and got into his pickup truck and drove to Alabama.

Following Judy's directions Henderson parked his truck in a wooded area adjacent to the Haney home and then walked through the woods and up to the front door of the house. Henderson put his loaded shotgun down on the porch and knocked on the door. Jerry, who was in bed, heard the knocking and went to the door. Henderson told him that he had brought Judy and the children back to Alabama, but that the truck had run out of gas and they were sitting on the side of the road and so Jerry agreed to help Henderson get some gas.

Jerry changed his clothes and came outside locking the front door behind him at which time Henderson fired a first shot hitting him in the chest. The blast knocked Jerry to the ground and while he was on the ground, Henderson shot him again, this time grazing his ear. After the second shot Jerry got to his feet and ran around to the back of his house collapsing on the back porch steps and begging for his life. Henderson placed the shotgun on Jerry's bottom lip and fired the third and final shot.

Henderson then rolled Jerry onto his stomach and took his wallet out of his back pocket. On the way back to his pickup truck he broke the light on the front porch. At approximately 11:00 p.m. Henderson stopped in Oxford, Alabama and called his wife and Judy from a Waffle House restaurant to tell them that Jerry was dead. When Henderson arrived back home he took approximately $100 out of the wallet and Judy took her husband's Social Security card. Judy paid Henderson about $30 for his expenses on the trip and kept the remainder of the cash. The wallet was later destroyed. The shotgun was thrown into the river and never recovered.

On January 2 Judy contacted her brother-in-law, Lieutenant Billy Haney of the Talladega Police Department, and requested that he go check on her husband because she had been trying to call him but had been unable to get an answer. The lieutenant went to the residence where he discovered his brother's body.

Jerry's body was taken to the Department of Forensic Sciences for an autopsy. The autopsy showed one shotgun wound to the left lower arm that penetrated the arm and entered the left chest, a wound that grazed the left ear, and a wound to the mouth that caused it to be torn at the corners. This later wound killed Jerry, fracturing almost every bone in his skull, fracturing his first two cervical vertebrae, and driving a tooth into his spinal cord.

When the murder investigation officially commenced Henderson was already the key suspect. On January 30 Henderson reported to police that his pickup truck had been broken into and his shotgun had been stolen, but the circumstances surrounding the alleged theft were very suspicious. For the next three years the authorities searched for clues and finally in the fall of 1987 Martha Henderson agreed to turn State's evidence.

On September 9, 1987, law enforcement officials placed a "Nagra unit" (sound recording device) in the back seat of Martha's car to tape-record conversations between her and her husband. That night the Hendersons got together and talked about the murder while sitting in Martha's car and every word was tape-recorded.

Henderson was arrested three days later in Rome, Georgia for capital murder. Very early the next morning he confessed to the Haney murder while inside Georgia's Floyd County jail. Henderson's entire confession was tape-recorded.

Henderson was convicted of murder for hire and murder during the course of a robbery in the Circuit Court of Talladega County. The jury voted 10-2 in favor of death by electrocution.[29] Henderson did not ask Governor Bob Riley for clemency. In 1989 Judy Haney was tried for capital murder and sentenced to death. On October 9,

---

[29] On July 1, 2002, the State of Alabama enacted law that allowed death row inmates to be executed by lethal injection unless they chose electrocution.

1997, her sentence was reduced to life without parole because one of her attorneys was drunk on the day before she was sentenced (*Haney v. State* (Talladega Cnty. Cir. Ct. 1997) Case No. 87-559; *Henderson v. State* (1990) 583 So.2d 276).

———

Alexander Rey Martinez, a 31-year-old Hispanic male, was voluntarily executed by lethal injection at the Texas State Penitentiary in Huntsville, Texas on June 7, 2005. Martinez was found guilty of the 2001 murder of Helen Joyce Oliveras Paul, a 45-year-old white female. Martinez, who was 25-years old when he committed the capital crime, was sentenced to death on December 16, 2002.

In 1994 the five foot one inch, 220 pound Martinez was convicted of attempted murder for which he was sentenced to 7-years' imprisonment. On August 23, 2001, some three weeks after his parole, Martinez gave a videotaped confession stating that he had arranged on the telephone a meeting with prostitute Helen Paul. Martinez agreed to pay Paul $200 but he "told her that just to get her there" adding that he really planned on trying "to get it for free." He met Paul at a mall and they got into her car and began driving.

As they were driving Martinez attempted to negotiate the price and Paul became upset. Martinez told Paul to pull over so he could use the phone and when she stopped he dragged her out of the car and cut her throat with a knife. He said he killed Paul because he did not like the way she was talking to him and he did not mention anything about sexual contact.

The next day Martinez gave a written statement that was largely consistent with the first statement except that he also stated that he took $150 in cash and some cocaine from Paul after he killed her. He reiterated that he agreed to the price for Paul's services on the phone again stating that he "never intended to pay her that much money." He stated that he "didn't have any money at all," and again did not mention having sexual contact.

In a third interview Martinez admitted killing Paul in his room at his mother's house. He stated that he had not been truthful about where he killed her because he was trying to protect his mother. In this interview, most of which was tape-recorded, Martinez stated that he had sex with Paul before stabbing her and that Paul had "complied" with the sex. Martinez also stated that he did not pay her and never intended on paying her. He said he stabbed her when she "started tripping" about the money. She wanted to be paid around $300 and when Martinez told her he would not pay her Paul started to leave. Martinez said he grabbed her and "put the knife to her."

Cesar Rios, a cellmate of Martinez's at the Harris County Jail, testified for the State that Martinez told him about the offense during the course of two different conversations.[30] Martinez told Rios he contacted Paul through a phone number for an escort service. On the phone he agreed to Paul's price of $300 that would make her trip across town worthwhile. Martinez told Rios that he really only had $30 and explained that when Paul arrived at his house she sat down on the floor in his room and they began discussing money.

---

[30] Rios acknowledged his own pending criminal charges for unauthorized use of a motor vehicle and aggravated assault. Because he was a "habitual offender" Rios stated that the punishment range for the offenses was 2 to 20 years and 25 to 29 years or life, respectively. Rios testified that he could not read and write and that he did not learn any of the facts of the case from any source other than Martinez. At the end of his testimony Rios stated that the prosecutor had offered to drop the unauthorized use and habitual criminal charges against him in exchange for his testimony, the result being that Rios would plead to aggravated assault with a punishment range of 2 to 20 years.

Paul wanted the money first and when it became apparent that Martinez did not have it, she got mad and tried to leave. Martinez attempted to stall her and she again asked him to see the money. Martinez then said Paul "started going off on him." He told Rios that he had a knife in his pocket and when Paul said she was leaving and started gathering her things Martinez put the knife to the side of her neck. He said she was still sitting on the floor and he pushed her back, got on top of Paul to have sex, and pushed the knife into her neck. According to Rios, Martinez told him he was "inside of" the victim attempting to have sex with her when she kicked him off of her.

Paul was bleeding and began begging him not to kill her and to call an ambulance. She told him that if he killed her there would be no one to take care of her dog. Martinez told her to be quiet so as not to wake the others in the house and tried to figure out how he could kill her without making too much noise. Martinez finally sliced her across her throat and after she was dead, put a towel over her sliced throat and had sex with her. He told Rios he also played with sex toys he found in Paul's bag. When he was done he stated that he folded Paul up and put her in a trash bag. For about three days Martinez kept Paul's body in his closet before disposing of it and her things. Martinez also described cleaning up his room and replacing the carpet.

Other evidence was consistent with and corroborated Martinez's confessions and Rios's testimony. Houston police officers testified that the blood spatters and stains found in Martinez's room were consistent with Martinez's version that Paul was stabbed while sitting on the floor next to his bed. Paul's body was found in a trash bag at the vacant lot where Martinez stated he had taken it. The condition of the body and the way in which it was wrapped was consistent with Martinez's descriptions.

Martinez's brother described the stains on the carpet and an unpleasant odor in the room. He testified that he assisted Martinez in replacing the carpet in his brother's room. The medical examiner testified that although Paul's body was in an advanced state of decomposition when found and was partially "skeletonized" he concluded that stabbing to the neck was the cause of death based on hemorrhage in the neck area and cutting lesions to the bones in the neck.

On October 11, 2002, a Harris County grand jury indicted Martinez for capital murder. Martinez was convicted the same year, and on March 3, 2004, the Texas Court of Criminal Appeals affirmed his conviction and sentence. Shortly thereafter Martinez dropped his appeals (*Martinez v. Dretke* (5th Cir. 2004) No. 03-51067; *Martinez v. State of Texas* (2004) 129 S.W.3d 101).

———

Robert Dale Conklin, a 44-year-old white male, was executed by lethal injection at the Georgia Diagnostic and Classification Prison in Jackson, Georgia on July 12, 2005. Conklin was found guilty of the 1984 murder of George Grant Crooks, a 28-year-old white male. Conklin, who was 23-years old when he committed the capital crime, was sentenced to death on June 16, 1984.

On April 8, 1984, Conklin, a five foot seven inch, 150 pound McDonald's manager made the following statement: "I first met George Crooks [a six foot two inch, 200 pound lawyer] at a rest stop off of I-20 by Douglasville. Over a period of time we established a relationship. We would see each other every couple or three weeks. I moved out to my apartment on Copeland Road. Every now and then he would come over and spend the night or I would go over there and spend the night. We would usually get high, have sex and go to sleep.

"On Monday night, he came over, we got stoned. He didn't drink but I did. He was in Alcoholics Anonymous and would not drink, but he did get high that night. We got high by smoking pot. Later on that evening we went on and

107

went to bed and I wanted to go to sleep and he wanted to play. He kept messing with me and it turned into a wrestling match. I got tired of it, told him to quit and he wouldn't. This went on for quite a while, an hour to an hour and a half, I guess. At this point I was getting pretty mad because he wouldn't leave me alone, so eventually he had me pinned on the bed sitting on my stomach. I was wrestling trying to get free. I was mad but he thought it was all a big joke. Eventually I got an arm free and I did hit him and he hit me back. He was still sitting on me.

"We were there struggling and I reached over and grabbed a screwdriver. I swung the screwdriver and it stuck into him. He rolled off the bed and I followed him screwdriver in hand. I held him down and I stuck the screwdriver in his ear, I wiggled it around and I realized what I had done and got scared.[31] I went ahead and got a blanket and I tried to stop him from bleeding but I think he was already dead. So I wrapped him up in the blanket and I drug him into the bathroom. Since he was bleeding, I tried to put him in the bathtub and I couldn't. He was too heavy and the shower curtain was in the way. So I went ahead and got a screwdriver downstairs, took the shower curtain down. I was able to go ahead and get his body into the bathtub. He was still bleeding and everything.

"At this point I panicked. There was blood all over the place, I think it was on the sheets, I'm pretty sure on the blanket, walls and all over the bathroom. At this point, I

---

[31] Conklin mentioned only two wounds having been inflicted prior to Crooks's death, admitting at trial that after he stabbed Crooks once, Crooks rolled off the bed. Conklin then sitting on top of Crooks "stuck [the screwdriver] in his ear," and stabbed Crooks a number of additional times while Crooks continued to struggle, saying "give me the screwdriver." Dr. Saleh Zaki conducted Crooks's autopsy and testified that eight stab wounds on the right side of Crooks's neck were in his opinion inflicted prior to death.

stopped and tried to think about what to do. I came to the conclusion that since I was on parole [for armed robbery and burglary], it wouldn't be in my best interest to get caught and have it discovered that I had killed this person. So I decided I had to get rid of the body some way.

"I couldn't move him, he was too big, too heavy, so I thought if I let the blood drain out he would be lighter, so I went ahead and got a steak knife from downstairs and tried to cut his throat and bleed him into the bathtub. That did not work too good. So I went ahead and tried to tie his feet up several ways so his feet was up and his head was down. Tried to use a neck tie but it broke. Eventually I just propped his feet up and left him like that with the water running. I went ahead and cleaned myself up and got the blood off of me. I tried to figure out what to do. I was scared and since I was on parole I didn't want to go to the police.

"I decided I had to get rid of the body some way, so I sat down and planned what to do. I couldn't pick him up and carry him, he was too big, and I didn't want to involve anyone else. So I decided I had to get rid of the body somehow and to get rid of his car and his possessions and everything else. By now it was Tuesday morning. I don't know what time. So I went ahead and took his keys and his wallet, honest face card, and I got into his car. I then went ahead and went to his apartment so I could get anything there that would connect me with him. I took a card with my name and number on it and the tape out of his answering machine then put another fresh tape in.

"Since I had his Honest-Face card and his checkbook, I drove around to several grocery stores and started to get cleaning supplies. The idea was to get cleaning supplies and the stuff to finish cleaning up the place at the apartment. While doing this I realized there was no way I could get rid of the body because I couldn't pick him up, so I thought if I were to cut him in half I could put him in a couple of garbage bags that I could remove him from the apartment. I also bought some other things, food, knives and other things, and I wrote some checks. After I did this, I brought all the stuff back to the apartment. He still hadn't lightened any from the bleeding all that much, so I used one of the knives to go ahead and cut his throat some more. It was a lot sharper than the steak knives. I realized I had to get rid of his car some how, so I drove it downtown.

"On the way downtown it ran out of gas so I pushed it into a parking lot. I think it was Sears in Buckhead. I wiped it down and took everything out of it and tried to catch a bus back to where I live; caught the wrong bus on the wrong road. I was on Paces Ferry Road. So I rode that bus to Paces Ferry Crossing and I caught a cab back to my apartment. When I got there I went ahead and went to work to cut him in half so I could get him out of there. After I had done that, he was still too big to move, too heavy, so I decided I had to cut him in smaller pieces. All of this I did in the bathtub. For most of the day I went ahead and worked on him. It was a big mess, I'm telling you.

"I decided there would be less of him to move if I could put some of him down the garbage disposal. Fortunately, he would not fit, so I cut him up in even smaller pieces. These I was able to stuff into the garbage disposal, but it turned out that the garbage disposal would not accept him. So I pulled all that out, took it back upstairs to the bathroom and cleaned up the kitchen and everything the best I could. I then went ahead and cut the rest of him up in small enough pieces to put in the bags. Before I could get all of this done I got a call from a friend of mine who was in the neighborhood and he said he was going to stop over. Since normally I tell him to come over, I told him to come on over. It was D-- M-- and his wife.

"I cleaned up everything downstairs before he got there the best I could. Between 3:00 o'clock and 5:00 that evening, I had gone to a meeting for work. I was gone for a couple of hours. And D-- came over about 7:00 or 8:00 o'clock. Shortly after he was there, another friend showed up, S-- L--. And D-- and his wife left and S-- and I sat around and drank beers. After a while S-- left and I went back upstairs, finished putting him in the bags. I found that I couldn't even carry all the bags, so I went to K-Mart and bought a garbage can. I think it was also at Handy City I bought a pushcart to put the can on so I could move the can. I went ahead and filled up the garbage can with these bags and they would not all fit, so I left some of the bags with George in them outside.

"Later on that night it started to rain, so I went ahead and took the trash can with the cart, took it to the dumpster, unloaded all the bags.[32] Before I did this I cleaned up the bathroom. I also took the sheets, blankets and other stuff and put that in the trashcan with him. I don't remember if it took two or three trips. I know it took at least two trips to get all that out there.

"I then went back and cleaned the apartment some more trying to get the blood and everything else up. Eventually I fell asleep on the couch and I woke up the next day. I had to be at work so I went ahead and took a shower, got ready for work and I was running late so I didn't finish cleaning up everything. I went out to my car, got into my car and drove around the building the way I usually go. But when I turned the corner, I noticed there was a tape across the road and people were digging stuff out of the dumpster.

---

[32] Crooks's body was found in parts in nine garbage bags as follows: (a) head with most of the neck, and both hands; (b) right upper torso, shoulder, and arm; (c) lower legs with feet attached; (d) buttocks and pelvic bones; (e) thigh muscle and skin; (f) left upper torso, shoulder and arm; (g) rib cage (with internal organs removed) and spine; (h) two thigh bones (from which the musculature had been removed and put in bag e, above) and the genitalia; and (i) lungs, heart, and portions of the liver, kidney, spleen and intestines.

"I didn't know if they would connect me with it or not but I decided it would be to my best interest not be around. So instead of going to work, I went ahead and drove around to try to figure things out awhile. I decided that it wouldn't be a good idea to go back to the apartment unless I knew for sure that I wasn't a suspect. Then I decided that it would be best that I left altogether and assume that I was a suspect until I found out otherwise.

"I went ahead and got all my money from my bank account using my bankcard. I then went downtown, parked my car at the Holiday Inn and wandered around town. I checked the bus station and eventually decided to buy a ticket for Miami. After I had been in Miami a couple, or was it two days, I decided it was not where I wanted to be so I hitchhiked back to Atlanta where I found out I was being sought. I had no place to go and I was broke and hungry. I went back to my apartment where I found police had already been. I stayed there anyways because I didn't think anyone would be by until that Monday.

"It was last night, Saturday night, I was discovered and chased. I didn't get to take anything that I had planned on taking when I left, I just left as quickly as possible. So after hiding all night I went back to the apartment to get the stuff that I had left. It wasn't there so I went ahead and got what I could and decided to catch a bus downtown again. On the way to the bus stop I was caught and here I am."

On June 15, 1984, a Fulton County Georgia jury convicted Conklin of malice murder finding that the murder was outrageously or wantonly vile, horrible, or inhumane, and that the murder involved depravity of mind. Conklin's attorney was given only 37 days to prepare for trial, and the trial judge refused to afford Conklin $2500 in state funds to hire an expert that the Eleventh Circuit Court of Appeals believed was crucial to his mitigating defense ruling that the trial as a whole was not fundamentally unfair or outside the bounds of the Constitution. The Georgia Board of Pardons and Paroles rejected Conklin's last-minute plea for clemency. Conklin requested and was given a last meal consisting of filet mignon wrapped with bacon; de-veined shrimp sautéed in garlic butter with lemon; baked potato with butter, sour cream, chives and real bacon bits; corn on the cob; asparagus with hollandaise sauce; French bread with butter; goat cheese; cantaloupe; apple pie; vanilla bean ice cream and iced tea (*Conklin v. State* (1985) 254 Ga. 558, 331 S.E.2d 532; *Conklin v. Schofield* (2004) 366 F.3d 1191).

———

Sharieff Imani Sallahdin, a 37-year-old black male formerly known as Michael Lannier Pennington, was executed by lethal injection at the Oklahoma State Penitentiary in McAlester, Oklahoma, on July 19, 2005. Sallahdin was found guilty of the 1991 murder of Bradley Thomas Grooms, a 20-year-old white male. Sallahdin, who was 23-years old when he committed the capital crime, was sentenced to death on September 17, 1993.

On October 21, 1991, James Principe and Bradley Grooms were working the late shift at a 7-11 convenience store located in Lawton, Oklahoma at Fort Sill Boulevard and Rogers Lane. At approximately 5:00 a.m. that morning Principe and Grooms were stocking shelves with Grooms located toward the front of the store. During this time a black male entered the store, went to the bathroom, and left. This male was wearing a black and white outfit with matching top and pants. Principe later described the pattern as cow-like with black and white spots.

About one minute after the male left the store Principe heard a loud bang while still stocking shelves in the back of the store. He stood up from his crouched position and noticed another black man wearing sunglasses standing just inside the door of the store looking in the direction of Grooms. Principe immediately heard Grooms exclaim, "Oh shit" and with that Principe ducked down and made his way to the back of the store.

As Principe was running he looked back and saw the man again taking a step towards Grooms. At that point Principe got a good look at the shooter and noticed he was wearing a black trench coat. As he continued moving to the back of the store Principe heard another shot. Principe ran to the bathroom and locked himself inside. While locked in the bathroom Principe heard several more shots. He then heard the front door buzzer and some voices. Principe heard the door buzzer again, and then came out of the bathroom and contacted police. He then observed Grooms lying motionless between the first two aisles of the store. Principe later identified Sallahdin as the man who did the shooting.

During a canvass of the neighborhood for witnesses an individual was discovered who could shed some light on what occurred while Principe was hiding in the bathroom. Lynn Renee Smith, who had stopped at the 7-11 just after the shooting to get a cup of ice, had known Sallahdin for about three years and had seen him earlier that evening at the Peacock Lounge. As Smith pulled up to the store she noticed Sallahdin behind the cash register thinking he must work at the store. Sallahdin asked her what she wanted and when she told him, he gave her a cup and she got some ice. She did not see anyone else while she was in the store and she noticed that it appeared to be unusually quiet.

Upon leaving the store Smith drove to her sister's house located approximately 50 yards from the 7-11 and backed into the driveway. As Smith looked towards the 7-11 she saw Sallahdin wearing a black trench coat leave the store and drive away in his car. Smith also testified that Sallahdin was wearing a black baseball style cap that he had on backwards. She further noted that he had on sunglasses that were not mirrored and described Sallahdin as being about five feet five inches tall. Smith did not recall seeing Sallahdin wearing the black trench coat in the store.

The neighborhood canvass turned up two other witnesses. Sylvia Smith, unrelated to Lynn Smith, and living in the neighborhood in the area of the 7-11, heard a gunshot between 4:30 a.m. and 5:00 a.m. When Smith looked out of her window, she saw two black males running up the street away from the 7-11.

Jose Rodriguez, living almost next door to Sylvia, left for duty at Fort Sill, the home of the U.S. Army Field Artillery, about 5:15 a.m. on the same morning. Rodriguez stated that he also saw two individuals running but was unable to describe the second runner and only able to recall that the first individual appeared to have on a knee length black coat.

After leaving the store, Sallahdin, who was an army soldier stationed at Fort Sill, returned briefly to the barracks and changed clothes. He then went to the airport and took the next available flight to Dallas with an ultimate destination of Akron, Ohio. The following day, the 22nd, Sallahdin was taken into custody by Ohio authorities at the home of his wife. While in custody Sallahdin volunteered information as to the location of the shotgun, which was then located in an orange duffel bag in the basement of the Akron residence along with a green compass pouch containing four shotgun shells.

Subsequent ballistics tests conducted on the shotgun revealed that the five expended shells from the scene and one expended shell found in the orange duffel bag were fired from the shotgun found in the orange duffel bag. Another search was conducted the next day in the area where the duffel bag had been recovered and this time police recovered a black baseball style cap, a three quarter length trench coat, and a gray and black sports sweatshirt.

The medical examiner, Dr. Boatsman, testified that the cause of Grooms's death was a shotgun wound to the chest. Twelve pellet wounds were found in Groom's left back and an exit wound in the back right area of his neck. An examination of the scene indicated that nothing was missing from the store after the incident. However, the cash register drawer had been pulled and pried upon and also apparently fired at since four large holes were in the front drawer area.

During the homicide investigation police had learned that Sallahdin was absent without leave from his unit. They also learned from Priscilla Jordan, Sallahdin's girlfriend in Lawton, that Sallahdin owned a shotgun, which he kept in an orange duffel bag. With that information police revisited the personnel at Sallahdin's battery and obtained information that led them to the K-Mart store where Sallahdin had purchased a Maverick .12-gauge shotgun.

At trial Sallahdin described the morning of the 7-11 shooting. According to Sallahdin he had decided to go home to Akron even though his discharge papers had not yet been processed. He testified that in order to raise some money he made a deal to buy some firearms to take home to sell. This deal was entered into with a man known only to him as "T."

Somewhere near the Peacock Lounge "T" and two other black males got into Sallahdin's car and rode around awhile to make sure they were not followed. Eventually they directed Sallahdin to stop near the 7-11 on Fort Sill Boulevard. Sallahdin parked near a massage parlor and pawnshop close to the store. One of the men exited the vehicle saying he was going to get the stuff.

After some time passed Sallahdin decided to go into the 7-11 to purchase some Lactaid milk. He took $1500 with him leaving his sawed-off shotgun in the car. While Sallahdin was in the store, "T" walked in carrying the gun and immediately began shooting. Sallahdin jumped behind the checkout counter as "T" came behind the counter telling Sallahdin not to worry and just give him the money he knew Sallahdin had on him to purchase the guns. Sallahdin gave "T" the $1500 as "T" focused his attention on the locked cash register, got mad, and shot the cash register several times trying unsuccessfully to yank it open. "T" then ran out of the store with Sallahdin's shotgun.

Sallahdin, who claimed he remained in the store in a state of shock, looked over and saw Grooms motionless and assumed he was dead when Lynn Smith entered the store and asked for the cup of ice. After Smith left Sallahdin got a grip on himself and ran out of the store. As he was running toward the car, Sallahdin saw his shotgun lying on the ground and picked it up as a reflex action. He then drove off in his car and went back to Fort Sill. Sallahdin stated that he did not call police because he feared "T" who was a notorious gang member; "T" was neither found nor identified.

A Comanche County jury convicted Sallahdin of first-degree malice aforethought murder and fixed punishment at death[33] afterwhich he converted to Islam and had his name change (*Pennington v. State* (1995) 913 P.2d 1356; *Sallahdin v. Gibson* (2002) 275 F.3d 1211; *Sallahdin v. Mullin* (2004) 380 F.3d 1242).

———

Kevin Aaron Conner, a 40-year-old white male, was voluntarily executed by lethal injection at the Indiana State Prison in Michigan City, Indiana on July 27, 2005. Conner was found guilty of the 1988 murder of two white males: Tony Moore, 29, and Bruce Voge, 19. Conner, who was 22-years old when he committed the capital crime, was sentenced to death on November 3, 1988.

---

[33] Sallahdin argued on appeal that the trial court erroneously denied him an opportunity to present mitigating evidence that he was experiencing psychiatric effects from anabolic steroid use at the time of the crime. According to Sallahdin the steroids taken to enhance his weight lifting and bodybuilding regimen altered his normal behavior and therefore the trial court wrongly prevented him from explaining what transformed him from a disciplined soldier into a fleeing killer.

In the early morning of January 26, 1988, Conner and friends Tony Moore, Bruce Voge, and 19-year-old Steve Wentland were drinking together at Moore's house in Indianapolis, Indiana after which Conner, Wentland, and Moore went for a drive. While still in the vehicle Moore argued with Wentland and stabbed him. When Wentland left the vehicle and ran Moore pursued him in the vehicle and Connor followed on foot. Moore struck Wentland with the vehicle, and Conner then beat Wentland and stabbed him multiple times.

Conner and Moore left the mortally wounded Wentland and drove to Conner's workplace. While there Conner later told police that he and Moore argued about what they should have done and Conner shot Moore with a sawed-off shotgun killing him. Conner then drove to the house where Voge had remained and shot Voge with the same shotgun as he lay on the couch. Conner disposed of the bodies with the help of friends and then fled the scene.

On January 30 Conner was arrested in Amarillo, Texas and subsequently returned to Indiana to be tried on three murder charges in the Marion Superior Court. Conner's trial lasted from October 3 to October 7. The jury found him guilty of murdering Wentland, Moore, and Voge, with the State seeking the death penalty alleging multiple murders as the aggravating factor.

On October 9 the jury unanimously recommended a death sentence for the murders of Voge and Moore and the court followed the jury's recommendation. Conner was also sentenced to 60 years' imprisonment for the murder of Wentland. Conner refused to seek clemency from Governor Mitch Daniels, writing in a letter to the governor: "Killing a person is far more honest and human than imposed repression under the guise of justice in the penal system." Conner's last meal came from Dairy Queen: four chili dogs, onion rings, a banana split and an Oreo-cookie Blizzard ice-cream drink. He also smoked two cigars, an exception to the prison's no-smoking policy (*Conner v.*

State (1991) 580 N.E.2d 214; *Conner v. State* (2005) 125 S.Ct. 1930).

David Aaron Martinez, a 29-year-old Hispanic male, was executed by lethal injection at the Texas State Penitentiary in Huntsville, Texas on July 28, 2005. Martinez was found guilty of the 1997 murder of Kiersa Alexandra Paul, a 24-year-old white female. Martinez, who was 21-years old when he committed the capital crime, was sentenced to death on December 1, 1998.

On July 23, 1997, a jogger found Kiersa Paul's body along at the Zilker Park Greenbelt trail in Austin, Texas. A pair of unbuttoned boxer shorts covered her body and her legs were spread open. Further investigation revealed injuries consistent with strangulation, blunt force injury to the head and nose, gouge marks on the neck, bruising of both nipples, cuts on her neck, breast, and stomach, and forceful sexual intercourse.

Paul had told her sister the previous night that she intended to meet an individual named Wolf at the Austin Greenbelt. Martinez, whose nickname was "Wolf," told friends that he intended to meet a girl that evening along a Greenbelt Trail in the park. He returned to his friends' house with a bicycle he did not own. After executing a search warrant police determined that Martinez possessed Paul's bicycle and bicycle bag. They also seized a Swiss army pocketknife owned by Martinez. Forensic tests determined that hairs found on Paul were consistent with Martinez's hair and that Martinez's pocketknife contained blood that matched Paul's DNA. Semen collected from Paul's underwear matched Martinez's DNA.

Martinez, who had no prior criminal record, was indicted in Travis County for the capital murder of Paul on December 9. On October 29, 1998, after the jury deliberated for all of 15 minutes Martinez was found guilty, and on December 1 the jury finding that he would commit future criminal acts of violence, was a continuing threat to society, and that no sufficient mitigating circumstances existed, recommended a death sentence. On May 10, 2000, the Texas Court of Criminal Appeals affirmed his conviction and sentence (*Martinez v. Dretke* (2004) 99 Fed.Appx. 538).

―――

George Everette Sibley Jr., a 62-year-old white male, was executed by lethal injection at the Holman Prison in Atmore, Alabama on August 4, 2005. Sibley was found guilty of the 1993 murder of Roger Lamar Motley, a 39-year-old white male. Sibley, who was 51-years old when he committed the capital crime, was sentenced to death on June 10, 1994.

Sibley and his common law wife, Lynda Cheryle Lyon, a 45-year-old white female, lived in Orlando, Florida, when in August 1992 they were arrested and charged with aggravated battery and burglary in a stabbing incident involving Lyon's 79-year-old former husband. Sibley and Lyon entered a plea of *nolo contendere* ("I will not contest it") to these charges and a sentencing hearing was set for September 7, 1993. After failing to appear for sentencing hearing on September 10, Sibley, Lyon, and her 9-year-old son Gordon fled the state in Sibley's Mustang knowing that the court had issued a writ of arrest.

On October 4 Sibley parked the Mustang near Big B Drug in Pepperell Corners Shopping Center in Opelika, Alabama. Lyon was using a pay telephone outside the store and Sibley stayed near the car with Gordon. A passerby, Ramona Robertson, heard Gordon ask for help. Worried that the child was in danger, she kept an eye on Sibley's Mustang as it moved to a different location in the parking lot near the entrance to Wal-Mart.

When Sergeant Roger Motley of the Opelika Police Department came out of a store in the shopping center, Robertson reported to him what she had observed. Motley, a uniformed officer, had been running an errand for the police department. After the situation was reported to him Motley approached the Mustang with Sibley in it and at that point Sibley got out of the car. Meanwhile, Lyon was using another pay phone, this one near the entrance to Wal-Mart.

Prior to approaching Sibley Motley radioed to the Opelika Police Department as to his activities, which was tape-recorded and later admitted as evidence at trial. Motley approached Sibley and asked for his driver's license. Sibley stated that he did not have one because he had no contacts with the State.[34] Motley then requested identification from Sibley who pulled a 9-millimeter Glock from a concealed holster and began firing at Motley. Motley attempted to get away from Sibley and ran behind his vehicle for cover where he began to return fire at Sibley.

Sibley fired numerous shots at Motley who was able to fire his weapon three times at Sibley. Lyon heard the shooting and ran toward the patrol car. She pulled a 9-millimeter Glock from her purse and began firing at Motley from his rear. Motley was finally able to get into his patrol car and radio for help. The patrol car started to move through the parking lot in an erratic manner hitting several vehicles as it moved eventually coming to a stop near Big B Drug.

Motley was mortally wounded having sustained several gunshot wounds. The fatal shot went through his chest from the front at a slight downward angle. The bullet was never recovered and tests were inconclusive, as to which 9-millimeter Glock fired the fatal shot.

Sibley, Lyon, and Gordon then sped away from the scene and after a high-speed chase the Mustang was stopped at a roadblock on Wire Road in Auburn, the largest city in eastern Alabama. After a four-hour standoff in

---

[34] Sibley carried "exemption papers" instead of a driver's license in support of his Libertarian beliefs opposing government interference in his personal, family, and business decisions.

which no shots were fired Gordon was released and Sibley and Lyon surrendered to police.

A search of the Mustang uncovered numerous weapons and large quantities of ammunition. After surrendering Sibley was taken to the emergency room for treatment of a gunshot would to his arm. While in the emergency room and after having been advised of his *Miranda* rights Sibley made an oral statement in which he stated he had shot the police officer. Another statement, which was reduced to writing, was taken from Sibley at the police department in which he admitted shooting at Motley.

Sibley testified at trial wherein he acknowledged shooting at Motley several times claiming that it was done in self-defense. He admitted firing three shots at Motley before Motley had drawn his police weapon adding that he was face-to-face with Motley at the time he fired his last two shots. At the time of the incident the parking lot was crowded with vehicles and people, twelve of who testified at trial as to being eyewitnesses to the shooting.

Sibley was tried in a Lee County Circuit Court. The jury found him guilty of capital murder and unanimously recommended the death penalty afterwhich the trial judge sentenced him to death. Lyon was tried approximately three months later, also convicted of the same murder, and also sentenced to death. She waived her appeals and on May 10, 2002, she was executed by electrocution. After Lyon's death, Sibley who for years had refused to file any appeals, requested a stay that was denied by both the Supreme Court of the United States and Governor Bob Riley on the day of execution (*Block v. State (*1996) 744 So.2d 404; *Ex parte Sibley* (2000) 775 So.2d 246; *Sibley v. Alabama* (2005) 545 U.S. 1156; *Sibley v. State* (1996) 775 So.2d 235).

Gary Lynn Sterling, a 38-year-old black male, was executed by lethal injection at the Texas State Penitentiary in Huntsville, Texas on August 10, 2005. Sterling was found guilty of the 1988 murder of John Wesley Carty, a 72-year-old white male. Sterling, who was 20-years old when he committed the capital crime, was sentenced to death on February 9, 1989.

On May 17, 1988, the six foot one inch, 176-pound Sterling was arrested in Hillsboro, Texas in connection with the killing of 72-year-old William Porter and his 71-year-old brother, Leroy Porter. The Porter brothers were murdered in the nominal 75-person town of Pelham, some 35 miles northeast of Waco.

While in custody Sterling stated that he wanted to tell the proper authorities about two additional murders in Navarro County. Upon contacting the Navarro County authorities and after being warned by a magistrate, Sterling led the authorities to the location of the bodies of John Carty and Delores 52-year-old Delore Smith. The bodies were found in an isolated area near Corsicana, a town 25 miles east of Pelham.

In a written statement Sterling admitted that on May 13 he killed Carty and Smith by striking them both in the head with a bumper jack. Smith's purse and glasses were later found in Sterling's home. Sterling said that he had taken Carty's money, wallet, and automobile, and sold the automobile to buy crack cocaine.

On July 14, 1988, a Navarro County grand jury indicted Sterling for the capital murder of Carty; he was not charged with Smith's murder. The weekend before he was tried Sterling pleaded guilty to the Hill County murder of the Porter brothers for which he was subsequently sentenced to life imprisonment. On April 22, 1992, the Texas Court of Criminal Appeals affirmed his conviction and death sentence. The Texas Board of Pardons and Paroles voted 7-0, rejecting both a clemency petition and a request for a reprieve. One hour before Sterling's execution, Justices of the Supreme Court of the United States Stevens, Ginsburg, and Breyer voted to grant a stay (*Sterling v. State* (1992)

830 S.W.2d 114; *Sterling v. Texas* (2005) 545 U.S. 1157; 126 S.Ct. 20).

———

Kenneth Eugene Turrentine, a 52-year-old black male, was executed by lethal injection at the Oklahoma State Penitentiary in McAlester, Oklahoma on August 11, 2005. Turrentine was found guilty of the 1994 murder of Anita Louise Richardson, a 39-year-old black female. Turrentine, who was 41-years old when he committed the capital crime, was sentenced to death on October 4, 1995.

For three months preceeding June 4, 1994, Turrentine and his estranged girlfriend, Anita Richardson, had been experiencing problems in their relationship that caused Turrentine to move out of their Tulsa, Oklahoma home to live with his 48-year-old sister, Avon Stevenson, also in Tulsa. While separated from Richardson and living with Stevenson, Turrentine began to believe that Richardson was having an affair with two other men and that his sister knew of these affairs because she was both a friend and confidant of Richardson. Turrentine also believed that Richardson and Stevenson were cheating him out of money to support their drug habits.

On June 3 Turrentine telephoned his ex-wife, Catherine Turrentine, and told her that he was at Richardson's house and that things were "about to come to a head." That same day he asked his ex-wife to return to him a .22-caliber pistol but she refused. He made the same request the next morning and this time his ex-wife gave Turrentine the loaded pistol. Later in the day Turrentine confronted his sister at her Green County home about Anita's supposed affairs and an argument ensued. Stevenson apparently laughed in Turrentine's face during this argument and called him a "punk." In response Turrentine placed the .22-caliber pistol to Stevenson's head and fired, killing her.

Turrentine then drove to Richardson's house where the two began to argue. As they argued they moved from the front to the back bedroom of the house and after more argument and struggle, Turrentine told Richardson that he would kill her children. Richardson pleaded with Turrentine, "Kenneth, no, no" and Turrentine shot Richardson in the head. She died at the scene. Turrentine then shot Richardson's children, 13-year-old Martise D. Richardson and 22-year-old Tina L. Pennington, in the head.[35]

Afterwards Turrentine talked to a 9-1-1 operator and declared he had shot his "ol lady." When officers arrived at the scene they immediately took Turrentine into custody and advised him of his *Miranda* rights. Turrentine waived his rights telling the officers that he had shot his sister, his estranged girlfriend, and his girlfriend's two children. A medical examiner later confirmed that all four victims had died from gunshot wounds to the head.

---

[35] Martise Richardson came running into the room where Turrentine was struggling with his mother and began hitting Turrentine. Initially found by paramedics lying across his mother's lap, one of the first arriving paramedics testified that Martise was alert and reached up and grabbed the paramedic's arm when he tried to put the oxygen mask on him. When Martise was moved from the apartment for transportation to the hospital he waved his arm and hit the spot where he had been shot. He was pronounced dead later at the hospital.

Tina Pennington, who was blind and disabled, was crying and screaming during the altercation between Turrentine, Richardson, and Martise. Tina was still conscious after being shot and followed Turrentine outside who told her to go back inside and wait with her mother for an ambulance. Tina was lying on the bed when paramedics arrived and the paramedics testified that upon their arrival that she was alive and breathing with her teeth clenched. Tina was transported to the hospital for further treatment where she died two days later never having regained consciousness.

Turrentine had no prior criminal history. He was tried before a jury in Tulsa County District Court and convicted of four counts of first-degree murder. The jury returned sentences of death for the murder each of Richardson and her children, and returned a verdict of life without the possibility of parole for the murder of Stevenson. On December 1, 2004, the Tenth Circuit Court of Appeals overturned the death sentence for Richardson's children because of an improper jury instruction.[36] The five-member Oklahoma Pardon and Parole Board unanimously denied clemency (*Turrentine v. Mullin* (2004) 390 F.3d 1181; *Turrentine v. State* (1998) 965 P.2d 955).

————

Robert Alan Shields Jr., a 30-year-old white male, was executed by lethal injection at the Texas State Penitentiary in Huntsville, Texas on August 23, 2005. Shields was found guilty of the 1994 murder of Paula Stiner, a 27-year-old white female. Shields, who was 19-years old when he committed the capital crime, was sentenced to death on October 16, 1995.

Shortly before 6:00 p.m. on September 21, 1994, Paula Stiner's husband, Tracy, arrived at their Texas Galveston County home from work and discovered her body in the laundry room. Stiner's body lay on its right side on the floor of the laundry room with her back to the washer and dryer. The room and Stiner's body were covered in blood. The

---

[36] In the jury instruction: "A person may *not* be convicted of MURDER IN THE SECOND DEGREE if he/she engages in conduct imminently dangerous to another person that shows a depraved mind in extreme disregard of human life, although the conduct is not done with the intention of taking the life of or harming any particular individual" the Court ruled that the italicized word "not" should not have been included because it deprived Turrentine of his right to be considered for a lesser offense.

breakfast area of the house was in disarray, and the contents of Stiner's purse were strewn about. There was also a hammer on the floor of the breakfast area.

As Stiner's husband searched the house he noticed that several items, including several pair of socks, shirts, a book bag, and a kitchen knife, were missing. He testified that he later learned that at 11:37 a.m., a time when his wife would have been at work, a telephone call had been made from his home to the home of one of Shields's friends in Spring, an unincorporated community some 20 miles north of Houston.

Dr. William Korndoffer, Galveston County's Chief Medical Examiner, testified that Stiner had suffered a blunt trauma to the head and had been repeatedly stabbed in the throat, chest, and torso. Stiner also suffered a number of defensive wounds, which indicated that she had struggled with her assailant before she died.

Detective Michael Wayne Tollett of the Friendswood Police Department testified that he was notified of Stiner's murder around 6:16 p.m. and arrived at the Stiner residence shortly thereafter. Tollett testified that police lifted Shields's fingerprints from the laundry room and that bloody shoe prints at the scene were consistent with Shields's shoes. Tollett found blood on the purse, the carpet, and a large amount of blood in the laundry room. Shields's fingerprints were found on Stiner's checkbook, on the door leading from the laundry room to the garage, and in Stiner's car. Tollett also found a screwdriver on the carpet below a broken window and a wooden-handled screwdriver outside. A cigarette butt found at the scene had saliva on it consistent with Shields's saliva. Stiner's car was also missing.

The Shields family lived next door to the Stiners. Shields's mother testified that a police officer informed her of Stiner's murder when she returned home on the 21st. The next day Shields's mother noticed that some items were out of place in her garage: cushions had been arranged to form a makeshift bed and some drinks were nearby. Shields's mother also found her son's pager and one of his shirts near the cushions although Shields had not lived with his parents for several months and was not welcome in their home without at least one parent present.

When Shields's mother learned from neighbors that a wooden-handled screwdriver like one that she and her husband owned had been used to break into the Stiner home she began to suspect that her son was involved in the crime. She contacted police and gave them Shields's friends' phone numbers where he might be reached.

On September 24 Shields was arrested in The Woodlands, a planned community 7 miles north of Spring. At the police station police noticed cuts on Shields's hands. There was also a cut on his right chin and what appeared to be blood on his shoes, which police took to the lab for analysis. Shields's underwear was also saturated with blood.

Stiner's husband identified several of the items in Stiner's car as having been in his home before her murder. The bloody shoe impression at the crime scene matched the shoes that Shields wore at the time of his arrest and the blood obtained from his underwear and from a paper towel at the Stiner home was consistent with his blood. Evidence showed that Shields had used Stiner's credit card after the murder to purchase a suit.

Mark Lang, the manager of Dejaiz's Men's Clothing in Willowbrook Mall, was working on the 21st. He testified that Shields came into the store around 6:15 p.m. and purchased a suit with a credit card in the name of Paula Stiner. Shields signed the credit card slip in the name of Stiner's husband. When Lang noticed a horizontal cut on Shields's finger, Shields told Lang that he had cut his finger while splicing wires at work. Shields also had a bandage around his middle finger on his left hand.

Several of Shields's friends testified for the prosecution. Troy Sterner testified he knew Shields in

1994 when Shields was staying in vacant houses in The Woodlands. Shortly after the murder Sterner saw Shields with cuts on his hand. Shields told Sterner that he had cut them while working at a store. Gina Cykala testified that on the day of the murder she saw Shields at McDonald's at around 8:45 p.m. driving a big white car that she had never seen before. Shields told Cykala that he had borrowed the car from a friend. Colin Checketts also testified that on the 21st, Shields was driving a white car. Shields told Checketts he had obtained the car from a friend, Ray Holt, and wanted to sell it for $500. He told Checketts that he had cut his hands while working at a store and then gave Checketts the suit that he had just purchased. David Chastain and Jarrod Moore testified the same.

On October 27, 1994, Shields, who had a prior arrest for grand theft auto, was indicted in Galveston County for capital murder. Convicted in 1995 Shields put on no witnesses at trial. The jury answered the special issue question of future dangerousness in the affirmative and recommended a death sentence. On February 25, 1998, the Texas Court of Criminal Appeals of Texas affirmed his conviction and sentence. The Supreme Court of the United States denied a stay on the day of execution (*Shields v. Dretke* (5th Cir. 2005) No. 04-70008; *Shields v. Dretke* (2005) 545 U.S. 1160).

Timothy Johnston, a 44-year-old white male, was executed by lethal injection at the Eastern Reception Diagnostic and Correctional Center in Bonne Terre, Missouri on August 31, 2005. Johnston was found guilty of the 1989 murder of Nancy Johnston, a 27-year-old white female. Johnston, who was 28-years old when he committed the capital crime, was sentenced to death on July 26, 1991.

At 2:28 a.m. on June 30, 1989, paramedics arrived at the St. Louis, Missouri home of Timothy Johnston and his wife, Nancy Johnston, in response to a 9-1-1 call seeking assistance for a "severe sick case." The 9-1-1 operator also dispatched Officer Matthew Rodden of the St. Louis Police Department to the residence. Rodden arrived at the Johnston residence at the same time as the ambulance carrying the paramedics. A male voice from inside the house directed these emergency personnel to "hurry up, inside. She is in here. She needs help." The officer and the paramedics stepped over the bloody sidewalk and porch into the house.

Just inside the doorway in the living room, Johnston was found bent over a woman lying on the floor with her otherwise nude upper body draped with a shirt and her face and torso horribly injured, swollen, and bloody. A six-inch gash ran across her forehead to the socket of her right eye. Someone had yanked large patches of hair from her head and she was not breathing. Rodden had to remove Johnston before paramedics could assess the woman's condition.

Paramedics declared the woman dead at the scene. An autopsy performed later that morning revealed extensive blunt-trauma injuries over much of her upper body; a broken nose; bruised and torn lips; scrapes to the back of her head and on her face; separation of a portion of the scalp from the skull; a broken right collarbone; a four-inch tear in her liver; bruising and tearing in the heart and spleen; breaks in nearly all of her front ribs and in four of the back ribs; and a variety of relatively "minor" scrapes and bruises over much of her body.

The medical examiner determined the cause of death as the collapse of the support structure around the heart and lungs rendering those organs unable to function because they could not bear the weight of the muscle, tissue, and bone pressing on them. Bleeding under the skin confirmed the woman had remained alive through most of the beating.

A purse near the woman identified her as Johnston's wife. When informed that his wife was dead, Johnston flew into a rage throwing him against the walls of the living room, knocking lamps and small items from their places, and overturning furniture. He ordered the officer and the paramedics to leave his house, screamed that he knew that a motorcycle gang that wanted "to get back at him" had killed his wife, and said that he would take care of everything that needed to be done.

Now at an obvious murder scene, Rodden did not leave and by this time other officers had arrived at the Johnston residence. One of those officers, Officer John Ruzicka, had seen Johnston earlier in the evening when he had responded to a call reporting an assault in progress at the intersection of South Broadway and Eichelberger. When he had arrived at that location at approximately 1:30 a.m. Ruzicka had discovered a dark-colored, two-door car stopped in the middle of the southbound lanes of Broadway. Ruzicka approached the car, noted the broken windshield on the driver's side, and told the driver to "hold on a minute." The driver ignored him and sped off. Ruzicka gave chase briefly but returned to the place of the assault to interview witnesses.

Marty Bounds, one of those witnesses, had stopped when he saw a car abandoned in the middle of Broadway and noticed a man "beating on someone" on the sidewalk next to a house. He could not determine the gender of the person being beaten until the attacker ripped her shirt from her. The attacker kicked the victim "like if you would kick a football, stomping like *** a tin can, if I was trying to flatten it."

Bounds tried to interrupt the attack verbally but the attacker responded only with profanity. Bounds drove his truck toward the attacker in an attempt to break off the beating and when this had no effect, Bounds drove his truck in circles in an attempt to attract enough attention that someone would call police. Naomi Runtz, awakening to the sound of a fracas outside her window, saw a man kicking and stomping someone and called 9-1-1. Streetlights illuminated the scene sufficiently well so that Bounds, Runtz, and Ruzicka later identified the attacker/driver as Johnston.

Johnston apparently remembered Ruzicka from their previous encounter. When Ruzicka arrived at the murder scene Johnston renewed his vulgar demands that the officers leave. The officers decided to handcuff Johnston and take him to a police car to protect the officers, the crime scene, and Johnston himself.

Johnston then began kicking the inside of the car. Detective James Maier arrived, saw Johnston flailing about, and ordered him removed from the car in an attempt to calm him. Maier then noticed blood and hair on Johnston's steel-toed motorcycle boots. When Johnston did not calm down Maier directed other officers to take Johnston to the police station.

Officers on the scene learned that Michael Federhofer, Nancy Johnston's 11-year-old stepson, also lived in the house. Police checked the house to see whether Federhofer was also a victim and to determine whether any members of the motorcycle gang to which Johnston had referred remained in the house.

After reviewing the crime scene Maier returned to the police station where he informed Johnston of his *Miranda* rights. Maier told Johnston that he believed Johnston was involved in the murder. Johnston denied involvement but became severely agitated. Maier left Johnston alone for nearly one hour and when he returned Johnston told a story that members of a rival motorcycle gang had dumped his wife's badly beaten body on the driveway. Johnston brought Nancy into the house and called 9-1-1. She died before help could arrive.

Maier told Johnston that eyewitness accounts differed substantially from the story Johnston told and Johnston began to cry. After a short delay in the interrogation while technicians took fingernail scrapings from Johnston, Johnston called his wife a "whore" and indicated that he had grown tired of her infidelities. Johnston also said that he was "dead meat" and told Maier he would confess.

Johnston recounted that he and Nancy had gone to a local bar on his motorcycle before midnight where they had had an argument afterwhich he left the bar and returned to their residence. He claimed that he called several friends on the telephone hoping, he said, that they would help him calm down. Still angry after his friends failed to calm him he grabbed a revolver and shot up the house and a television. Nancy came home in the midst of this tirade and attempted to drive away in her mother's car, which was parked in the driveway.

Johnston ran out and jumped on the hood of her car as Nancy tried to drive away. Nancy stopped the car on Broadway after he had kicked in the windshield and she tried to run away. Johnston chased her, knocked her to the ground, and punched her a few times. According to Johnston, he and Nancy decided to return home but the argument resumed once they arrived afterwhich he resumed hitting and kicking her, only to take her inside and call 9-1-1.

Police found Federhofer the next day in the company of his grandmother. The boy confirmed parts of Johnston's story adding that he saw Johnston hitting his stepmother while she was still in the car when the two returned home. Johnston saw Federhofer on the porch and ordered the boy to help him get Nancy into the house. Federhofer told Johnston to "leave her alone." Johnston told Federhofer to "shut up or I'll kill you" and moved toward the boy. Federhofer ran away and spent the night with his grandmother.

A neighbor, Robyn Romanchuk, told police that she saw a man standing over a woman, kicking her repeatedly, and calling her "slut," "bitch," and "whore." She heard Federhofer, whom she knew because he played with her

133

son, scream, and saw him run away. She recognized the voice as that of the man who lived with Nancy. Romanchuk watched as the man continued kicking the woman. She saw the man drag the woman behind some bushes, beat her with a lawn chair, then go into the house, leaving the woman lying outside, and return carrying a new, unidentified weapon with which he hit the still body repeatedly. Romanchuk then saw him drag the woman over the porch and into the house.

On July 24 Johnston was indicted. On May 16, 1991, a jury found him guilty of first-degree murder and armed criminal action, and two days later recommended the death sentence because the murder involved torture and depravity of mind and was, as a result, outrageously and wantonly vile, horrible, and inhuman. Johnston received a life sentence for armed criminal action. In July the St. Louis City Circuit Court sentenced him. The day before Johnston was executed Governor Matt Blunt denied clemency (*State v. Johnston* (1997) 957 S.W.2d 734).

————

Frances Elaine Newton, a 40-year-old black female, was executed by lethal injection at the Texas State Penitentiary in Huntsville, Texas on September 14, 2005. Newton was found guilty of the 1987 murder of Adrian Newton, a 23-year-old black male, Alton Newton, a 7-year-old black male, and Farrah Newton, a 21-month-old black female. Newton, who was 21-years old when she committed the capital crime, was sentenced to death on October 25, 1988.

At 8:27 p.m. on April 7, 1987, Deputy R.W. Ricks was dispatched to an apartment complex at 6126 West Mount in Houston, Texas in response to a possible shooting. Newton was at the location along with her cousin Sondra Nelms. Lying on a couch in Newton's apartment, Ricks found the body of Newton's husband Adrian Newton with a bullet wound to the head, and the bodies of their children

Alton and Farrah Newton, both of whom had died from gunshot wounds to the chest. There were no signs of forced entry into the apartment, nor any signs of a struggle.

Earlier the same evening between 7:00 p.m. and 7:30 p.m. Newton arrived in an automobile at Nelms's residence at 6524 Sealy. Newton asked Nelms to come over to Newton's apartment to visit. Before leaving Nelms's house Newton took a blue bag out of her car and put it in an abandoned house that belonged to her parents located next door at 6520 Sealy. Upon arrival at Newton's apartment Nelms and Newton found Newton's husband and her two children dead.

Later that evening homicide detective Michael Talton spoke with Nelms who took him to the house at 6520 Sealy. Inside he found a blue bag containing a blue steel Raven Arms .25-caliber automatic, which he turned over to a crime scene officer.

The gun's owner, Michael Mouton, had loaned the gun to his cousin, Jeffrey Frelow, five or six months prior to the murders. Frelow had known Newton since junior high school and began to have a sexual relationship with her some one to two months prior to the murders. Frelow identified the gun and indicated that he kept it in a chest of drawers in his master bedroom. Because Newton often did Frelow's laundry she had access to the drawers and to the gun.

On April 8 Newton accompanied Detective Michael Parinello during a search of her apartment where she pointed out the clothing she wore the day of the murders. Parinello collected the clothing and delivered it to the Department of Public Safety Crime Laboratory to test for possible gunpowder residue.[37]

---

[37] A ballistics expert for the State established that the .25-caliber automatic pistol recovered by Talton was the murder weapon, and a forensics expert for the State established that
(*continued*)

Newton's brother-in-law, Sterling Duane Newton, was also living at the apartment where the murders occurred and was present on the evening of April 7. When Sterling arrived at the apartment at 5:30 p.m. or 6:00 p.m. Newton was there. Newton requested that Sterling leave the apartment to give her some time alone with her husband to talk over their marital problems. Sterling remained at the apartment for approximately one to one and one-half hours before leaving.

Ramona Bell, a long time acquaintance of Newton's husband, had been dating him for some time prior to April 7. Bell knew that Newton and her husband were on bad terms. Bell testified that on the 7th she called Newton's husband from work at approximately 6:45 p.m. and Newton answered the telephone. Bell then spoke to Newton's husband for about 15 minutes. During the telephone conversation he told Bell that he was tired and was going to go to sleep but not until Newton left because he did not trust Newton.

Alphonse Harrison, a friend of Newton's husband, had seen him earlier in the day on the 7th and the two made plans to get together that night. Harrison testified that he called Newton's husband between 7:00 p.m. and 7:15 p.m. that evening and Newton answered the telephone. Harrison never got to talk to Newton's husband because Newton put him on hold and left him holding for possibly 45 minutes. Harrison hung up but continued to call back and finally got an answer around 9:00 p.m. when Nelms

---

(*continued*)

nitrites were present on Newton's skirt. The forensics expert opined that the nitrites came from gunpowder residue and were consistent with someone shooting a pistol in the lower front area of the skirt. He further testified that another possible possible source of nitrites would be fertilizer, and a forensic expert for Newton confirmed that nitrites could come from fertilizer.

answered the telephone and told him that Newton's husband had been shot.

Claudia Chapman was working for a State Farm Insurance agent when she met Newton in September 1986. Newton came in for automobile insurance and Chapman talked to her about purchasing life insurance. On March 18, 1987, Newton purchased a $50,000 life insurance policy on herself, another on her husband, Adrian, and a third on her daughter, Farrah. According to the insurance applications Newton was the primary beneficiary on the latter two policies, which became effective immediately. Both Newton and her mother had made claims on the policies as of the time of trial.

On July 17 the five-foot three-inch tall Newton was indicted in Harris County for capital murder. On October 24, 1988, the jury convicted Newton of capital murder and recommended a death sentence the following day. On June 17, 1992, the Texas Court of Criminal Appeals affirmed her conviction and sentence. In a 7-0 vote, two days before Newton was executed, the Texas Board of Pardons and Paroles recommended that Governor Rick Perry not commute her death sentence to life in prison to which the governor complied (*Newton v. Dretke* (2004) 371 F.3d 250).

———

John W. Peoples Jr., a 48-year-old white male, was executed by lethal injection at the Holman Prison in Atmore, Alabama on September 22, 2005. Peoples was found guilty of the 1983 murder of Paul G. Franklin, a 34-year-old white male, Judy Charon Franklin, a 34-year-old white female, and Paul G. Franklin Jr., a 10-year-old white male. Peoples, who was 26-years old when he committed the capital crime, was sentenced to death on December 7, 1983.

The Franklins, Paul, Judy, and their son Paul Jr. resided in a house on a peninsula that extends into Lake

Logan Martin near Pell City, Alabama. Paul owned as many as five vehicles including a red 1968 Chevrolet Corvette, and had a very close relationship with Rose Franklin, his mother in Birmingham. Paul and Rose would talk by telephone "every" day, and on July 6, 1983, they spoke at about 6:30 p.m. and again for five minutes at about 8:30 p.m.

On July 7 the Franklin's housekeeper arrived at the Franklin residence as she had for the past three years to find the house unlocked and no one home. She found the lights and the color televisions turned on and the family dog "laying" in the washroom. She began her housekeeping chores as usual, when sometime between 8:30 a.m. and 9:00 a.m. Rose telephoned. After talking with Rose, the housekeeper returned to work, and while getting the mop and pail, discovered that Judy's Buick Regal was downstairs in the garage. This was unusual in that the Buick was usually parked outside and Paul's red corvette was kept inside the garage "fastened up all the time." The housekeeper also noted a puddle of oil where the Corvette was supposed to be.

As the housekeeper proceeded with her cleaning she found under the bed in the master bedroom, Paul's pants folded in his usual but peculiar manner still containing his keys, billfold, and money clip. Noticing it unusual that the bed in the guest bedroom was unmade, she began vacuuming when "a voice" told her, "Rosa, get the hell out of here and now," whereupon she "dropped everything right then and there" and left.

At about 2:00 p.m. Rose arrived at the residence finding no one home and the doors unlocked. Paul was supposed to have made arrangements for her car to be serviced at a local garage, but when she telephoned the garage from the residence, she found that no appointment had been made even though the servicemen did come get her car and service it. In the meantime Rose waited at the residence hoping the family would return. When no one arrived she began calling family members—her son Hugh Franklin, in Blakely, Georgia, and Dean Choron, Judy's mother in Birmingham. She also called the sheriff's office.

At about 7:00 p.m. Choron arrived at the residence, and a sheriff's deputy came a short time later. Choron noticed Judy's purse on the kitchen bar, and saw clothes hanging on a dresser that her daughter had been wearing the previous day. The deputy made a "short investigation" staying there about an hour and a half getting information and determining if anything was missing. Based on this investigation the deputy put out a police broadcast that the family was missing, and later that night when he obtained a tag number for the missing Corvette, issued a report of the missing car entered in the National Crime Information Center (NCIC). Both mothers were asked to remain in the house until Sunday afternoon.

On the night of July 8 Officers Marvin Roye and Ed Traylor of the Alabama Bureau of Investigation (ABI), and Investigator Owen Harmon of the St. Clair Sheriff's Department continued the investigation at the residence, and although they were unable to determine if anything was missing, Traylor noted an oily shoeprint from a shoe or boot that had a "vibram lug type sole."

On July 10 further investigation disclosed the name "John Peoples" written in eyebrow pencil on the top of a clothes hamper in the bathroom. The name which was later determined to have been written after July 2 was covered by a piece of toilet tissue lying over the name and the end of a towel on a towel rack draped over the clothes hamper. Choron had recognized the handwriting as being her daughter's, and Rose informed the officers that Peoples was someone she knew had worked for her son around the house. She also told them that Peoples, who she described as being a "big robust type fellow, a big man," had borrowed money from her son in the past and had lately been trying to borrow more money. Both mothers left the residence that day leaving authorities with a house key.

On July 11 the officers learned that on the previous Friday, a large man named John Peoples had attempted to sell a red Corvette with a "59 tag" to Regal Pontiac Company in Sylacauga. Peoples was described as being about six foot four and weighing 240 pounds.

On the same day Childersburg Police Chief Ira Finn received a telephone call from Paul Wesson, a Childersburg druggist, concerning a man being at the drug store trying to sell a red Corvette. Finn knew the car was listed "on the NCIC machine," and when he gave the druggist the tag and registration numbers of the car, the druggist told him that was the car the man at the drug store was trying to sell. Finn notified officers to go to Wesson's Pharmacy.

At 1:29 p.m. Assistant Police Chief Lewis Finn arrived at the drug store where he found Peoples and the red Corvette. Finn walked in the drug store and asked Peoples if the car was his, and he replied that it was. Outside Finn informed Peoples he would have to come to the police station. Peoples drove the Corvette to the station while officers followed in a police car.

At the police station Peoples was taken into Chief Finn's office, and the chief told him the Corvette had been reported stolen from Pell City and that the three family members were missing. Peoples replied, "Well, by god, I didn't steal the car. I've got a bill of sale for it." He then threw a piece of paper on the chief's desk. The chief looked at it without picking it up, and replied, "Well, that ain't too much of a bill of sale. It's not notarized." Peoples responded, "Well, I've got a goddamn tag receipt," and he threw another piece of paper on the desk. He was then told he would have to wait until the arrival of ABI officers, whom Chief Finn had already notified.

Upon receiving the call in Talladega from Chief Finn, Harmon and Traylor immediately drove to Childersburg, arriving around 2:15 p.m. about 20 minutes after Peoples had been brought in. The officers talked to Chief Finn for some 20 to 30 minutes. Finn gave the officers a "bill of sale"—it read, "I Paul Franklin trade John Peoples one 1968 Corvette for 50 percent ownership of the C.J. Supper Club."[38] The document was signed, "Paul G. Franklin, John W. Peoples, and Judy Franklin." Two sets of handwritten figures appeared at the bottom of the document: "1946785406573 and 59A7093 59-5560."

At about 2:45 p.m. Peoples was given a *Miranda* warning to which he told the officers he understood his rights. Attorney Ray Robbins telephoned while the officers were questioning Peoples. Traylor talked with Robbins who told him that Peoples's father had contacted him and "he just called to see what was going on with" his son. Peoples then talked to Robbins and told him that he "didn't need him or an attorney at that time, that [the officers] were talking to him about the car that he had purchased from Paul Franklin, and that if he decided he needed him later he would call him back."

After talking with his attorney Peoples gave the officers a statement in which he admitted he and his cousin, Timothy Millard Gooden, a 24-year-old white male, had gone to the Franklin residence on the night of July 6 in Peoples's Toyota pickup truck, but that they left the Franklins at home alive and well about 12:00 p.m. or 12:30 p.m. that night. The officers asked Peoples if he would give them permission to search "his Toyota pickup he was riding in when he went over to Paul Franklin's residence," and to search both his residence in Talladega and the Corvette. Peoples said, "that would be fine."

---

[38] Curtis Jackson, the man who actually owned the C.J. Supper Club, came to the police station and told the officers the establishment belonged to him and that the only right, title, or interest Peoples had in it was "operating rights from June the 15th to July the 15th."

A permission to search form was then read to Peoples, which informed him he had the right to refuse to allow the searches. At approximately 4:30 p.m. Peoples signed the form afterwhich he left the Childersburg police station with the officers taking him to his father's residence. There the officers searched his Toyota pickup truck; nothing was taken from the truck.

They then went to Peoples's apartment in Talladega, where Peoples unlocked the door for the officers. Upon searching the apartment the officers found, in a dirty clothes box, a shirt and a pair of pants that appeared to have bloodstains on them. When the officers found the clothes Peoples "just slid down the wall and was kind of sitting on his heels," and when confronted with the apparent bloodstains, Peoples said they were from barbecue sauce "that he got on there on the 4th of July when he was barbecuing down at the club." However, "at this point [Peoples] got very nervous and upset *** started sweating just around the lower part of his chin, sweat was just a-dripping off."

At 9:00 p.m. on July 11 Peoples arrived at the St. Clair County Jail in Pell City where he was again given a *Miranda* warning and read a waiver-of-rights form, which he read and signed. He was then interviewed until about 1:30 a.m. at which time the decision was made by the assistant district attorney of St. Clair County to formally place him under arrest for theft by deception of the Corvette.

Peoples was wearing "what appeared to be pigskin type boots with a vibram lug type sole," similar to the shoeprint found in the Franklin home. The officers asked him for the boots he was wearing and before he was locked up Peoples took them off and gave them to the officers. The next morning Harmon appeared before a magistrate and swore out a theft warrant, which was later read to Peoples. Bond was set at $25,000.

Sometime after the warrant had been read to him Peoples sent a note to the officers requesting that they come and talk to him, that it was "important." Roye responded and again read him the *Miranda* warning. Peoples then made a statement to the effect "he could clear this thing up about 90 percent" and that he "could furnish *** two names" but that he wanted to wait until his lawyer arrived before he furnished the information. Robbins arrived and after talking with Peoples told the officers that his client "didn't have anything that would help [them]." Routine mugshots and fingerprints were made that afternoon.

About noon the next day Robbins returned to participate in an interview of People's wife afterwhich a discussion ensued between Robbins and Assistant District Attorney Dennis Abbott. The discussion lasted less than an hour and was prompted by an earlier request by Peoples that he take a polygraph test.

According to Abbott, Robbins told him that Peoples "had already told us all that he knew and there might be one or two little things that we didn't already know, but it wouldn't help us any in our investigation." Abbott then asked Robbins if he would recommend that Peoples take the polygraph test that he had previously requested. Based on Peoples's prior statements Abbott's offer was that if a polygraph test confirmed that he was being truthful, Peoples could post bond, a preliminary hearing would be set, and, if there were no further incriminatory developments, he would "probably walk" after the preliminary hearing because there would not be sufficient evidence to bind him over to the grand jury. Robbins then stated that he would recommend that Peoples take the polygraph test because he believed his client was telling the truth.

At about 5:00 p.m. on the 13th Peoples and Robbins were brought from the county jail to the sheriff's office. Robbins told Roy that Peoples had some information to add to his prior statement. In the presence of his attorney, Harmon, and Traylor, Peoples stated that the Franklin

143

family was dead. Traylor then asked Peoples if he would take them to the bodies. Abbott was called to come to the sheriff's office, and when he arrived, Robbins said, "John Peoples is going to tell ya'll some more. All of them are dead."

Peoples then took police to the bodies of the Franklin family in Talladega County, in a wooded area just off County Road 377. All three bodies were in the same stage of advanced decomposition. On July 15, four days after Peoples was arrested, Gooden directed officers to the location where the bodies of the Franklin family had been found two days earlier under the guidance of Peoples.

Unexpended rounds of .22-caliber rat shot and a gun sight elevator were found lying near the bodies. Mud-grip tire tracks were found leading off the paved road, and a "mashed" path of grass indicated that Paul's body had been dragged through the grass. Also, the bottoms of the yellow pajamas he was wearing were pulled down around his ankles, consistent with his body having been dragged. Both Judy and Paul Jr. had been blindfolded.

Judy's skull had been fractured: "There was a large fragmented skull fracture 4½ by 4 inches in diameter. There were ten separate pieces of skull in this area." She had been also shot: "The upper arm near the armpit on the right showed a perforated wound going from this arm through the arm and a few perforations were present in front of her armpit in this area. Went through the robe and skin and soft tissue in this area and minute, very small pellets were recovered from the wound." The pathologist opined that Judy died from blunt force trauma due to a blow to the head.

Paul Jr.'s skull was also crushed. There was a "large fragmented skull fracture in the back of the left side of the head *** virtually the entire left side of the head *** [an] area 6½ by 4." The skull fracture was very similar to Judy's skull fracture and there were approximately 15 fragments in the fractured area. The impact side of Paul Jr.'s skull was a patterned injury consistent with having been inflicted by the rifle Peoples had shown the two deputies. The pathologist opined that Paul Jr. died from blunt trauma to the skull. The pathologist further opined that Paul's death "was not accident or natural or suicide."

At about 8:30 p.m. on July 19 Peoples sent a signed note to the sheriff of St. Clair County: "To whom it may concern I John Peoples are asking to see the sheriff of St. Clair County on the date of July 19, 1983 it is important and he is the only one I will talk to ***."

When St. Clair County Sheriff Lewis Brown went to the jail, Peoples indicated he also wanted to talk to Talladega County Sheriff Jerry Studdard who was then summoned to the jail. Brown told Peoples to call his lawyer and got the number for him. Peoples placed the call and unable to contact his attorney told the two sheriffs his attorney was not at home. Brown then told him to call another attorney, and so Peoples said he wanted to call attorney George Sims. Brown then called information and got Sims's home telephone number but when Peoples was given the number, he said, "Well, that's all right, I don't need a lawyer. I'll just talk to y'all."

Brown began advising Peoples of his *Miranda* rights and when Peoples interrupted, saying, "You don't have to read those rights, I've probably had those rights read to me over a thousand times" Brown continued to read the warning and again ask if Peoples wanted to call a lawyer. Peoples answered, "No, I don't want to call a lawyer, I just want to talk to ya'll. I don't want you taping anything or I don't want ya'll writing down any kind of statement, I just want to talk to ya'll." He was asked if he understood his rights, to which he said, "Yes." He was then asked, "Having these rights in mind, do you wish to talk to us now?" Peoples replied, "Yes, I do."

The sheriffs then talked to Peoples and asked him to write a statement that Peoples wrote out and signed on a form containing both a *Miranda* warning and a waiver of rights. The statement read: "The case I am in I did do it. Concerning the Franklin family I did do it." After he had written the statement, signed it, and had it witnessed by the sheriffs, Peoples said, "Man, I am glad I told somebody that. It's really a load off my shoulders. I am really glad I told you." The statement was admitted into evidence at trial.

On July 22 Peoples was removed from St. Clair County and transported to the Talladega County Jail. While being booked Peoples said to Deputy Terry Brewer, "Terry if you'll get Ricky, I'll show ya'll where the gun is." Brewer got Deputy Rick Daniels, and they took Peoples across the street to an investigator's office, where they met with Studdard.

Peoples was then given a *Miranda* warning to which he said he understood his rights and signed the waiver-of-rights form. He also wrote on the form: "I already have a lawyer, but I do not wish to talk to him or have him present with me at this time." He then took the officers "out in the Brecon area" and showed them a gun wrapped in a towel and concealed in some bushes. The gun was bent and broken.

On August 3 a Talladega County grand jury indicted Peoples on five counts of capital murder. Convicted on all counts the jury recommended the death penalty by a vote of 11-1. Peoples asked to be electrocuted as his original death sentence had stipulated but his request was denied. The State argued that Peoples had missed the 2002 deadline to request the electric chair and thus lethal injection, the State's default method since July 1, 2002, was to be applied. The day before he was executed Governor Bob Riley denied clemency.

Gooden testified for the prosecution in a plea deal wherein he received a life sentence with the possibility of

146

parole[39] (*Peoples v. Campbell* (2004) 377 F.3d 1208; *Peoples v. State* (1986) 510 So.2d 554; *Peoples v. State* (1990) 565 So.2d 1177).

---

[39] According to Gooden on July 6 he came home from work and his wife gave him a message from Peoples prompting him to go to Peoples's house. There, Gooden asked Peoples if he was "going to get the car that day." Peoples said, "yes," and told Gooden he would pick him up "around dark."

About 8:00 p.m. or 8:30 p.m. Peoples picked up Gooden in Peoples's Toyota pickup truck with its large mud-grip tires. The two then drove to the Franklin residence. At the Franklin residence Peoples got out, and Gooden left in the truck and went to a nearby store and bought cigarettes. Gooden then drove back to the Franklin residence and knocked on the door, which was answered by Peoples. Gooden went in and had a seat. Peoples sat at a table with Paul and Judy "with a bunch of papers on the table with a notebook pad." Peoples got up, asked Gooden to sit there with the Franklins, and "went to the back of the house." He returned accompanied by "the little boy."

Peoples asked Paul "about selling the car" and Paul told him he was going to keep "the car" for the little boy for when he grew up. Peoples "got kind of pissed off about it" and again asked Paul to sell him the car to which Paul again declined. Peoples then "went to the back room and when he come back, he had some sheets or towels and [Paul's .22-caliber Winchester] rifle in his hand."

Peoples then gagged and blindfolded Judy and the boy, and while Gooden watched them, Peoples took Paul downstairs. When Gooden heard a commotion downstairs, he started down the stairs with Judy and the boy. Judy "nudged" Gooden in the side, and when he took her gag off and asked, "What's wrong," she said she wanted to go to the bathroom. Gooden let her go to the upstairs bathroom while he stood at the end of the hall, and when she came out, he took her and the boy back downstairs after replacing her gag and blindfold.

Downstairs Paul was lying on the floor by the pool table in the big family playroom. Peoples then told Gooden to go get the truck and bring it "to the basement door where the Corvette was

(*continued*)

147

Herman Dale Ashworth, a 32-year-old white male, was voluntarily executed by lethal injection at the Southern Ohio Correctional Facility in Lucasville, Ohio on September 27, 2005. Ashworth was found guilty of the 1996 murder of

---

(*continued*)

sitting." While Gooden got the truck Peoples "got some blankets and stuff and throwed a blanket over the man." The hands of Judy and the boy were then tied, and they were locked in the truck. Gooden and Peoples then "pushed the car out and jumped the car off," and Peoples "put the man in the car with the blanket over him and [Peoples and Gooden] left."

Peoples and Gooden then "came back to I-20, came back up to 77, come down 77 to Jackson's Trace" and "pulled off in a wooded area." Peoples dragged Paul from the car, dragging him backwards in a "bear hug," and then he came back out of the woods. "[Peoples] walked up and he got the woman and little boy out of the truck. She started asking [Peoples], said, what are you doing. He said it didn't matter, like that. They went down in the woods and the woman was crying and begging [Peoples], saying please don't ***." Gooden also testified that he heard a gunshot and the woman still screaming, and "a few minutes later, everything got quiet."

When Peoples re-emerged from the woods, he told Gooden "to meet him over there where he used to run a store on 77." Peoples then put the gun and blanket back in the Corvette and left. Gooden complied and later met Peoples at the specified location. The two then returned to the Franklin residence, where Peoples went in and stayed for about 10 or 15 minutes before coming out carrying a telephone and two drinking glasses. The two then returned to the pickup truck. Gooden drove the pickup truck home, and Peoples and his wife went to Gooden's home about 2:00 a.m. to get the truck. Peoples showed Gooden some money, which Gooden counted—in excess of $1100—and then gave back to Peoples. Gooden did not get any of the money and when Gooden gave Peoples the truck keys, Peoples said, "I'll fix you up later." Gooden "didn't see him no more after that."

Daniel L. Baker, a 40-year-old white male. Ashworth, who was 23-years old when he committed the capital crime, was sentenced to death on June 17, 1997.

On September 10, 1996, Ashworth went to the Wagon Wheel Bar in Newark, Ohio and began drinking. Around 4:30 p.m. or 5:00 p.m. Ashworth's cousin, Louis Dalton, met Ashworth at the bar to have a few drinks. Dalton stayed for a couple of hours and before he left Ashworth asked him whether he could borrow some money. Dalton told him no. Lloyd Thompson, owner of the Wagon Wheel, saw Ashworth in the bar around 8:00 p.m. or 9:00 p.m. Ashworth asked Thompson whether he could borrow $10 and Thompson said no.

Thompson later saw Ashworth talking to a man whom Thompson had not seen before but who was later identified as Daniel Baker. People in the bar, including Baker, were buying Ashworth drinks. Ashworth told Thompson that he thought Baker was gay and he was going to get rid of him even though Thompson had not observed anything that would indicate that Baker was gay or had made any homosexual advances.

Thompson saw Ashworth and Baker leave together. He also saw Ashworth later in the evening but never saw Baker again. When Ashworth returned to the bar he appeared to have over $40 with him. He also appeared to have a swollen right hand. Ashworth asked Thompson to cover for him if the cops came in.

Around 9:30 p.m. Dalton received a call from Ashworth. Ashworth told him that he had been in a fight and "kicked the shit out of this guy." Ashworth said that he kicked him until he could not kick him any more, and also mentioned that his hand hurt.

Tanna Brett, Ashworth's girlfriend, saw Ashworth that evening outside the TNT Bar and Wagon Wheel Bar. As they were talking to each other Brett grabbed Ashworth's right hand. Ashworth fell to his knees in pain and told Brett that he hurt his hand in a fight with a guy. Ashworth then took her behind the Legend Bar to the Salvation Army loading dock where Brett observed a man lying on his belly; she did not see any blood. Brett heard what sounded like snoring coming from the man. She did not observe any belongings on the ground. They stayed less than a minute. Brett did notice that Ashworth had blood on one shoe.

Brett and Ashworth proceeded to the TNT Bar where Ashworth bought a "bucket of beer." Brett noticed that Ashworth had a $5 bill, a few singles, and a $10 bill. Ashworth told Brett that he thought he should go back and finish the guy off because he did not want to be recognized. Brett begged him not to go back and Ashworth told her he was going over to the Wagon Wheel Bar.

Brett stayed at the TNT until "last call," around 2:15 a.m. She then went over to the Wagon Wheel but Ashworth was not there. Brett proceeded to the Legend Bar to look for him, and when she got near the Legend she heard a noise that sounded like something hitting metal. She walked toward the noise that was coming from the Salvation Army loading dock.

Brett saw the same man lying on his back with his head against the garage door. This time there was a lot of blood and she observed papers and articles strewn about. Brett could hear the man breathing and saw him move his hand a little bit. She left because it made her sick to her stomach. Brett returned to the Wagon Wheel, grabbed Ashworth and said, "You robbed him." Ashworth did not say anything; he just looked at the floor. She saw dark spots on his pants.

Around 3:45 a.m. on September 11 Baker's body was found on the Salvation Army loading dock. There was blood around Baker's head and upper shoulder area, so much blood, in fact that it had seeped underneath the garage door. Items belonging to Baker were strewn about the area. Bloody footprints surrounded the area and were found on Baker's chest. While police were investigating the crime scene a 9-1-1 call came into the police station around 4:13 a.m. The caller said that he had beaten a man badly and left him on the loading dock of the Salvation Army. The call was traced to a public telephone located less than one mile from where Ashworth was living since April, the home of his cousin Ron Sillin.

Police went to Sillin's home, knocked on the door, and rang the doorbell, but no one answered. They called Sillin and obtained permission to enter finding Ashworth asleep in the back bedroom. Police woke him and asked him to come down to the police station for questioning. He ultimately agreed and dressed. After being informed of his *Miranda* rights Ashworth agreed to make a taped statement.

Ashworth said he had been drinking at the Wagon Wheel starting around 3:30 p.m. on the 10th. Around 8:00 Baker arrived and the two started talking together. Upon Baker's suggestion the pair went over to the Legend Bar where they had a beer, and then Ashworth suggested going back to the Wagon Wheel.

On the way back to the Wagon Wheel, Baker told Ashworth that he wanted to show him something. They went around the corner where Ashworth claimed Baker "reached down and grabbed me on my butt." Ashworth told him to stop, that he was not "that way," but Baker would not stop. Ashworth said that he kept trying to move away from Baker and they ended up on the loading dock. Baker kept moving toward him and again tried grabbing him. Ashworth began to hit him with his fist and "freaked out." Baker did not fight back but kept coming at him saying, "it's okay," it'll be all right." Ashworth said that he eventually picked up a six-inch wide, five-foot long board and struck Baker with it.

After Baker fell down Ashworth kicked him. Ashworth took the wallet out of Baker's pants but denied keeping the wallet. He said he just took the money, about $42, and the remaining contents of the wallet spilled out.

Ashworth said that he went back to the Wagon Wheel Bar and drank and then went to the TNT Bar and drank some more. He then went home but did not remember how he got there. He woke up Sillin and asked him to take him up to Tee Jaye's Restaurant to get something to eat. On the way back Ashworth asked Sillin to stop so he could use the telephone because he was worried about Baker, but Sillin told him not to worry about it.

After Ashworth got home he said that he began to worry and walked back to the pay phone and called 9-1-1. He told the operator that he had hurt someone, that the person needed some help, and described the location, but he did not identify himself. He then went back home and went to bed. Ashworth never admitted going back to the loading dock a second time.

During his statement to police Ashworth indicated that the clothes he had worn were at his house and that he was wearing the shoes he had on during the encounter with Baker. The shoes had blood on them and police confiscated them. The officers asked for Ashworth's consent to obtain the clothing he had worn and he gave it. Police also obtained a search warrant. The pants they recovered had blood on them and in the front pants pocket police found Baker's driver's license and credit cards. The soles of Ashworth's shoes matched the bloody footprints found at the scene and on Baker's shirt.

The coroner found that Baker had died as a result of numerous blunt force injuries noting that the injuries he observed were typical of those he was more likely to see as a result of a car accident or an airplane crash. In his 20-years of practice he had seen only one other case with such severe injuries as a result of a beating suggesting that with such injuries death would normally occur in 10 to 20 minutes.

On September 20 Ashworth was indicted in Licking County for aggravated murder. Ashworth was arraigned ten days later, and after first pleading not guilty, changed his plea to guilty and waived his right to present mitigating evidence. After being found competent to stand trial a three-judge panel accepted Ashoworth's guilty plea and sentenced him to death. Ashworth did not apply for clemency which both the Ohio Parole Board and Governor Bob Taft subsequently denied (*State v. Ashworth* (1999) 85 Ohio St.3d 56).

———

Alan Lehman Matheney Jr., a 54-year-old white male, was executed by lethal injection at the Indiana State Prison in Michigan City, Indiana on September 28, 2005. Matheney was found guilty of the 1989 murder of Lisa Marie Bianco, a 34-year-old white female. Matheney, who was 38-years old when he committed the capital crime, was sentenced to death on May 11, 1990.

Lisa Bianco was afraid of her husband, Matheney, and so when she decided to end years of beatings and other abuse by divorcing him on June 19, 1985, she got an order of protection warning him to stay away from her Mishawaka, Indiana home. Matheney, however, was not dissuaded and he continued to intimidate her. Bianco continued to complain, and on July 3 Matheney abducted the couple's two young daughters, Brooke, 6, and Amber, 2. On August 23 Matheney was arrested more than 650 miles away in Wilmington, North Carolina, and extradited back to Mishawaka where Bianco pressed charges.

After posting $1000 bail Matheney was released. Matheney beat up Bianco again, was arrested again, and released again. Finally in 1987, facing charges that included illegal confinement, rape and assault, Matheney plea-bargained his way to a reduced charge that resulted in an 8-year prison sentence.

In January 1989 while Matheney was in state prison Bianco learned that Matheney was eligible for a pass under the prison's furlough program. Bianco appealed to the local prosecutor for help and Matheney was denied that furlough. "We told them it was not appropriate or wise to release him," recalled St. Joseph County Prosecutor

Michael Barnes. "We said we wanted to be notified if and when he ever came up for another pass."

On March 4 Matheney received an eight-hour pass from the prison authorizing him to travel to Indianapolis. However, neither Bianco nor Barnes was notified. Matheney headed north to St. Joseph County where Bianco lived. Stopping at his family's house in Granger, Matheney telephoned Bianco who told him she would file more charges against him and that he would never get out of prison. Matheney then took an unloaded shotgun from a friend's house, drove the nine miles to Bianco's house where he parked a few houses away, walked to her backyard, and broke in through her back door.

Bianco told her children to call a neighbor for help, and wearing only her underpants, ran outside with Matheney in pursuit. Brooke ran next door to the home of Denise Sloan who called police. Sloan watched Matheney catch up with Bianco in the middle of the street where he repeatedly beat her with the shotgun using such force that the gun broke. Bianco died as a result of severe blunt trauma to the head afterwhich Matheney surrendered to police.

Matheney was charged with one count of intentional murder and one count of burglary. At trial Matheney asserted he was legally insane and so he was examined by various mental health professionals. No one testified that Matheney had been legally insane when he murdered Bianco, but Dr. Helen Morrison, an expert for the defense, testified that he suffered from some sort of paranoid personality disorder (pervasive distrust and suspicousness interpreting other people's motives as malevolent) or schizophrenic disorder (delusions or hallucinations).

The jury unanimously recommended the death sentence and the Lake Superior Court followed the jury's recommendation. Matheney failed to attend his clemency hearing and in so doing negated the need for the Indiana Parole Board to make a recommendation; thereafter Governor Mitch Daniels denied clemency (*Matheney v.*

Anderson (2001) 253 F.3d 1025; *Matheney v. State* (2005) 833 N.E.2d 454).

———

Ronald Ray Howard, a 32-year-old black male, was executed by lethal injection at the Texas State Penitentiary in Huntsville, Texas on October 6, 2005. Howard was found guilty of the 1992 murder of Bill Davidson, a 43-year-old white male. Howard, who was 18-years old when he committed the capital crime, was sentenced to death on July 14, 1993, and again on January 26, 1999.

On April 11, 1992, outside Edna, some 100 miles southwest of Houston, Texas, Howard was driving an automobile that he had stolen three days earlier when Department of Public Safety Trooper Davidson noticed that the right headlight of the vehicle was broken. Davidson pulled Howard over to the side of the road, called in the license plate, and got out of his police car.

As Davidson approached the driver-side window Howard shot him in the neck with a 9-millimeter pistol and drove away. Davidson told police who arrived at the scene that a lone-black male was the shooter. Law enforcement officers arrested Howard later that night, and three days later Davidson died.

On April 30 a Jackson County grand jury indicted Howard for capital murder. At the time of the murder Howard was on probation having received in 1991 a 6-year probated sentence for burglary of a motor vehicle. Given the multiple confessions by Howard to police, the grand jury, and fellow inmates, numerous eyewitnesses, and evidence that at the time of his arrest Howard possessed hollow point bullets matching the firearm used to kill Davidson, Howard's counsel did not contest the State's evidence at the guilt phase of his trial.

On July 13, 1993, the jury convicted Howard of capital murder and the following day, he was sentenced to death. On December 18, 1996, the Texas Court of Criminal

Appeals overturned his sentence finding that the trial court erroneously dismissed a prospective juror over her ability to impose a death sentence. In January 1999 Howard was again sentenced to death, and on December 19, 2001, the Texas Court of Criminal Appeals affirmed the judgment (*Howard v. Dretke* (5th Cir. 2005) No. 04-70021).

––––

Luis Ramirez, a 42-year-old Hispanic male, was executed by lethal injection at the Texas State Penitentiary in Huntsville, Texas on October 20, 2005. Ramirez was found guilty of the 1998 solicitation of the murder of Nemecio Nandin, a 29-year-old Hispanic male. Ramirez, who was 34-years old when he committed the capital crime, was sentenced to death on May 4, 1999.

On April 8, 1998, Edward Bell, a 36-year-old white male, murdered Nemecio Nandin at a house owned by Lana Riordan in the nominal 850-person town of Miles, Texas. Nandin had been shot twice in the head with a shotgun and buried on the property.

Nandin, a firefighter and part-time washer/dryer repairperson was dating Ramirez's ex-wife, Dawn Holquin. Ramirez and Holquin were divorced in late 1995 and Holquin had begun dating Nandin in 1997. Ramirez had been jealous of Holquin's boyfriends, and Ramirez's daughter testified that Ramirez was visibly upset about his ex-wife's relationship with Nandin.

In the days before Nandin's murder Ramirez was seen meeting with Bell at Riordan's house. Bell and his girlfriend, Lisa McDowell, had previously lived in the house. After the murder Nandin's truck was discovered at a local Wal-Mart. McDowell testified that she left Bell alone without a car at Riordan's house between 11 a.m. and noon on the day of the murder and that Ramirez dropped Bell off at McDowell's aunt's house between 3:30 p.m. and 4:00 p.m. that afternoon. As McDowell drove Bell back from her aunt's house back to Riordan's house later that afternoon she saw Bell throw two latex gloves out of the car window. Police later recovered the gloves and a set of keys fitting Nandin's truck.

A subsequent search of McDowell's car revealed Bell's wallet containing two of Ramirez's business cards and handwritten notes including directions to Holquin's house, Holquin's address, Holquin's uncle's address, and descriptions of Holquin's and her uncle's cars. Police also discovered in the car a pair of jeans and a glove spattered with Nandin's blood.

Shortly after the murder but before his arrest in Tyler, 330 miles east of Miles, Bell described Nandin's murder to Timothy Hoogstra. Bell told Hoogstra, at whose home he was staying at the time of the murder, that Ramirez had hired him to kill a firefighter for $1000. Bell also told Hoogstra that he and Ramirez had gone to Riordan's house, called Nandin for a washer repair, handcuffed Nandin when he arrived, and shot him with a shotgun, burying him on the Riordan property. Testimony indicated that Ramirez had purchased the same brand of handcuffs years earlier.

Ramirez's girlfriend, Ginger Herring, testified that on the day of the murder Ramirez had packed a bag and left his home between 12:30 p.m. and 1:00 p.m. and returned around 3:00 p.m. or 3:30 p.m. Other evidence showed that Ramirez and Bell were seen together after the murder and that on at least one occasion Bell, who had no apparent means of support, returned from such a meeting with cash.

On June 4 Ramirez was indicted for the capital offense of solicitation of capital murder. On May 7 Ramirez was convicted, and seven days later he was sentenced to death. On February 13, 2002, the Texas Court of Criminal Appeals affirmed his conviction and sentence. Ramirez, who had no prior criminal record, denied involvement in Nandin's murder: "I did not murder him. I did not have anything to do with his death." On January 18, 2000, Bell was convicted of Nandin's capital murder and sentenced to life imprisonment (*Ramirez v. Dretke* (2005) 398 F.3d 691).

————

William J. Williams Jr., a 48-year-old black male, was executed by lethal injection at the Southern Ohio Correctional Facility in Lucasville, Ohio on October 25, 2005. Williams was found guilty of the 1991 murder of four black males: William Dent, 23, Eric Howard, 20, Alfonda Ray Madison Sr., 21, and Theodore Wynn Jr., 23. Williams, who was 34-years old when he committed the capital crime, was sentenced to death on August 13, 1993.

In the late 1980's Williams controlled the drug trafficking at the Kimmelbrooks housing project in east Youngstown, Ohio. Incarcerated in the California State Penitentiary from January 17, 1989 to April 28, 1991, Williams paroled to Ohio returned to find that Alfonda Madison, William Dent, Eric Howard, and others had taken over the drug trade at the Kimmelbrooks project.

Williams wanted to regain control of the drug business and so he decided to rob and kill Madison and the others. Williams had three juvenile accomplices: his 16-year-old girlfriend, Jessica M. Cherry, her 16- or 17-year-old brother, Dominic M. Cherry, and his 17-year-old best friend, Broderick Boone. Before the murders Williams outlined his plan to his three accomplices. During this meeting Williams drew interior and exterior diagrams of Madison's house. He ordered Dominic to burn the diagrams but Dominic burned only one. Williams also supplied each accomplice with a gun. He purchased Jessica's gun from a neighbor.

On August 27, 1991, Williams bought walkie-talkies at a Radio Shack store. The devices had a combined microphone-earphone earpiece that left the user's hands free. Williams also bought batteries and duct tape. Williams, Dominic, and Boone later tested the walkie-talkies.

On September 1 Jessica met with Madison and discussed a drug deal. Later that night Williams and his three juvenile accomplices arrived by car at the home Madison shared with Howard. Williams armed the three juveniles with guns and a walkie-talkie and sent them inside while he waited outside with a walkie-talkie. Once inside the house the trio drew their guns on Madison. After receiving word via walkie-talkie that the situation was secure, Williams armed with a semiautomatic, entered the house carrying a duffel bag containing handcuffs, duct tape, and gloves. Williams handcuffed and bound Madison and put tape over his mouth.

About 30 to 45 minutes later Theodore Wynn Jr., a recently discharged Air Force sergeant, came to the door looking for Madison and Howard. Jessica answered the door and told Wynn that Madison was not home and Howard was asleep. As Wynn walked back towards his car Williams told Jessica to call Wynn back into the house because Wynn could identify them. Inside the house Williams held Wynn at gunpoint and handcuffed him.

Upon Williams's orders Jessica walked to a pay phone and called and asked for Dent for the purpose of luring him to the house. When Dent arrived accompanied by Howard, Williams and his accomplices ambushed them and forced them to lie down in the bathroom. Williams strangled Madison and Wynn and then instructed Jessica to turn up the stereo to muffle the sound of gunfire. Going from room to room Williams shot each of them in the head with a gun that belonged to Madison.

The group left Madison's home but Williams, according to Jessica, went back in "to make sure they were all dead." Back at Williams's apartment he later embraced his juvenile accomplices and rewarded them with drugs. He also warned them not to tell anyone what they had done or he would kill them.

On September 24 Dominic turned himself in and gave a statement about the murders. Officers then arrested

Jessica and Broderick, who also gave statements. Thereafter Jessica, Dominic, and Broderick were held at the Mahoning County Juvenile Justice Center.

Williams was arrested in connection with the murders, and on October 14, shortly after being arrested, he escaped from jail. Williams remained a fugitive from justice, and on November 12 a Mahoning County grand jury indicted him on four counts of aggravated murder, four counts of kidnapping, and one count of aggravated burglary.

On January 12, 1992, Williams armed and dressed in a police uniform appeared at the Justice Center with two other accomplices, Paul R. Keiper Jr., a 22-year-old white male, and a juvenile named Eric Fields. After deceiving a receptionist the trio was permitted to enter. Williams held the receptionist and a deputy sheriff hostage demanding to see Jessica, Dominic, and Broderick, and after lengthy negotiations Williams surrendered to authorities.

The Mahoning County grand jury reindicted Williams on twelve counts of aggravated murder, four counts of kidnapping, and one count of aggravated burglary. Each aggravated murder charge included two felony-murder death specifications and one death specification for multiple murders. On Williams's motion, the court transferred venue to Summit County where he was convicted on all counts and specifications.[40]

The trial court merged the twelve aggravated murder counts into four and the three specifications per count into a single multiple-murder specification. Following the sentencing hearing the jury recommended death for each

---

[40] Keiper testified at trial that Williams planned to kill the three juveniles because Williams knew that they had made statements to police regarding the murders. He was subsequently convicted of kidnapping, burglary, and impersonating a police officer, and was last listed as "offender at large" for violating parole.

aggravated murder and the court sentenced him to death. On November 1, 1995, the court of appeals affirmed, and on June 11, 1997, the Ohio Supreme Court affirmed his conviction and death sentence. On September 30, 2005, the Ohio Parole Board recommended 7-0 that Govenor Bob Taft deny Williams clemency, which the governor did the day before the execution (*State v. Williams* (1997) 79 Ohio St.3d 1, 679 N.E.2d 646).

Marlin Gray, a 38-year-old black male, was executed by lethal injection at the Eastern Reception Diagnostic and Correctional Center in Bonne Terre, Missouri on October 26, 2005. Gray was found guilty of the 1991 murder of two white females: Julie Kerry, 20, and Robin Kerry, 19. Gray, who was 23-years old when he committed the capital crime, was sentenced to death on December 9, 1992.

Julie Kerry and her sister Robin made arrangements with their cousin, Thomas Cummins, a 19-year-old white male, to meet them shortly before midnight on April 4, 1991. Cummins, who was visiting at his grandparents' home in St. Louis, Missouri, sneaked away shortly before midnight to meet the girls at a prearranged location. The Kerry sisters were intent on showing Cummins a graffiti poem the girls had painted on the Chain of Rocks Bridge that had been abandoned some years earlier. The bridge spans the Mississippi River at St. Louis and was a site of drinking and partying by trespassers since its abandonment. The three arrived at the bridge, climbed through an opening in the fence, and entered the Missouri side of the bridge.

Earlier that same evening Gray, and three other black males, Reginald B. Clemons, 19, Antonio D. Richardson, 16, and Daniel Winfrey, 15, met at the home of a mutual friend in St. Louis. Gray was the oldest and largest of the group. At Gray's suggestion the four left for the Chain of Rocks Bridge to "smoke a joint" that Gray had acquired from someone at the house where the four met. The group had been at the bridge sometime before Cummins and Kerry sisters arrived.

As the Kerrys and their cousin were walking toward the Illinois side of the bridge they encountered Gray and his three companions. After a brief exchange of greetings Winfrey asked for cigarettes that were supplied by one of the Kerry sisters. As he had done earlier for his cohorts Gray demonstrated to Cummins and the girls how to climb down a manhole on the deck of the bridge to a metal platform that leads to a concrete pier that supports the bridge. Gray told Cummins the platform was a good place to be "alone with your woman." The two groups then separated with Cummins and the Kerrys walking eastward toward Illinois and Gray's group walking toward Missouri.

As they walked away Clemons suggested that the group rob Cummins and the Kerrys. Gray smiled, clapped his hands, and replied, "Yeah, I feel like hurting somebody." The four then turned and began walking back toward the east end of the bridge. While walking, Clemons and Gray engaged in some conversation. When Gray handed Winfrey a condom, he responded saying he "wasn't going to do anything." At that point Gray and Clemons pushed Winfrey against the bridge railing and said, "You're gonna do it." Winfrey then agreed to "do it."

Gray's group continued walking toward the Illinois side and soon came upon Cummins and the Kerrys. The girls were watching a campfire that had been built by someone on the Illinois side of the river when Richardson went to that side of the bridge and yelled something at the people by the campfire. The Kerrys and Cummins then began walking back toward the Missouri side of the bridge.

Gray and his three associates followed at a close distance and as they passed a bend in the bridge, Gray, on a prearranged signal, put his arm around Cummins and walked him back 10 to 15 feet telling him, "This is a robbery. Get down on the ground." Cummins complied and

Gray told him that if he looked up he would kill or shoot him. At the same time Clemons, Winfrey, and Richardson grabbed the Kerry sisters. The girls screamed and one assailant said, "Do you want to die?" ordering them to stop screaming or that he would "throw you off this bridge."

Winfrey then held Robin on the ground covering her face with her coat, and Richardson held Julie while Clemons ripped off her clothing and raped her. While Clemons and Richardson were raping the girls Gray went to Cummins, who was still lying face down on the ground and stated, "I've never had the privilege of popping somebody *** if you put your head up or try to look, I'm going to pop you."

Gray then went to where Winfrey was holding Robin on the ground and told him to watch Cummins. With Clemon's assistance Gray tore off Robin's clothing and raped her. Clemons then forced Cummins to surrender his wallet, wristwatch, some cash and keys, and upon finding a firefighter's badge, became agitated thinking that Cummins might be a police officer.

One of the assailants then forced Cummins to get up and while holding Cummins's head down so he could not see who it was, walked him a short distance on the bridge and made him lie down again where Gray and Winfrey warned him not to talk to police. One of the assailants showed Cummins his driver's license and said, "We know who you are and if you tell anybody, we're going to come and get you." Cummins then heard two voices discussing whether he would live or die.

While Gray was raping Robin, Richardson forced Julie into the manhole and followed her. When Gray finished the rape he went to Winfrey who was still watching Cummins and asked where Richardson had gone. Winfrey pointed toward the Missouri side of the river as Gray then ran off in search of Richardson and Julie, running past the manhole. According to Gray he thought Richardson had taken her "to the end of the bridge where he could take her by the river and maybe drown her or somethin'."

Clemons, after completing his rape of Robin, forced her down the same manhole where Richardson had taken Julie. Clemons then returned to Cummins and putting Cummins's coat over his head, forced him down the same manhole where Richardson and the two girls were located. Clemons then followed, as did Winfrey who was told by Clemons to go find Gray instead, and which he did.

Clemons ordered Cummins and the Kerrys to step out onto the concrete pier below the metal platform. The three were told not to touch each other as Clemons or Richardson pushed Julie and then Robin from the pier of the bridge, causing the girls to fall 50 to 70 feet to the water below. Cummins was told to jump and believing his chances of survival were better if he jumped instead of being pushed, he jumped.

Winfrey then caught up with Gray. The two were returning back onto the bridge and were near a rock pile at the entrance of the bridge when Clemons and Richardson met them. Clemons said, "We threw them off. Let's go." The group ran to their car, drove to a gas station in Alton, Illinois, and bought food and cigarettes with the stolen money. They then drove to an observation point over the Mississippi River called the Chair, where they sat and watched the river. While there, Clemons remarked, "They'll never make it to shore." Gray praised Richardson for being "brave" to push the Kerry sisters off the bridge.

Robin's body was never recovered and Julie's body was found three weeks later in the river by the sheriff of Pemiscot County, Missouri. Cummins survived and although he was the original suspect, he later testified against Gray at the trial[41] in which a jury convicted Gray of

---

[41] Cummins never mentioned Gray and his accomplices. The photographs of Cummins taken shortly after he claimed to have jumped from Chain of Rocks bridge showed his hair to be

two counts of first-degree murder as an accomplice to the killings and which the court sentenced him to death.[42] The Board of Probation and Parole recommended against clemency and Governor Matt Blunt denied clemency.

On July 2, 1993, Richardson was indicted for first-degree murder, convicted by a jury, and sentenced to death. On October 28, 2003, because a judge and not a jury had sentenced him, the Missouri Supreme Court commuted Richardson's sentence to life without parole. Clemons was also found guilty of first-degree murder and sentenced to death. Winfrey pleaded guilty to second-degree murder and forcible rape for which he was sentenced to 30 years' imprisonment in exchange for

---

clean and dry and the police report described his hair as "dry and neatly combed." The self-described firefighter, paramedic, and expert in lifesaving techniques also admitted pushing Julie away when she attempted to hold on to him in the water.

After Gray's trial Cummins filed a civil lawsuit against the City of St. Louis and detectives, Chris Pappas and Joseph Brauer. Cummins claimed police had beaten him into making a statement, threatened him, and denied him his right to counsel. He received $150,000 in a confidential settlement to resolve the case.

Pappas and Brauer also interrogated Gray, who maintained since his arrest and interrogation that on April 8, 1991, he was beaten into giving an audiotaped statement to the police in which he admitted to raping the girls.

[42] Gray did not do the killing or directly participate in it. However, he did participate in the planning of the robbery, the planning and execution of the rape, and he did twice threaten to kill Cummins showing murderous intent. Gray also continued in the criminal enterprise after the threats to kill the victims were made, and he knew that Julie and Robin had been threatened with death complimenting his friends on the killings after they had occurred. Under Missouri law such a person may be guilty of first-degree murder and therefore eligible for the death penalty without being the actual killer.

testifying for the State in the other three trials (*Gray v. Bowersox* (2002) 281 F.3d 749); *State v. Clemons* (1997) 946 S.W.2d 206; *State v. Gray* (1994) 887 S.W.2d 369; *State v. Richardson* (1996) 923 S.W.2d 301).

———

Melvin Wayne White, a 55-year-old white male, was executed by lethal injection at the Texas State Penitentiary in Huntsville, Texas on November 3, 2005. White was found guilty of the 1997 murder of Jennifer Lee Gravell, a 9-year-old white female. White, who was 47-years old when he committed the capital crime, was sentenced to death on June 14, 1999.

On August 4, 1997, White attended a neighborhood barbecue in Ozona, Texas where he consumed several alcoholic drinks. Between 10:30 p.m. and 11:00 p.m. White went home and was visited by Jennifer Gravell, a little girl who lived two doors away. White abducted Gravell and took her in his truck to a roadside rest area where he bound her hands behind her back with electrical tape, stuffed a sock in her mouth, and sexually assaulted her with an object, possibly a screwdriver. White also admitted that he penetrated Gravell's vagina with his finger.

The following day White killed Gravell by repeatedly striking her head with a tire tool afterwhich he dumped her body behind a water tank in a field outside of town. In a trashcan in White's house investigators discovered Gravell's underpants, sandals, and a ball of electrical tape with her hair in it.

White later told police where they could find Gravell's body. Shoe prints found at the crime scene matched the shoes White had been wearing at the barbecue and later found in White's home. Blood on the shoes matched Gravell's DNA. Blood on the right rear quarter panel of White's pickup truck also matched Gravell's DNA. Tire tracks at the crime scene were similar to those of White's pickup truck.

On August 15 White was indicted for capital murder. Two years later he was tried and at the punishment phase the prosecution presented evidence that White had forced his daughter to perform oral sex having penetrated her with his finger when she was 12 years old. White's daughter testified that two years later her father had offered her $50 per week if she would provide him with sexual favors upon demand.

Further evidence demonstrated that when White was between 10 and 12 years old he touched the genitals of a 4-year-old relative, and another witness testified that White allowed teenagers to have parties at his house where alcohol was served, and during a party he touched a teenage girl's breast. A third witness testified that White had watched her engage in sex with his son and later described the events in detail.

Dr. Windell Dickerson, the chief psychologist employed by the Texas prison system, opined that if one believed that White had raped his daughter then White posed a very serious risk for further violent conduct. Dickerson concluded that White was "at substantial risk" or "considerable risk" of committing criminal acts of violence that would constitute a continuing threat to society. He stated "the possibility of White doing something else in or out of prison is substantially greater than it is for an individual who is doing okay in their life."

Dickerson further testified that research indicates that sex offenders "tend to commit multiple kinds of sex offenses." He informed the jury that women serve among the prison staff, and in most units of the prison system there have been escapes from prison including one from death row. Dickerson warned that alcoholic beverages are available inside prison even though their consumption violates prison rules.

On June 10, 1999, a Pecos County jury found White guilty of capital murder and four days later, following a separate punishment hearing, recommended the death penalty. On January 31, 2001, the Texas Court of Criminal Appeals affirmed his conviction and sentence (*White v. Dretke* (5th Cir. 2005) No. 04-70024).

———

Brian D. Steckel, a 36-year-old white male, was executed by lethal injection at the Delaware Correctional Center in Symrna, Delaware on November 4, 2005. Steckel was found guilty of the 1994 murder of Sandra Lee Long, a 29-year-old white female. Steckel, who was 25-years old when he committed the capital crime, was sentenced to death on January 8, 1997.

In August 1994 Steckel met Sandra Long when she had gotten into a verbal dispute with Steckel's friend and Long's neighbor, Tammy Johnson. On September 2 Steckel gained access to Long's Driftwood Club Apartment in Wilmington, Delaware by asking her if he could use her telephone. Once inside Steckel pretending to use the phone unplugged it from the wall. He then demanded sexual favors from Long, which she refused.

The six foot three inch, 195-pound Steckel beat Long and threw her onto a couch pinning her beneath him. During the struggle Long bit Steckel's finger causing it to bleed. Steckel then attempted to strangle Long with a pair of nylons that he had brought with him. When his attempts to strangle her with the nylons failed Steckel grabbed a sock and continued to strangle her with the sock.

Long eventually fell unconscious, and while unconscious Steckel sexually assaulted her, first using a screwdriver that he brought with him, and then by raping her anally. Long remained unconscious while Steckel dragged her to the bedroom and set the bed on fire using a lighter that he had brought with him. Steckel also set fire to the curtain in Long's bathroom.

After setting the fires Steckel departed to have a few beers with a former coworker, Larry Day. Steckel drove to Day's residence during lunchtime and after Day came home for lunch he returned to work leaving Steckel alone with his wife. Steckel then asked Day's wife to drive him to a liquor store to purchase beer and on the way to the liquor store the two went past Long's now burning apartment.

Upon passing the apartment Steckel became visibly angry and slouched down in his seat asking why she went this way to which Day's wife said, "What's the matter with you, you're acting like you killed someone." Steckel then denied killing anyone and instructed Day's wife to proceed to the liquor store. While driving she noticed that Steckel's finger was bleeding but she dismissed the wound.

In the meantime police, firefighters, and passers-by responded to Long's burning apartment building. Two men, Johnny Hall and Lane Randolph, who worked as tree climbers, were driving past the apartments and stopped to render assistance. When they approached the building they heard Long, who had regained consciousness, screaming for help. The two tried in vain to extricate Long from the building, grasping her arm briefly, but the temperatures and smoke from the fire prevented them from completing the rescue. Long died in her apartment and her body was badly burned.

Later that same day the News Journal received an anonymous phone call from a male who identified himself as the "Driftwood Killer." The man named his next victim as Susan Gell. The News Journal immediately contacted police and police brought Gell into protective custody. Gell had previously reported to police that she had been receiving harassing phone calls with a "very lurid, very sexual" content. The calls were later traced to Steckel.

Based on the phone calls to the News Journal and the connection to Gell the authorities began to suspect Steckel of Long's murder. Steckel was arrested in connection with an outstanding harassment warrant for the phone calls to Gell. Upon his arrest Steckel was visibly intoxicated and agitated so police did not question him immediately.

When Steckel awoke the next morning he asked police, "So I killed her?" Police then advised him of his *Miranda* rights and offered him breakfast. Steckel waived his rights and was then interviewed by police. During this interview Steckel confessed in detail and recounted his attempts to strangle Long, his rape of Long, and the fires he set. Steckel told police he had taken the nylons, screwdriver, and lighter with him for use in the attack. He also told police that he discarded the screwdriver in a nearby dumpster. Steckel further confessed to harassing Gell and calling the *News Journal* and threatening Gell.

With Steckel's permission he was taken to Dr. Martin W. Scanlon, a forensic dentist who examined the wounds on his finger. Scanlon opined that the wound had been caused within 24 hours by Long's teeth. And while some portions of Steckel's confession lacked credibility, many of the details were confirmed by subsequent investigation by police including the autopsy of Long, the fire department's discovery of the points of origin of the fire, DNA testing of blood found on Long's apartment door matching Steckel's, and the discovery of the nylons, lighter, and screwdriver used in the attack.

Steckel's trial commenced on September 18, 1996 and lasted until October 1, 1996. On October 2 the jury convicted Steckel of three counts of first-degree murder, two counts of second-degree burglary, one count of unlawful first-degree sexual penetration, one count of unlawful first-degree sexual intercourse, one count of first-degree arson, and one count of aggravated harassment. Following an 11-1 jury recommendation Steckel was sentenced to death (*State v. Steckel* (1996) 708 A.2d 994; *Steckel v. State* (1998) 711 A.2d 5).

————

Hastings Arthur Wise, a 51-year-old black male, was voluntarily executed by lethal injection in the Capital Punishment Facility located in the Broad River Correctional

Institution in Columbia, South Carolina on November 4, 2005. Wise was found guilty of the 1997 murder of Charles Griffeth, a 56-year-old white male, David W. Moore, a 30-year-old white male, Earnest Leonard Filyaw, a 31-year-old-white male, and Esther Sheryl Wood, a 27-year-old white female. Wise, who was 43-years old when he committed the capital crime, was sentenced to death on February 2, 2001.

At about 3 p.m. on September 15, 1997, Wise, a six foot four inch, 250 pound ex-convict, drove into the employees' parking lot at the R.E. Phelon manufacturing plant in Aiken County, South Carolina as the work shifts were changing. Several weeks earlier Wise had been fired from his job as a machine operator at the plant. As Wise exited his vehicle he walked to the guard station and shot 49-year-old Stanley Vance, the security officer on duty, once in the upper abdomen with a semiautomatic pistol.

After tearing out telephone lines in the guard station Wise entered the plant's human resources office where he shot Charles Griffeth, the personnel manager, twice in the back, killing him as he sat at his desk. Wise then held his pistol to the head of a secretary as he exited Griffeth's office, tore out the secretary's telephone line, and continued into the plant.

Wise next walked to the tool and dye area where several employees were working. He fired his pistol repeatedly at several tool and die machinists, killing David Moore and Earnest Filyaw, and wounding 44-year-old Lucius Corley and 60-year-old John Mucha. Mucha was shot in the chest and suffered extensive and severe internal injuries that required multiple surgical procedures. Wise then walked toward another area of the plant as employees, who gradually had become aware of the shootings in the plant, fled the building. He then fatally shot Sheryl Wood, a quality assurance employee, in the back and leg as she stood near a doorway.

Wise continued firing his pistol at other employees in other areas of the plant. Witnesses observed Wise reload his pistol several times as he progressed through the plant. Investigators recovered four empty, 8-round magazines at the scene, plus four full magazines, and 123 additional rounds in Wise's possession. Some witnesses related that Wise was "screaming something" unintelligible during the shootings.

Wise then walked to an upstairs office shooting through glass windows and doors. He entered an office, lay down on the floor, and swallowed or attempted to swallow an insecticide. Police found Wise lying there semiconscious, arrested him, and transported him to a hospital.

Wise was tried in 2001 in Aiken County with jurors selected from Beaufort County because of similar demographics. The trial judge ruled that Wise was competent to stand trial and although Wise's attorneys had evidence of the presence of LSD in his body when the shootings occurred, Wise told the judge, "I was in total control of my faculties at the time."

Wise did not present witnesses or evidence during the guilt or sentencing phases. Wise, in fact refused to allow his attorneys to call thirteen mitigation witnesses to present evidence that life imprisonment without parole was the appropriate sentence. Wise's refusal prompted the trial judge to again have him examined by a psychiatrist who again testified that he was competent. The court sentenced Wise to death for the four murders and 60 years in prison for the shootings of Vance, Corley, and Mucha. His last meal included a lobster tail; he had no last words (*State v. Wise* (2004) 596 S.E.2d 475).

Charles Daniel Thacker, a 37-year-old white male, was executed by lethal injection at the Texas State Penitentiary in Huntsville, Texas on November 9, 2005. Thacker was found guilty of the 1993 murder of Karen Gail Crawford, a

36-year-old white female. Thacker, who was 24-years old when he committed the capital crime, was sentenced to death on June 3, 1994.

On the evening of April 7, 1993, during a telephone conversation with a friend, Karen Crawford said that she was going to go to the store for dog food. Later that same evening a resident of her apartment complex in Houston, Texas informed the maintenance supervisor, Arkan Hall, that Crawford's keys were hanging from her mailbox which was located in a common area near the apartment offices. Hall went to Crawford's apartment but she did not answer the door. He then noticed her car with her dog inside parked near the mailroom. While checking the area of the mailroom and pool Hall found the women's restroom locked. He beat on the door and a man's voice answered from the inside. The man became quiet when Hall asked why he was using the women's restroom.

Hall attempted unsuccessfully to force open the door of the restroom. He then telephoned the apartment manager, Emily Vaughn. She and her husband Terrence Cowie arrived at the scene and the three discussed what to do. Suddenly, the rest room door opened and Thacker, a parolee, emerged.

A fight ensued when Hall attempted to stop him. Hall attempted to cut Thacker with his pocketknife but Thacker sprayed him with mace and got away. Thacker sprayed Cowie as well and then pushed his way through one of the two exit gates. Hall and others nearby chased Thacker down the block and tried to cut off his escape.

In the meantime Vaughn found Crawford lying unconscious face down on the restroom floor. One shoe and one leg of her jogging pants were pulled off and the other pants leg was pulled down to her ankle. Hall and another man administered CPR detecting a heartbeat and no breathing. Some faint brain activity was detected when she arrived at the hospital but it ceased within 24 hours.

Medical examiners concluded that Crawford's death was the result of strangulation. Crawford's neck was bruised on the front and left side and her face and eyes exhibited a condition known as pinpoint hemorrhaging. It was determined that a chokehold or "hammerlock" was the probable method of strangulation. No evidence of a completed sexual assault was found.

In the early morning hours of April 8 a police canine unit found Thacker hiding in a yard near Crawford's apartment complex. A truck containing papers bearing Thacker's name was found parked outside the offices of Crawford's apartment complex. Several witnesses identified Thacker loitering about the mailroom just before the murder. Other witnesses also saw him running near where Crawford was found. A pubic hair matching a sample from Crawford was found in Thacker's underwear.

In April 1993 Thacker was indicted for capital murder. The State conceded that it did not have evidence of Thacker's intent to kill Crawford and instead presented evidence that in 1988 Thacker was convicted of sexual assault and robbery for which he was sentenced to 12 years' imprisonment. On May 4, 1994, Thacker was found guilty and five days later he was sentenced to death. On September 18, 1996, the Texas Court of Criminal Appeals affirmed his conviction and sentence on direct appeal (*Thacker v. Dretke* (2005) 396 F.3d 607).

Steven Van McHone, a 35-year-old white male was executed by lethal injection at the Central Prison in Raleigh, North Carolina on November 11, 2005. McHone was found guilty of the 1990 murder of Mildred Johnson Adams, a 53-year-old white female, and Wesley Dalton Adams Sr., a 51-year-old white male. McHone, who was 20-years old when he committed the capital crime, was sentenced to death on March 7, 1991.

On the evening of June 2, 1990, Wesley Jr., his wife Wendy Adams, and their 2-year-old son, Alex, joined Wesley Adams Sr. and his wife Mildred Adams to go on a fishing trip. At approximately 12:30 a.m. the next day they returned to their Surry County, North Carolina home. McHone, who resided with the family, was at home alone when they arrived.

After their arrival Wendy began getting Alex prepared for bed, and while doing so, she overheard McHone arguing with his mother and stepfather.[43] McHone said that "he wanted his money and he couldn't go on living like that." Wendy, Wesley Jr., and Alex went to bed. Approximately 10 or 15 minutes later Mildred opened the door to their room and asked Wesley Jr. if he had taken the handgun from the camper. Wesley Jr. said that he had not moved the gun, which the family kept in the camper solely for protection from animals. Mildred responded, "then it's missing" and she closed the bedroom door.

Wesley Jr. then got up and began to get dressed so that he could find out why McHone had been arguing with their parents, but before he left the bedroom he and Wendy heard three gunshots. Wesley Jr. told Wendy "to stay down and keep Alex covered." He then went out into the

---

[43] Cheryl Adams McMillian, McHone's half-sister, testified that one day while McMillian was at work, Mildred called her and said, "You've got to come. He's going to kill me." McMillian told her mother to calm down and tell her who she was talking about. Her mother responded, "Stevie. He's got a knife."

McMillian testified that when she arrived at home shortly after her telephone conversation with her mother she was told that McHone had chased her mother around the dining room table and into the kitchen with a knife. McMillian also testified that the last time her mother expressed fear of McHone was when she told her, "I am afraid of him. I am afraid to be alone with him. When Wes is not around, I have to watch what I say to keep him from getting so upset. He has told me that he is going to kill me."

hallway to find out what had happened. Wendy heard someone coming up the basement stairs and then heard Wesley Sr. tell Wesley Jr. to call 9-1-1.

Wesley Jr. testified that while he was talking on the telephone with the 9-1-1 operator, he turned and saw McHone and Wesley Sr. enter the back door. They were wrestling and McHone had a pistol. Wesley Jr. immediately dropped the telephone and disarmed McHone. Wesley Jr. went back to the telephone and McHone and Wesley Sr. began wrestling again. They struggled out of the living room and headed down the hallway, out of Wesley Jr.'s sight.

Approximately one minute later Wesley Sr. reappeared in the kitchen doorway and said, "Your mother is facedown out back. You have got to get help for her, your mother's facedown. I don't know how badly she's hurt." As Wesley Sr. approached Wesley Jr., McHone came to the doorway carrying a shotgun. When Wesley Sr. realized that McHone was bringing the gun up into a firing position and aiming it at Wesley Jr., he immediately moved toward McHone to reach for the gun. McHone fired the shotgun into Wesley Sr.'s chest and the force of the discharge threw him into Wesley, Jr.'s arms knocking them both to the floor. Wesley Jr.'s leg was injured as a result.

After shooting Wesley Sr. McHone raised the gun in the direction of Wesley Jr. who managed to get up from the floor and take the weapon from him. When the struggle ended Wesley Jr. told McHone to stay down and not to move. McHone began crying and saying, "Oh, my God. What have I done." Wesley Jr. turned away from McHone to see if his wife was safe. McHone then stopped crying and reached for the shotgun and Wesley Jr. struggled with McHone again. This time he was able to keep the weapon from him.

McHone suddenly began to curse Wesley Jr. and told him, "I killed him. Now I want you to kill me because I don't want to spend the rest of my life in jail. Just shoot me.

Just get it over with." McHone continued to curse Wesley Jr. in a very loud voice and stated that Wesley Jr. was gutless and "if [he] didn't kill him and he got out of jail he'd hunt [Wesley Jr.] down and hunt his family down and finish [them] off."

William Kent Hall, a member of the first response team organized by the volunteer fire service, testified that when he arrived at the Adams's residence Wesley Sr. was lying on the kitchen floor with a large chest wound and no pulse. Tommy Wayne Baker, also a member of the first response team, found Mildred on the ground in the backyard. She appeared to have been shot in the back of the head and although she was still alive she died from the gunshot wound.

Officer Jimmy Inman, a deputy sheriff with the Surry County Sheriff's Department, arrived at the crime scene shortly after 2:00 a.m. When Inman entered the house, McHone yelled, "Why did I do it? What have I done?" McHone was taken outside and placed in the patrol car. Inman smelled alcohol on McHone's breath.

Officer Terry Miller, another detective with the Surry County Sheriff's Department, testified that when he entered the residence, McHone stated, "I know what I've done, and I'll have to pay for it. Why don't you just shoot me and get it over with." Miller said that although McHone had been drinking, he was not drunk.

McHone was convicted of first-degree murder of his mother and stepfather and assault with deadly weapon with intent to kill his stepbrother. He was sentenced to death on each of the first-degree murder convictions after a jury trial. Governor Mike F. Easley denied clemency some three hours before his execution (*State v. McHone* (1993) 435 S.E.2d 296).

———

Robert Dale Rowell, a 50-year-old white male, was executed by lethal injection at the Texas State Penitentiary in Huntsville, Texas on November 15, 2005. Rowell was found guilty of the 1993 murder of Raymond David Mata, a 34-year-old Hispanic male. Rowell, who was 38-years old when he committed the capital crime, was sentenced to death on April 7, 1994.

Rowell had a $500 cocaine habit and a lengthy criminal record that included prison time for armed robbery and voluntary manslaughter. In the early morning hours of May 10, 1993, he went to the Houston, Texas home of Irvin Wright, a grossly overweight 52-year-old white male. Angie Perez and her husband, Raymond Mata, were also living in Wright's home, a purported crack house. Perez opened the door for Rowell, who said he was going to get dope and money from Wright. Holding a gun, Rowell told Perez and Mata he would shoot them if they tried to leave.

After Rowell went into Wright's room Perez heard a thumping sound followed by Wright screaming for Rowell to stop hitting him. After about three minutes Wright and Rowell went to Perez's and Mata's bedroom. Wright was staggering, covered in blood when Rowell ordered Wright, Mata, and Perez to get into the bathtub where he then shot them. Mata, who had also been struck on the back of his head with a hammer-type instrument, died from a gunshot wound. Wright later died in the hospital and Perez, who was shot in the left arm and her leg, was left paralyzed.

Police arrested Rowell at the steering column repair shop where he worked. Officers searched his work area and found a .22-caliber revolver with six spent cartridge casings in the chamber, the gun case, and Wright's bank bag.

On March 1, 1994, a Harris County grand jury indicted Rowell for capital murder. Perez testified against him at trial and evidence was presented that Rowell had killed a fellow inmate while in the penitentiary by stabbing him multiple times in the chest with a shank, a homemade knife. On December 18, 1996, the Texas Court of Criminal

Appeals affirmed his conviction and sentence (*Rowell v. Dretke* (2005) 398 F.3d 370).

———

Shannon Charles Thomas, a 34-year-old black male, was executed by lethal injection at the Texas State Penitentiary in Huntsville, Texas on November 16, 2005. Thomas was found guilty of the 1993 murder of Maria Elda Isbell Rios, a 10-year-old Hispanic female, and Victor Roberto Rios, an 11-year-old Hispanic male. Thomas, who was 22-years old when he committed the capital crime, was sentenced to death on November 8, 1996.

On Christmas Eve 1993 Thomas and his friend Keith Bernard Clay, a 25-year-old black male, entered the Baytown, Texas home of Roberto Rios, the "Vato Man," a small-time dealer of marijuana and cocaine. Thomas and Clay robbed the 32-year-old Rios, bound him in duct tape, and then murdered him by shooting him three times with a 9-millimeter pistol and stabbing him in the neck with a pair of scissors. Thomas then went upstairs and executed Rios's two children, Maria Rios and Victor Rios, by shooting each child in the head through a pillow, as they lay side-by-side on the floor.

The murders remained unsolved for over one year until police received information from Joseph "Boo" Jones, a friend of Clay and Thomas. After his arrest Thomas gave police two written statements: in the first statement he acknowledged purchasing narcotics from Rios the day of the murders but denied any knowledge of the killings; in the second statement he asserted that Clay had acted alone in killing the Rios family after Thomas had left the residence.

Thomas was indicted for capital murder. At trial there was no physical evidence linking Thomas to the crime. The State showed the jury that Thomas possessed a gun similar to the murder weapon and three witnesses testified that Thomas had asked them to participate in robbing Rios, two of whom stated that Thomas had admitted the murders. One of them, Jones, agreed to tape-record a conversation with Thomas at the request of police in which Thomas made incriminating statements about the murders.

Other evidence put Thomas at the scene of the crime including a statement by Earl Guidry, a postal worker who saw two men leaving the Rios home near the time of the killings. Guidry tentatively identified Thomas after undergoing hypnosis and participating in several photograph identification arrays and one live line-up. Another witness testified that he saw a car resembling Clay's near the Rios residence shortly before the murders.

A Harris County jury convicted Thomas of the murder of Rios's children afterwhich the judge sentenced him to death. The Texas Court of Criminal Appeals affirmed his conviction and sentence, and the state Parole Board did not consider his clemency petition because it was filed 15 days too late.

Clay, who confessed to only "roughing up" Roberto Rios, was charged and not prosecuted. Clay was, however, found guilty of the January 4, 1994, murder of Melathethil Varughese, for which he was executed on March 20, 2003, by the State of Texas, and for which Thomas was charged and not prosecuted (*Thomas v. Dretke* (5th Cir. 2004) No. 04-70006).

———

Elias Hanna Syriani, a 67-year-old Asian (Arabic) male, was executed by lethal injection at the Central Prison in Raleigh, North Carolina on November 18, 2005. Syriani was found guilty of the 1990 murder of Teresa Yousef Syriani, a 48-year-old Arabic female. Syriani, who was 52-years old when he committed the capital crime, was sentenced to death on June 12, 1991.

On July 28, 1990, the Syrianis were living apart, Syriani in a motel, and his wife Teresa with their three children in their home in Charlotte, North Carolina.[44] On that day Syriani had come by and asked his 8-year-old son, John Syriani, to go out with him. According to John he and his mother went to the Crown gas station and were on their way home when they saw Syriani's van stopped ahead.

As Teresa approached the turn onto the main street before their house, Syriani moved the van to block their way, got out of the van, gestured, and chased Teresa's car. She put the car in reverse and Syriani opened the door and started stabbing her and she started screaming. John tried to push his father's hands off Teresa, but the boy could not stop him.

John ran home to get his 15-year-old sister, Rose, and told her, "Dad is killing Mom." Rose called police and John ran to a friend's house. He and his friend ran back to Teresa's car, which was now in a neighbor's driveway. John saw Syriani kneeling at the open door and stabbing into the car. Syriani then walked back to the van and yelled in Arabic, "Go home bastard," to his son. Frightened, John ran back down the street where neighbors took him into their home.

Rose then ran to Teresa, saw Syriani enter his van, look at her, and drive away. When Rose reached her mother, Teresa said, "Ma Ma [Arabic for honey], shut up."

---

[44] Syriani, an Assyrian Christian, was born in Jerusalem. When his father, a laborer, became sick, the 12-year-old Syriani left school and went to work to help his mother support his three sisters and two brothers. Syriani learned the machinist trade and entered the Jordanian Army at 19 afterwhich he worked in a garage and then as a singer on a radio station. He married Teresa in Amman, Jordan when was 36 and she was 24. It was an arranged marriage. Teresa returned to the United States and Syriani followed. The Syriani's first lived in Washington, D.C. where Syriani worked as a busboy and learned English at night. The Syriani's later moved to Chicago where he worked as a machinist.

In addition to John and Rose, at least two neighbors watched from their homes as Syriani stabbed Teresa and walk away.[45]

At around 11:37 p.m. Charlotte Police Department Investigator Hilda M. Griffin arrived at the scene to find Teresa alive, sitting in the car with her head laid back, blood everywhere. Teresa tried to speak, but Griffin could not tell what she was saying. When Griffin arrived at the fire station where Syriani had stopped for first aid, he had already been arrested, and his van had been searched. He

---

[45] David Wilson testified that he lived in the same neighborhood as the Syrianis and knew John but only knew Syriani by sight. Around 11:20 p.m. on July 28 Wilson was at home when he heard children hollering. He looked out his window and saw a van parked across the street with the interior lights on and the door open. He watched Syriani come toward the van, get into the driver's seat, and fumble with something. Then he saw Syriani go back down the street and cross the street to a car in the driveway next to Wilson's house. Syriani leaned over inside the car and Wilson saw the car shaking. Wilson then went outside and saw Syriani get back in the van. He also saw two young boys, John and John's friend. Wilson heard a young woman hollering, "somebody help my mother" and he went to the car where he saw a woman covered in blood. A neighbor wiped her face. She looked to him "like somebody [who] had been shot in the face with a load of buckshot."

Thomas O'Connor testified that he lived near the Syrianis but did not know them. Around 11:20 p.m. on July 28 he received a phone call from a neighbor prompting him to look out his window. O'Connor saw a man standing at a car halfway in a driveway holding what appeared to be a screwdriver and "stabbing into the car." O'Connor ran outside, yelling, and made eye contact with the man. The man kept stabbing into the car. O'Connor ran back inside to phone police and then returned outside to watch the van pull away, stop, and the man with a screwdriver in hand get out and walk toward the car. After seeing O'Connor the man turned back to the van and drove away.

appeared sober. There was blood all over him but only some light scratches on his arm and shoulder. Griffin testified that a team searched for, but never found, the murder weapon.

Teresa died 28 days later. According to James Sullivan, a forensic pathologist and medical examiner, Teresa's August 24 autopsy showed seven healed wounds located on her left cheek, five wounds on the left side of her neck, five wounds on her right cheek and around her mouth, and five wounds to the back of her right hand and arm. There were visible healed wounds in the mouth where her jaw had been fractured, and several of her teeth had been fractured or lost. Several of the wounds had been sutured and all of the wounds had a linear or rectangular configuration.

In Sullivan's opinion the chronic penetrating brain wound caused Teresa's death. A three-inch deep puncture wound to the right temple, to the right of Teresa's right eye, penetrated her brain going through the right temporal lobe and into the deep central area of her brain. A narrow instrument, like a squared-off pick, screwdriver, or knife, caused the wound and Sullivan opined that it would have taken a substantial amount of force to penetrate an adult's skull.

John Syriani testified that the family had lived in the house in Charlotte since 1986 except for a week in the summer of 1988 when police took him, his sisters, and his mother to a Battered Women's Shelter. Afterwards Teresa and the children stayed with Teresa's sister in New Jersey for about one month. When Syriani came to take them back they returned to Charlotte. In July 1990 the family lived in a motel later moving back to their home when Syriani moved out.

John testified that Syriani worked long hours and always carried a screwdriver as part of his work tools. Before the family moved to Charlotte, Teresa had never worked, had dressed according to Arabic tradition, and had worn no makeup or lipstick. According to John, Syriani and Teresa had argued mostly over the children. In 1988 or 1989 Teresa decided she did not like staying at home and wanted to get a job.

Teresa occasionally worked nights at her second job at a gas station, and when she did John's older sister babysat. Beginning in 1990 Syriani and Teresa argued more frequently as Syriani did not like the fact that Teresa was working. Syriani wanted Teresa to stay home with the children. In July 1990 Syriani moved into a motel.

John recalled seeing Syriani slap his mother when he was five and hit his mother in "the ear" on Easter Sunday 1989. He also recalled seeing his mother "screaming and running out of the house" while Syriani stood at the door in the summer of 1988. John testified that Teresa was a good mother and that she and Syriani argued about three times a week, Syriani sometimes calling Teresa a "whore."

Rose Syriani maintained that her parents were always arguing and that her father would jump and yell at Teresa. Sometimes her father "would go downstairs around three o'clock in the morning *** and just start breaking things downstairs." During arguments between January and July 1990 Teresa would say she would quit her job if Syriani would buy food the children liked to eat.

Rose recalled a time when Syriani started yelling at her in Arabic and grabbed her around her throat saying that he was going to kill her. Rose remained angry with her father from 1988 to 1990 because he constantly disciplined the children who were not allowed to play outside after 5:00 p.m.

When Syriani thought Rose had scratched his new van, he grabbed her and started to kick her. Crying, she ran out of the house. She testified: "He got me on the floor and kicked me *** into the ground. People were walking by and my mom pulled his leg off me." Syriani told Teresa he would kill her if she ever left him, that she would not live without him, and that he would "fuck up our world." Rose also testified that she and her brother and sister were always scared of their father even though he provided well for them.

Sara Syriani, who was 13-years old at the time of Teresa's murder, testified that on one occasion her father threatened her mother with a pair of scissors. On Easter Sunday 1988 Syriani hit Teresa, yelled at her, pushed her down, and kicked her. On Sara's graduation from sixth grade, Syriani had yelled at Teresa, followed her upstairs, grabbed her by her hair, threw her down the stairs, and dragged her into the kitchen, ripping her shirt.

Kenneth C. Martin, an attorney, testified that Teresa had asked him to represent her in a domestic action against Syriani in November 1989. He prepared a complaint against her husband, which she only decided to file on June 27, 1990, and an *ex parte* (a decision made by a judge that does not require the participation of all the parties) domestic violence order was issued on July 5.

At trial Syriani recalled receiving papers from a lawyer about his wife's request for a divorce noting that in July 1990 Teresa came home with police officers who told him he had to leave his keys and move out of the home. Syriani packed his clothes and moved into a hotel room visiting the neighborhood several times thereafter.

Walid Bouhussein, a neighbor who lived two or three blocks from the Syrianis and had known them almost three and one-half years testified at trial that their families exchanged visits and ate together a number of occasions. He had never seen any arguments between the Syrianis and his children felt "a warmth" toward Syriani. Elias and Teresa, he said, were very nice people, neither appearing violent nor showing temper. Elias was very hospitable, a "mild-mannered man." However, Bouhussein did admit that Teresa had told his wife that her husband mistreated her.

In 1991 Syriani was convicted and sentenced in Mecklenburg County Superior Court. At his sentencing hearing Syriani testified that he had been out on bond for a short time during which he had arranged for the care of his children. He testified that he felt "real, very terrible" about what had happened, that he loved his wife and missed her very much, and that he was very sorry for what he had done. He reiterated that at the time of the confrontation with his wife he was very emotional and upset feeling he was going to lose his wife and family. Syriani testified that in his 11 months in jail he had never been cited for any misconduct or caused trouble for anyone.

On March 12, 1993, the North Carolina Supreme Court confirmed Syriani's conviction and sentence. On November 8, 2005, Syriani's three children met with Governor Mike F. Easley to plead for their father's life. The governor found "no convincing reason to grant clemency and overturn the unanimous jury verdict affirmed by the state and federal courts" and Syriani was executed the next day (*State v. Syriani* (1993) 428 S.E.2d 118).

————

Eric Randall Nance, a 45-year-old white male, was executed by lethal injection at the Arkansas Department of Correction Cummins Unit in Varner, Arkansas on November 28, 2005. Nance was found guilty of the 1993 murder of Julie Heath, an 18-year-old white female. Nance, who was 33-years old when he committed the capital crime, was sentenced to death on March 31, 1994.

Julie Heath was last seen alive on October 11, 1993. That evening she left her home in Malvern, Arkansas to visit her boyfriend some 23 miles away in Hot Springs. Heath's automobile was reported abandoned on Highway 270 west of Malvern near Interstate 30, just two miles from her home. On October 18 Heath's body was discovered on rural property just south of Highway 171 approximately seven and one-half miles from the location where her vehicle was found.

Heath's body was fully clothed with the belt buckle partially undone, the pants' zipper partially zipped, and the portion of the shirt covering the body's right shoulder torn. Donald E. Smith, a criminalist, testified that red pubic hairs found in the cab of Nance's pickup were microscopically similar to those taken from Heath's body. Officer Kirk McClenahan testified that Heath's body was discovered with her shirt turned inside out and with one shoulder pad on the outside. The medical examiner, Dr. Frank Peretti, testified that Heath's brassiere was pulled up around her neck and shoulder area, her socks and panties were inside out, her pants were partially zipped, and her shirt was inside out, although photographic evidence showed that the bra was not in that position when the body was discovered. Lastly, Kermit Channell, a forensic serologist, could neither confirm nor deny that sexual intercourse had occurred, that the exposure of Heath's body to the weather could account for lack of some evidence, and that enzyme-characteristic analysis showed blood recovered from Nance's vehicle was consistent with Heath.

Peretti also testified that it was likely that there was trauma to the skull and neck region of Heath's body based on the accelerated skeletonization and evidence of insect activity in that area as compared with the relatively intact remainder of the body. Although the autopsy failed to reveal the cause or manner of death, Peretti could not rule out death by knife wound and testified that examination of Heath's shirt showed defects consistent with a cutting wound.

At trial Nance's brother, Vernon Nance, and his sister, Belinda Christopher, testified that, after initially denying any involvement in the crime, Nance later stated that he had accidentally killed Heath. They testified that Nance stated that he gave Heath a ride into Malvern because her automobile had broken down on the road, that Heath saw his work knife (a box cutter) slide out of his pocket as they drove, that Heath asked him to put the knife away, that as he moved to put the knife in the glove compartment, Heath turned sideways in the seat and started kicking him, that he put his hand up to keep her from kicking and hitting him, and that the knife fatally lodged in her throat.

At trial after the State presented evidence of six prior felony comvictions stemming from Nance's rape and beating of two Oklahoma girls in 1982, the jury found Nance guilty of murder with attempted rape as the underlying felony. The state Parole Board voted 6-1 against clemency, which Governor Mike Huckabee later denied. On the day of Nance's execution the Supreme Court of the United States denied a stay by a vote of 6-3 (*In Re Eric Randall Nance* (2005) 546 U.S. 1029; *Nance v. Norris* (2004) 392 F.3d 284; *Nance v. State* (1996) 918 S.W.2d 114).

————

John R. Hicks, a 49-year-old black male, was executed by lethal injection at the Southern Ohio Correctional Facility in Lucasville, Ohio on November 29, 2005. Hicks was found guilty of the 1985 murder of Brandy Green, a 5-year-old black female. Hicks, who was 29-years old when he committed the capital crime, was sentenced to death on February 21, 1986.

Around 4:00 p.m. on August 2, 1985, Hicks acquired some cocaine in Cincinnati, Ohio. After snorting the drug Hicks desired more and took the VCR from the home he shared with his wife, Ghitana Hicks, and stepdaughter, Brandy Green. Hicks gave the VCR to a drug trafficker as security for a $50 cocaine purchase.

After consuming more cocaine Hicks realized he had no money with which to redeem the VCR. Recognizing that the missing VCR would lead to problems with Ghitana, he decided to rob 56-year-old Maxine Armstrong who was Ghitana's mother. Hicks knew that "if [he] robbed her he would have to kill her." Hicks went to Armstrong's Cincinatti apartment where Green was spending the night. Hicks found Green asleep on the couch, woke her, put her to bed, and at about 11:00 p.m. prepared to kill Armstrong, telling himself, "you go do it or you don't."

Hicks killed Armstrong by strangling her with a clothesline he had brought with him. He then stole approximately $300 and some credit cards from her apartment, retrieved the VCR from the drug dealer, and purchased more cocaine. Around 12:30 a.m. on August 3, after injecting the cocaine, Hicks "got to thinking again" and realized that Green could identify him as the last person to visit Armstrong and so he decided to return to the apartment to kill Green.

Upon returning to Armstrong's apartment he first tried to smother Green with a pillow. As Green was "bucking" and "fighting" he tried to choke her with his hands. When she continued to make breathing sounds he affixed duct tape over her nose and mouth. Finally killing Green, Hicks moved Armstrong's body into the bathtub so that he could dismember it for easier disposal.

After nearly severing one of her legs with a kitchen knife he gave up and returned to the bedroom where Green's body was located. He removed her underwear and digitally penetrated her vagina with his finger. He then stole a checkbook, a ring, a .32-caliber pistol, and a box of ammunition from the apartment, returned to his own apartment, and at 6:00 a.m. fled to Cincinnati.

On August 4 Hicks surrendered to police in Knoxville, Tennessee where he confessed to both murders. Hicks was returned to Cincinnati and made additional incriminating statements to two Cincinnati homicide detectives. On February 12, 1986, Hicks was found guilty of two counts of aggravated murder and one count of aggravated robbery. Nine days later he was sentenced to death for murdering Green to avoid detention and during the commission of a robbery. Hicks was also sentenced to life imprisonment for Armstrong's murder. On November 8, 2005, a tearful Hicks asked for clemency which both the eight member Ohio Parole Board and Governor Bob Taft

189

subsequently denied. On the day of Hicks's execution the Supreme Court of the United States denied a stay (*Hicks v. Collins* (2004) 384 F.3d 204; *Hicks v. Taft* (2005) 546 U.S. 1058; *State v. Hicks* (1989) 538 N.E.2d 1030.

———

Kenneth Lee Boyd, a 57-year-old white male, was executed by lethal injection at the Central Prison in Raleigh, North Carolina on December 2, 2005. Boyd was found guilty of the 1988 murder of Julie Curry Boyd, a 36-year-old white female, and Thomas Dillard Curry, a 57-year-old white male. Boyd, who was 40-years old when he committed the capital crime, was sentenced to death on October 25, 1988, and again on July 14, 1994.

On March 4, 1988, Boyd entered Dillard Curry's home in Stoneville, North Carolina, where Dillard's daughter and Boyd's estranged wife, Julie Boyd, was then living with their children: Chris, 13, Jamie, 12, and Daniel, 10. Inside the home Boyd shot and killed Dillard and Julie with a .357-caliber magnum pistol. The shootings were committed in the presence of the children and other witnesses, all of who testified for the State. Immediately after the shootings law enforcement officers were called to the scene. As they approached Boyd came out of some nearby woods with his hands up and surrendered to the officers.

After being advised of his *Miranda* rights Boyd gave a lengthy inculpatory statement in which he described the fatal shootings: "I walked to the back door and opened it. It was unlocked. As I walked in, I saw a silhouette that I believe was Dillard. It was just like I was in Vietnam. I pulled the gun out and started shooting. I think I shot Dillard one time and he fell. Then I walked past him and into the kitchen and living room area. The whole time I was pointing and shooting. Then I saw another silhouette that I believe was Julie come out of the bedroom. I shot again, probably several times.

"Then I reloaded my gun. I dropped the empty shell casings onto the floor. As I reloaded, I heard someone groan, Julie I guess. I turned and aimed, shooting again. My only thoughts were to shoot my way out of the house. I kept pointing and shooting at anything that moved. I went back out the same door that I came in, and I saw a big guy pointing a gun at me. I think this was Craig Curry, Julie's brother. I shot at him three or four times as I was running towards the woods."

Boyd testified at his 1988 trial that he remembered buying twelve beers the day of the murders and that he thought he drank all the beer because he "[didn't] let beer sit around." The Rockingham County jury found Boyd guilty of capital murder with the two murders as aggravating factors and recommended a sentence of death for each murder.[46]

On appeal the State's Supreme Court held that the trial court erred by excusing a juror after a private, unrecorded discussion between the juror and judge and awarded Boyd a new trial. In 1994 Boyd was tried again in the same county, found guilty, and sentenced to death for the second time. On July 31, 1996, the North Carolina Supreme Court confirmed Boyd's conviction and sentence. On December 1, 2005, the Supreme Court of the United States denied an application for stay of execution and Governor Mike F. Easley denied clemency (*Boyd v. North Carolina* (2005)

---

[46] In mitigation Dr. Patrico Lara testified that at the time of the murders Boyd suffered from an adjustment disorder with psychotic emotional features, alcohol abuse, and a personality disorder with predominate compulsive dependent features. Lara opined that Boyd's emotional condition was impaired and that Boyd suffered from some level of alcohol intoxication. Dr. John Warren also opined that at the time of the murders Boyd suffered from chronic depression, alcohol abuse disorder, dependent personality disorder, and a reading disability.

546 U.S. 1059; *State v. Boyd* (1996) 473 S.E.2d 327; *State v. Boyd* (1992) 418 S.E.2d 471).

———

Shawn Paul Humphries, a 34-year-old white male, was executed by lethal injection at the Broad River Correctional Institution in Columbia, South Carolina on December 2, 2005. Humphries was found guilty of the 1994 murder of Mendal Alton "Dickie" Smith, a 43-year-old white male. Humphries, who was 22-years old when he committed the capital crime, was sentenced to death on August 9, 1994.

On New Year's Eve night 1993 Humphries and his friend, Edward Gerald Blackwell, a 19-year-old white male, stole a 9-millimeter pistol and drove around drinking beer. Shortly after 7:00 a.m. on the 1st Humphries and Blackwell entered the Max Saver convenience store in the small town of Fountain Inn, South Carolina. Dickie Smith, the storeowner, asked Humphries whether he wanted something hot. Humphries flashed the stolen gun and replied that he wanted money. A video camera at the store recording the incident showed that Smith appeared to reach under the counter to pull out a gun and as he did Humphries fired a single shot in Smith's direction. The bullet struck Smith in the head, killing him afterwhich Humphries fled. When the shot was fired Blackwell fainted and fell to the ground in the store. Police arrested Blackwell at the scene, and later that day apprehended Humphries.

In 1994 a Greenville County jury found Humphries, who had prior convictions for burglary and larceny, guilty of capital murder. The State sought a death sentence based on the fact that the murder was carried out while in the commission of an armed robbery. During the sentencing phase the State made a comparitive worth argument that led to the jury recommending and the court imposing the death penalty.[47] The jury recommended the death penalty and the court imposed the sentence. On May 3, 2004, the U.S. Fourth Circuit Court of Appeals vacated the sentence citing "ineffective assistance of counsel" and on February 4, 2005, the District Court of South Carolina reinstated the sentence. The day before Humphries was executed the Supreme Court of the United States denied a stay, and on the morning of the execution, Governor Mark Sanford turned down a request for clemency. Accomplice Blackwell was convicted of murder, armed robbery, and criminal conspiracy, for which he was sentenced to life imprisonment (*State v. Humphries* (1996) 479 S.E.2d 52; *Humphries v. State* (2002) 570 S.E.2d 160; *Humphries v. Ozmint* (2004) 366 F.3d 266; *Humphries v. Ozmint* (2005) 397 F.3d 206; *Humphries v. South Carolina* (2005) 546 U.S. 1059).

---

[47] The State introduced evidence that Smith, one of eight children, had overcome extreme poverty and the loss of his father at an early age to contribute financially to the family while going to school. Smith finished high school, ultimately received an engineering degree and builder's license, marry Pat, and raise a daughter Ashley.

In mitigation Humphries was shown to have a similarly impoverished background in which he was raised by alcoholic grandparents and an abusive father who huffed paint and grew marijuana. Extreme poverty forced Humphries to dig in dumpsters to obtain food and clothing at the age of 7 to 8 years. By the time he was 12-years old, his father grew so abusive to him that his grandfather sent him to live with his mother who had abandoned him when he was a baby.

In closing the State noted that "in 1984 [Dickie] met Pat, and they fell in love, and they got married. That's the same year Shawn Paul Humphries committed two house break-ins at 13 ***. In 1988 Ashley is born. That's the same year Shawn Paul Humphries went to jail for two years."

Wesley Eugene Baker, a 47-year-old black male, was executed by lethal injection at the Maryland Diagnostic and Classification Center in Baltimore, Maryland on December 5, 2005. Baker was found guilty of the 1991 murder of Jane Frances Tyson, a 49-year-old white female. Baker, who was 33-years old when he committed the capital crime, was sentenced to death on October 30, 1992.

On June 6, 1991, Jane Tyson took two of her six grandchildren, 4-year-old Carly, and 6-year-old Adam, shopping for sneakers at the Westview Mall in Baltimore County. After shopping Tyson, Carly, and Adam, left the mall and entered the parking lot where Tyson had parked her red Buick. When they arrived at the car Carly sat in the rear seat and, as Adam was preparing to enter the front passenger seat and Tyson was preparing to enter the driver's seat, a man ran up to Tyson and shot her in the head.

Adam heard his grandmother scream and he saw the man shoot her. Adam then saw the man run to a blue truck and enter on the left side.[48] Tyson died at the scene from

---

[48] Adam did not testify at trial but Baker and the State entered into a stipulation that was read into the record: "If Adam Michael Sulewski, age seven, were called to the stand, he would testify that on June 6, 1991, he was six years old and the grandson of Mrs. Tyson, the victim in this offense. Adam would state that he was present with his grandmother when she was shot and that he, along with his grandmother and his four year old sister, Carly, were shopping at the Westview Mall.

"Adam would state that when they arrived at their grandmother's car, his sister got into the rear seat. He was standing on the passenger side, preparing to enter the right front passenger seat and his grandmother was getting in the vehicle through the driver's door when he observed a 'black man' run up to his grandmother. The next thing he remembered was hearing his grandmother screaming 'NO'. Adam would state, 'He shot her. I saw blood coming out of her mouth'. Adam would

the gunshot wound. An autopsy revealed that Tyson was killed by a single shot to the head, and forensic evidence indicated that the gun was in contact with her temple at the time of the shooting

On that same evening at approximately 8:30 p.m. Scott Faust was traveling behind the Westview Mall on the way to visit his father who lived directly behind the mall. As Faust was driving he noticed a blue Chevrolet Blazer truck and a red Buick parked side by side in the mall parking lot. Faust watched as two men jumped into the Blazer and sped away, then noticing that a person was lying on the ground next to the open driver's side door of the Buick. Faust drove closer to the Buick at which time he saw that the person laying on the ground was a woman and that she was bloody.

He watched as a little girl ran around the front of the Buick from the passenger's side and screamed, "Mom Mom's shot." Faust saw a woman run over and take care of the children. He then decided to pursue the Blazer. Faust caught up to the Blazer after several blocks and as he was sitting behind it at a stoplight, he wrote down the license plate number of the Blazer on a tissue box.

Faust then headed back to the crime scene at which time he gave police the tissue box with the license plate number on it. He also identified Baker as the passenger in the Blazer. This information was relayed to the Baltimore County Police Department. Two Baltimore County police

---

continue to state that after the shooting, he saw who he thinks were 'two good guys' chasing after the man who did the shooting. He would state that the 'black man' ran to his truck, which he described as being blue in color with black windows. He would further state that once the subject entered his truck on the left side, he 'took off' as fast as he could. The only other description Adam would give about the black male would be that he had short hair."

officers then saw the Blazer pass them at which time they pursued the vehicle. When the Blazer's path was blocked the two passengers of the Blazer fled on foot. The officers immediately apprehended Gregory Lawrence, the driver of the Blazer, who gave them the description of the passenger in the Blazer. A police officer then apprehended Baker nearby.

When Baker was apprehended the officer observed blood on Baker's right leg, including his pant leg, sock, and shoe. The blood was later tested by serology comparison and a positive DNA match was made to Tyson. No blood was seen on Lawrence's clothing. An identification card with Tyson's name was found on the floor of the passenger's side of the Blazer. The handgun that shot and killed Tyson was found between the front seats of the Blazer and Tyson's purse and wallet were found on the same path as that used by Baker when he fled. Baker's palm print and fingerprints were found on the exterior of the Blazer's passenger side and Baker's fingerprints were found on the driver's side door and window of Tyson's Buick.

On June 24, 1991, Baker was charged by indictment that was filed in the Circuit Court for Baltimore County. On October 26, 1992, after a jury trial in the Circuit Court for Harford County, Baker elected to be sentenced by the court and was found guilty of first-degree murder, robbery with a deadly weapon, and use of a handgun in the commission of a felony.[49] Baker was executed less than an hour after

---

[49] The U.S. Fourth Circuit Court of Appeals opined that evidence that Baker shot Tyson was not overwhelming: Adam's stipulated testimony was that the man he saw shoot his grandmother ran to the left, the driver's side, of the Blazer; Faust testified that he saw two people run from the Buick to the Blazer, and that Lawrence entered the driver's side; and the fingerprints on the Buick were from Baker's right hand. The court queried, "If Baker were right-handed, as is the majority of the population,

Governor Robert L. Ehrlich Jr. announced that he would not grant clemency. Accomplice Lawrence was convicted of murder and given a life sentence (*Baker v. Corcoran* (2000) 220 F.3d 276; *Baker v. State* (2002) 790 A.2d 629).

———

Stanley "Tookie" Williams III, a 51-year-old black male, was executed by lethal injection at the San Quentin State Prison in Point Quentin, California on December 13, 2005. Williams was found guilty of the 1979 murder of Albert Lewis Owens, a 26-year-old white male, and three Asians (Chinese): Yen-I Yang, a 76-year-old male, Tsai-Shai Chen Yang, a 63-year-old female, and Yee-Chen Lin, a 43-year-old female. Williams, who was 25-years old when he committed the capital crime, was sentenced to death on April 15, 1981.

On February 28, 1979, Albert Owens, the father of two, was murdered in a Whittier, California convenience store. Alfred Coward, known as "Blackie," testified after being granted immunity from prosecution and gave the following account of Owens's murder: At approximately 10:30 p.m. on the 27th Williams came to Coward's house. The two went to the home of James Garrett where Williams was staying, and Williams went inside returning with a sawed-off shotgun. A man named Darryl, who was wearing a brown corduroy jacket, accompanied him.

The three men made several stops including one to obtain "Sherms" (cigarettes containing PCP). They all shared a Sherm and then picked up Tony Simms, who was dressed in a green jogging suit and a cap. Williams shared a second Sherm with Coward and Simms and asked

———

one must wonder how it was possible for him to hold the gun to Tyson's head and leave his fingerprints on the Buick, especially in light of the fact that the incident took only a matter of moments."

Simms if he knew where he could "make money" in Pomona, a large city in Los Angeles County.

Taking two cars, the foursome made two unsuccessful restaurant and liquor store robbery attempts, and eventually went to a 7-Eleven store in Whittier where Owens, an employee and Army veteran, was sweeping the parking lot. Simms and Darryl went into the store followed by Owens, Williams and Coward. Coward testified he saw no one with a weapon except Williams, who approached Owens and told him to keep walking. Owens walked toward the back rooms of the store with Williams and Coward following him. Williams told Owens to lie down and Owens complied. Coward heard a gun being loaded, a shot, and glass breaking followed by two more shots. A television monitor in the store had been shot out and Owens had been shot twice in the back while he lay face down on the floor. The group then returned to Simms's house where the money was divided among the four.

The owner of the 7-Eleven store later testified that $120 was missing from the cash register. Simms asked why Williams had shot Owens and Williams explained he did not want to leave any witnesses, adding that the shotgun shells could not be traced and that he had retrieved a few of them.

Coward saw Williams later that morning at the home of Williams's brother. He stated Williams told his brother, "You should have heard the way he sounded when I shot him." Williams then made a growling noise and laughed hysterically for a number of minutes.

At about 5 a.m. on March 11 Robert Yang, who owned and lived in the Brookhaven Motel on South Vermont Street in Los Angeles, heard a woman scream and three or four shots. A few minutes later Robert left his bedroom and saw that the door separating the motel office from the living quarters was open. It appeared the door had been forced open from the outside. He discovered that his father, Yen-I Yang, his mother, Tsai-Shai Chen Yang, and his sister,

198

Yee-Chen Lin, who was visiting from Taiwan, had all been fatally wounded by shotgun fire. Yen-I Yang was shot once in the torso and once in the arm while he was laying on a sofa, Tsai-Shai Lin was shot once in the abdomen and once in the back, and Yee-Chen Lin was shot once in her face. The cash drawer was open and empty.

Police found two shotgun shell casings at the scene. A firearms expert testified that one of the shells could have been fired only from a .12-gauge shotgun identified as having been purchased by Williams in 1974.

Three witnesses provided testimony regarding Williams's involvement in the Brookhaven Motel incident. Samuel Coleman, testifying as an immunized witness, said that on March 10 he and Williams went to the Showcase Bar where he remained until it closed around 6 a.m. He last remembered seeing Williams about 2:30 a.m. but the next day Williams told him that he had robbed and killed some people on Vermont Street. Williams said he got approximately $50 and was going to use it to buy PCP.

James Garrett testified that Williams kept some of his possessions at the Garrett house and stayed there approximately five days a week. Early on the morning of March 13 Williams told Garrett and his wife Esther[50] that he had heard that some Chinese people had been killed on Vermont Street. He said he did not know how the killings had occurred but thought the killers were professionals because no shells or witnesses had been left. He went on to say that he heard the killings had occurred at 5 a.m. in

---

[50] Esther Garrett testified to essentially the same matters as her husband. In addition to the admissions testified to by James, Esther said Williams told them the killers were using the money to buy "juice" (PCP) and that the killers had picked up the bullets so there would be no evidence for police. After her husband left Williams told Esther he had committed the murder with his brother-in-law.

the morning, that two men had knocked down the door, and that the men had taken $600.

Williams, a 300 pound man with massive 22-inch biceps, later spoke about how the people were killed: "After the big guy knocked the door down, he went in the motel, and there was a guy laying on the couch, and he blew him away." Williams said the man on the couch and a woman at the cash register were shot twice, and another woman was also shot. Garrett testified that Williams told him he was the "big guy" adding: "I blew them away in the motel."

George Oglesby, also known as "Gunner," provided additional testimony. Oglesby was an inmate who was housed in the same cellblock as Williams, a few cells away. Oglesby pleaded guilty to second-degree murder but had not yet been sentenced.[51] Oglesby testified that in late April Williams asked him about the chances of escaping from Atascadero or Patton where he believed he might be sent. Oglesby also testified that Williams told him he, Blackie, and two others had robbed a motel and had shot the people inside—a man, a woman and a child, possibly a daughter.

At trial Williams presented an *alibi* defense for the Owens's murder. Beverly McGowan testified that on the night of Owens's murder she and Williams dined and spent the night together. Two witnesses corroborated Williams's noninvolvement in the Brookhaven Motel murders. Fred

---

[51] Oglesby was originally charged with first-degree murder, two counts of kidnapping, and one count of rape; special circumstances also were alleged. A supplementary probation report prepared on Oglesby indicated the charge eventually would be reduced to manslaughter because he was to testify in other cases. Oglesby also testified that he understood his attorney had spoken to the district attorney who was prosecuting Williams's case about reducing the charges against him to second-degree murder. He also hoped to receive protective housing in another state.

Holiwell, Williams's stepfather, testified that on Sunday morning, March 11, he arrived at the Showcase Bar around 3:30 a.m. He stated he thought he saw Williams there about 5 a.m. in the parking lot area. He remembered that he had seen his stepson there on this particular night because Williams had been involved in an altercation and had been cut across the chest.

Eugene Riley, an inmate in the same cell block as Williams, testified that on the morning of the 11th he saw Williams in the parking lot of the Showcase Bar about 5 a.m. and gave him a ride home around 5:30 a.m. and that Williams was smoking a sherm. The jury did not believe Williams and he was convicted of all four murders. Governor Arnold Schwarzenegger denied Williams clemency, and the Supreme Court of the United States denied a stay the day before his execution. Williams had no final words and did not request a last meal (*People v. Williams* (1988) 44 Cal.3d 1127; Schwarzenegger, A statement of decision (corrected version) request for clemency by Stanley Williams. 12 December 2005).

————

John B. Nixon Sr., a 77-year-old white male, was executed by lethal injection at the Mississippi State Penitentiary in Parchman, Mississippi on December 14, 2005. Nixon was found guilty of the 1985 murder of Virginia Tucker, a 45-year-old white female. Nixon, who was 56-years old when he committed the capital crime, was sentenced to death on March 26, 1986.

On January 22, 1985, Nixon brought his son, Henry Leon Nixon, and Gilbert Jimenez to the home of Thomas and Virginia Tucker in Rankin County, Mississippi. Upon entering the Tuckers' house Nixon pulled out a .22-caliber pistol and said, "I brought y'all something." Thomas, who had married Virginia six months earlier, three months after her divorce was finalized, immediately surmised that his wife's former husband, Elester Joseph Ponthieux, a 49-year-old white male, had hired the killers.

Thomas offered Nixon money to spare their lives but Nixon replied, "that's not what I'm after. The deal's already been made." Nixon gave the murder weapon to his son in the hope that he would kill Thomas before he escaped. Nixon's son then shot at Thomas who managed to escape despite receiving several gunshot wounds.

Thomas made his way to his nearby place of work and asked a coworker to check on Virginia. Meanwhile Nixon's son then returned the gun to Nixon who approached Virginia whom Jimenez had pinned to the floor. Nixon then placed the gun one inch behind Virginia's head and fired a shot into her brain before running away with his son and Jimenez. Virginia initially survived the gunshot only to be discovered on the floor gasping for breath, blood gushing from her head. She died in the hospital the following day.

Nixon, who had a 1958 statutory rape conviction in Texas, was arrested after being identified in a lineup by Thomas. His two-day trial in Rankin County took a jury 30 minutes to find him guilty and 90 minutes to determine the sentence should be death. On December 8, 2005, Nixon asked for clemency, and two days later Governor Haley Barbour denied the plea. Nixon professed innocence to the end: "I'm sorry for what I've done. I'm sorry to the world. I'm sorry for myself and I'm sorry to the family. I did not kill Virginia Tucker. I know within my heart, and it hurts to acknowledge, that it was a son of mine and a Spanish friend and another man from Jackson."

Henry Leon Nixon and Jimenez were convicted of conspiracy to commit capital murder and sentenced to 20 years' imprisonment. In a separate trial Ponthieux was convicted of capital murder and sentenced to life imprisonment (*Nixon v. Epps* (5th Cir. 2004) No. 02-60385; *Nixon v. Epps* (2005) 405 F.3d 318).

Inmates Executed in 2006

Clarence Ray Allen, a 76-year-old white male, who claimed Native American heritage, was executed by lethal injection at the San Quentin State Prison in Point Quentin, California on January 17, 2006. Allen was found guilty of conspiring in the 1980 murder of Josephine Linda Rocha, a 17-year-old white female, Bryon Schletewitz, a 27-year-old white male, and Douglas Scott White, an 18-year-old white male. Allen, who was 50-years old when he committed the capital crime, was sentenced to death on November 22, 1982.

In June 1974, when Allen was 44-years old, he decided to burglarize Fran's Market in Fresno, California. Allen had known the owners of the market, Ray and Frances Schletewitz, for over a decade. To carry out his plan he enlisted the assistance of his son, Roger Allen, and two other men, Carl Mayfield, and Charles Jones, the latter two, who were ostensibly employees in Allen's security guard business and worked for him and his son in various criminal pursuits.

On June 29 Roger invited Schletewitz's 19-year-old son, Bryon, to an evening swimming party at Allen's house. While he was swimming the Fran's Market keys were taken from his pants pocket. Later that night while Bryon was on a date arranged by Allen with Mary Sue Kitts, a 17-year-old white female, Allen, Mayfield, and Jones used Bryon's keys to burglarize his parents' market. They removed a safe and took it to the house of Jones's wife, Charlotte, where they opened it and divided the booty—$500 in cash and over $10,000 in money orders.

Allen, with help from his son Roger, Kitts, Allen's girlfriend Shirley Doeckel, and two additional persons, Barbara Carrasco and her stepson, Eugene "Lee" Furrow, cashed the stolen money orders at Southern California shopping centers using false identifications. Thereafter Kitts contacted Bryon and tearfully confessed that Allen had burglarized Fran's Market and that she had been helping to cash the stolen money orders with a fake identification and a wig provided by Allen.

Bryon went to Roger's house to confront him with this story. Roger admitted the Allen family had burglarized the store, and Bryon confirmed to Roger that Kitts had confessed to him. When Roger told his father of Bryon's accusation, based on Kitts's confession, Allen responded that Bryon and Kitts would have to be "dealt with."

Allen subsequently told the Schletewitzes he had not burglarized their store and that he loved Bryon like his own son while threatening them by hinting that someone was planning to burn down their house. Allen also intimidated them by having his son Roger pay Furrow $50 to fire several gunshots at their home one midnight.

Allen later called a meeting at his house and told Jones, Mayfield, and Furrow that Kitts had been talking too much and should be killed. Allen called for a vote on the issue of Kitts's execution, and it was unanimous that she should be killed as Allen had previously told those working with him that he would kill snitches and that he had friends and connections to do the job for him even if he was locked up. Allen added that the "secret witness program" was useless because a good lawyer could always discover an informant's name and address.

Allen had on numerous times referred to himself as a Mafia hit man. He kept a newspaper article about the murder of a man and woman in Nevada and claimed he had blown them in half with a shotgun. When discussing the plan to murder Kitts, Allen overruled Jones's suggestion that she be sent somewhere until "things died down." He also dismissed Doeckel's objection to a murder being committed in her apartment.

After the vote Allen developed a plan to poison Kitts by tricking her into taking cyanide capsules at a party to be held at Doeckel's apartment in Fresno. Shortly before the party started at Doeckel's apartment, Allen also told Furrow that it was just as easy to get rid of two persons as one if Furrow did not take Kitts's life. Allen sent Mayfield and Furrow to a winery to pick up the cyanide. Allen also put some stepping-stones from his house in the back of Jones's truck to be used to weigh down Kitts's body, which was to be dumped into a canal after the murder.

Allen left Doeckel's apartment shortly before Kitts arrived, having first arranged for his operatives to call him from a nearby phone booth to report on the progress of the execution plan. When Kitts arrived she refused to take the "pills" without wine, and Mayfield and Jones so informed Allen by phone. Allen then told Furrow to kill Kitts one way or the other because he just wanted her dead.

The partygoers later brought wine, beer, and "reds" to the apartment but Kitts still did not take the cyanide. Allen subsequently met Furrow outside the apartment and stressed, "he didn't care how it was done but do it." Allen told him he had people surrounding the apartment and that Furrow would be killed if he tried to leave. When Furrow and Kitts were left alone in the apartment, Furrow began to strangle her only to be interrupted by a call from Allen asking if he had killed her yet. Furrow answered, "no"; Allen ordered, "Do it" and hung up. Furrow then strangled Kitts to death.

Furrow called Allen and told him to come pick up Kitts's body. Jones, who was with Allen when he received the call, then announced he wanted nothing to do with the murder. Allen told him it was already done and that he was equally involved with the others. Allen, Doeckel, and Jones then went to pick up Kitts's body, which they wrapped and put in Allen's Cadillac trunk. He again warned Jones that they were all equally involved.

Allen and Doeckel, leading in the Cadillac, led Jones and Furrow, in Jones's car, to Allen's house where they transferred Kitts's body to Jones's car and then drove to the mountains with Allen in the lead. They all stopped after passing over the Friant Kern Canal where Allen instructed Furrow and Jones to tie stones with wire to Kitts's body. While Allen watched for traffic, Kitts's body was thrown into the canal.

When Mayfield asked Allen how "everything went" a few days later, Allen said, "everything went okay," meaning that Kitts had been killed. And when Mayfield asked how Furrow was doing, Allen said he was no longer in existence, explaining it is easy to go to Mexico, get someone killed, and have the body disposed of for only $50.

About six months after Kitts's murder, when Mayfield asked Allen if he was worried about others talking, Allen said he was not afraid, that "things would be taken care of" if that happened, that he would have snitches killed, and that he would take care of "secret witness" informers even if he was locked up.

Allen told Jones and others "talking was a spreading disease and that the only way to kill it was to kill the person talking." When Jones and others gathered at Allen's house, Allen stated that "none of [these] people talked," that "they first took what was coming," and that, if they did not, "he would get them from inside or outside prison." When Jones's home was burglarized some time after the murder and Jones told Allen about the burglary, Allen told Jones the burglary showed he could be easily reached. He later gave Jones a key that Jones discovered fit his residence, and told Jones in front of Jones's 5-year-old son he knew Jones "would like his kids to grow up without harm."

Allen made several statements to Doeckel after Kitts's murder, telling her, among other things, that Furrow was no longer around and repeating his claim that he had killed a woman in Las Vegas, Nevada. He also spoke often with

Carrasco, telling her he had "offed Kitts because she was opening her mouth about the money orders," that he involved Furrow in the murder because "he wanted to get him in deep so he couldn't talk about the armed robberies and other things that he knew," and that "he would have put Furrow in the same hole if Furrow didn't go along with the murder." Speaking about Kitts herself, Allen told Carrasco that they "had to ride her up, wet her down and [feed] her to the fishes." Kitts's body was never found.

In early 1977 Allen brought some new employees, Allen Robinson and Benjamin Meyer, into his crime family. He told Meyer he previously "had a broad helping them who got mouthy so they had to waste her" and that "she sleeps with the fishes." He warned Meyer, "If you bring anybody in my house that snitches on me or my family, I'll waste them. There's no rock, bush, nothing, he could hide behind." When Meyer asked what would happen if Allen was arrested and could not make bail, Allen replied, "you've heard of the long arm of the law before? Well don't underestimate the long arm of this Indian. I will reach out and waste you."

Some time later Allen told Meyer about Ray Schletewitz, stating that he kept $50,000 to $75,000 in a second safe in Fran's Market. He mentioned he had robbed Fran's Market by taking the first safe and that Ray was mad at him for the robbery, but that "the stupid son-of-a-bitch don't have no proof so he shouldn't be upset."

After holding meetings with his new men and his son, Roger, Allen drove all of them to "case" their first robbery project, a K-Mart store in Tulare, a small city in California's Central Valley. After the robbery Allen phoned Meyer to congratulate him on a fine job and to chastise Robinson for making mistakes. He told Meyer, "we are not going to have anything else to do with [Robinson] anymore, and we just might waste him," and that he would "be back to [him] for other robberies." Roger later contacted Larry Green to replace Robinson as the "inside man" for a number of robberies planned by Allen.

In March 1977 they committed an armed robbery that proved to be the beginning of the end. Green shot a bystander and police arrested him along with Meyer and Allen at the K-Mart store in Visalia, another Central Valley city. For his part in the crime Allen was tried and convicted of robbery, attempted robbery, and assault with a deadly weapon. The same year Allen was also tried for the Fran's Market burglary, conspiracy, and the murder of Kitts—a trial at which numerous witnesses, including Bryon Schletewitz, Mayfield, Jones, Furrow, Doeckel, Carrasco, and Meyer testified for the prosecution. On November 30 Allen was convicted of burglary, conspiracy, and the first-degree murder of Kitts, and sentenced to life imprisonment.[52]

While serving time in Folson Prison, Allen was found guilty of conspiring with Billy Ray Hamilton to murder witnesses who testified against him in Kitts's murder trial. Allen had met Hamilton, a convicted robber, in mid-1980. Nicknamed "Country," Hamilton became Allen's "dog," running errands and taking care of various problems in return for cash. Gary Brady, another inmate, would on occasion assist Hamilton in running errands for Allen.

---

[52] On February 18, 1972, the California Supreme Court declared the death penalty cruel and unusual punishment in violation of the state constitution. On August 11, 1977, the Legislature reenacted the death penalty under certain conditions. Under the new statute, evidence in mitigation was permitted, and the death penalty reinstated as a possible punishment for first-degree murder under "special circumstances": murder for financial gain, murder by a person previously convicted of murder, murder of multiple victims, murder with torture, murder of a peace officer, murder of a witness to prevent testimony and several other murders under particular circumstances. Not until April 21, 1992, did Robert Alton Harris, become the first person executed under the new law.

Brady was supposed to be paroled on July 28, 1980, and Hamilton was scheduled for parole the following month.[53]

After Hamilton and Brady had been helping Allen for some time, Allen said he had an appeal coming up and wanted certain people taken "out of the box, killed," because "they had been onto his appeal," and "messed him around on a beef." Allen mentioned the names "Bryant," (Bryon), Jones, and "Sharlene" (Charlotte) as witnesses to be killed, and offered Hamilton $25,000 for the job. Allen confided to another Folsom inmate, Joseph Rainier, that he had been convicted of first-degree murder on the basis of the testimony of "the guy who did the actual killing," and that he would like to see this individual as well as four other witnesses who testified against him killed.

Rainier saw Allen and Hamilton talking together in the prison yard bleachers and on the track every day for the four to six weeks before Hamilton's release on parole in late August 1980. Hamilton and Allen usually huddled close together when they were talking; both men would straighten up, separate, and stop talking whenever Rainier approached. After Rainier repeatedly asked Allen what was going on, Allen stated "[Hamilton's] going to take care of some rats for me." He later told Rainier, in front of Hamilton, that Hamilton was going to "get paid for the job" and that "Kenny was going to take care of transportation" for Hamilton after Hamilton's release. Allen said that he could probably "win his appeal" if the witnesses were killed

---

[53] Hamilton was released from Folson Prison on August 29, 1980. On September 2 Allen's son, Kenneth Allen, wired Hamilton $100 in San Jose. During the week preceding September 5 Hamilton and his girlfriend, Connie Barbo, had visited Kenneth and and his wife Kathy's home several times. A photograph of Hamilton was subsequently found there as Allen had access to photographs of Folson inmates.

and offered to kill witnesses who had testified against Rainier as well.

Allen asked Kenneth and Kathy to visit him, which they did with their baby on August 15. He told Kenneth that both Ray and Bryon were going to be murdered and that the other witnesses against him would also be eliminated so that he would prevail on retrial if he won his appeal, adding that Doeckel had agreed to change her testimony were he granted a new trial.

Allen explained that "Country" would do the killing (and simultaneously commit a robbery so he could have some money to tide himself over) and that he expected Kenneth to supply "Country" with guns and transportation. He stated that "Country" was a professional who would "do what you told him to do," and gave Hamilton's mug shot to Kenneth telling him to burn it after memorizing Hamilton's face. Allen's son agreed to find guns for Hamilton with the help of Kathy, who would evidently trade drugs for the guns, and he smuggled Hamilton's picture out of prison in his baby's diapers. Kenneth subsequently received a series of letters from his father detailing the evolving plan.

In the first letter written the day after the August 15 visit, Allen told Kenneth, "I rapped to my dog when I jammed back in here ***. [He] is looking forward to meeting you all and it's okay with him to smoke to your pad." Allen asked Kenneth to "send me the name of that dude that got off with such a light sentence, okay? *** and that lawyer, that sounds like just might be the play I have been looking for ***. I know with the right lawyer I could beat this beef I am riding. Keep the Allen faith because there is good times ahead."

Kenneth got another letter dated August 20 telling him of a second short visit from Doeckel, who was "willing to help me in court and tell it like it really was." Allen also wrote: "Hey, I hear a country music show is coming to town around September 3." "Show," Kenneth testified, was a code word for murder.

Kenneth received a third letter dated August 26 stating, "remember September 3, around that date y'all be listening to a lot of good old 'country' music, okay? Just for me. You know how I like 'country."

Yet another letter dated August 27, stated "now remember around September 3, have everything ready so y'all can go to that 'country' music show. I know y'all really 'enjoy' yourselves. I know you kids never liked 'country' music before. But I bet when you hear that dude on the 'lead' guitar you'll be listening to it at least once a week, ha. Anyway, forget about rock and roll and get lost in the country. Ha, ha."

At Kenneth's house Hamilton confirmed he was there to murder Bryon and Ray Schletewitz, and asked to see the weapons he would be using. He explained he would not kill Doeckel as yet because she was helping him locate the other hit list witnesses. Barbo joined Hamilton in Fresno, another Central Valley city. During the next few days Barbo told acquaintances she had a chance to get a few thousand dollars and a hundred dollars worth of "crank" for "snuffing out a life."

On September 4 Hamilton went to Kenneth's house and got a sawed-off shotgun, a .32-caliber revolver, and seven shotgun shells from Kenneth, all to be used to murder Ray and Bryon at Fran's Market. Hamilton discussed the market and said he knew there were two safes there, one in the wall and the other in the freezer. He left in the evening with Barbo telling Kenneth he was going to murder Ray and Bryon. That night, just before the 8 p.m. closing time, Hamilton and Barbo entered Fran's Market and bought several items. Joe Rios handled their purchases. At about 9:45 p.m. they returned to Kenneth's house explaining they aborted the execution because Barbo objected to killing a 15-year-old Mexican boy.

The next evening Hamilton took 13 additional shotgun shells and 6 more cartridges from Kenneth, and went with Barbo back to Fran's Market. At 7:57 p.m. Hamilton and

211

Barbo entered the store and one of the clerks locked the front door after they entered as the employees were closing the market. Bryon, and the store's employees Douglas Scott White, Josephine Rocha, and Rios were then the only people in Fran's Market.

Hamilton and Barbo went back to the meat counter where Rios wrapped several items for them. Rios began to sweep the aisles but kept an eye on the couple because he suspected they might shoplift. After watching them go down several aisles and put items in a shopping cart, however, he decided they were not planning to steal and he went back to the stock room at the rear of the store. Thereafter Hamilton brandished the sawed off shotgun and Barbo produced the .32-caliber revolver.

As Rios walked into the stockroom he saw Bryon, White, and Rocha walking in behind him followed by Barbo and Hamilton holding a sawed-off shotgun. Hamilton ordered all four employees to lie on the floor. He then directed White into the freezer to open the safe. White protested there was no safe there. Bryon then identified himself and offered to open the safe and led Hamilton to a room behind the freezer where the safe was located. Barbo held a revolver on the other employees.

From where he lay Rios could hear some scuffling between Bryon and Hamilton. He heard Hamilton say, "You better not get a gun," and then a loud bang. Hamilton emerged from behind the freezer and said to White, "Okay, big boy, where is that safe?" When White said he did not know Hamilton shot him in the neck. At that point Rios dashed to the bathroom and tried to lock himself in. Rocha was still sitting on the stockroom floor.

From inside the bathroom Rios heard another shot. The bathroom door then opened and Hamilton loaded his shotgun, aimed, and fired at Rios who managed to raise his left arm to cover his face sustaining severe injuries to the arm and elbow.

Hamilton said, "Let's go, babe," and Rios then heard Hamilton and Barbo go to the front of the store. Emerging from the bathroom Rios saw the three other employees lying on the floor. Hamilton and Barbo tried to leave by the locked front door as Rios raced out the back door. A voice called out to him to halt and a shot was fired but he kept running.

When Jack Abbott, who lived behind Fran's Market, heard the shots he got his shotgun loaded with shells containing No. 6 pellets and ran toward the store as Rios · ran out. Abbott went into the store where he saw White and Rocha. As Abbott was leaving he was shot in the left hip. He turned and saw the man who shot him standing in the doorway and shot back as the man ran toward his car. The man, who had the same physique as Hamilton, groaned and stumbled as he got in the car and drove away.

Just before 8:30 p.m. police arrived and found Barbo hiding in the bathroom and her revolver in the toilet tank. Rocha, White, and Bryon had died from massive shotgun wounds. The front door of Fran's Market was stained with blood later found to match Hamilton's blood type.

Hamilton phoned Kenneth later that evening and said that "he lost his kitten" and that "things went wrong at the store." They arranged to meet and exchange cars. Around 10 p.m. Kenneth sold Barbo's car, a Mercury Comet, to a friend. Bloodstains matching Hamilton's blood type were later found inside the Comet. Several days after the event Rios selected Hamilton's picture from a photographic lineup having seen Hamilton and Barbo on two successive evenings.

After Hamilton exchanged cars with Kenneth, Hamilton drove to Brady's home in Modesto, some 100 miles northwest of Fresno. While staying there for about five days Hamilton told Brady he had "done robbery" and he had "killed three people for [Allen]." He also had Brady's wife write a letter to Allen asking him for the money he was owed for the job, signed it "Country," and gave Brady's Modesto address as the return address.

On September 10 Hamilton was arrested in Modesto after robbing a liquor store across the street from Brady's apartment.[54] Police seized from Hamilton an address book

---

[54] At the time of his arrest Hamilton's lower left pants leg and his left shoe had small holes in them. His left foot bore several small circular injuries and contained five foreign objects the size of No. 6 shotgun pellets. He also had a several-day-old skin laceration between his right thumb and forefinger, a type of injury frequently caused by the recoil of a sawed-off shotgun. A Cadillac registered to Kenneth Allen was parked near the liquor store; it bore Hamilton's fingerprints and was stained with blood matching Hamilton's blood type.

Hamilton put on a defense of mistaken identity. The deputy sheriff who took Abbott's initial statement testified that Abbott had been unable to identify or describe the man who shot at him except as a "dark-haired male." Abbott said he had seen only a silhouette in the doorway when he looked to see where the shots were coming from.

Kathy's brother, William Proctor, testified he saw a third man with Kenneth and Hamilton at the Allen house on September 5. Proctor claimed the third man was tall and muscular like Hamilton. He also testified Hamilton was walking with a slight limp that day, as though he had a twisted ankle. Proctor asserted that Barbo was not present at the Allen home that evening.

Shane Callaway, also testifying for the defense, claimed he accidentally shot Hamilton in the foot on September 4. He stated Hamilton and Kenneth had come to his house to collect a debt that he owed Allen; he paid under duress, but said he would get even; Hamilton laughed; he then angrily pulled out a shotgun and accidentally caused it to discharge into Hamilton's foot. Callaway admitted he had been at the Allen house several times since the 5th and had talked with Kathy and was aware Kenneth had been charged in connection with the Fran's Market killings but he denied knowing the perpetrator had been shot in the foot and discussing any of the events at Fran's Market with Kathy.

containing a list of names and addresses of those who had

As Callaway left the courtroom he was arrested on two outstanding misdemeanors. The court then released Callaway on his own recognizance and directed him to the public defender's office where he conferred with an attorney.

When the court reconvened later that day Callaway, his public defender, Hamilton's defense counsel, and the prosecutor were present. The public defender informed the court that he had discussed both the misdemeanor warrants and possible perjury charges with Callaway. The public defender and the prosecutor agreed that Callaway, who had returned to testify from Utah without a subpoena, should be immune from arrest on the warrants, and be given immunity from prosecution for perjury in his earlier testimony in exchange for testifying for the prosecution.

Callaway then entirely recanted his earlier testimony for the defense, stating instead that on the September 3 or September 4 he had been working at a copper mine in Eureka, Utah until 7 a.m. or 8 a.m. The airport nearest to Eureka is less than 130 miles away and so he said he could not have reached Fresno on the 4th and in fact was not there that day. Callaway also testified that Kathy was a good friend, that he had spoken with her one and one-half months before the trial when he was living in Fresno, and that when he agreed to testify for Kenneth she gave him a letter containing the substance of what he was supposed to say. He flushed the letter down the jail toilet immediately after his arrest that day. Kathy supplied him with a description of Hamilton, whom he had never met, and thereafter was present when he first talked to the defense investigator at the Allen home. After his interview with the investigator, he decided not to testify and went back to Utah. When members of his family received anonymous telephone threats he agreed to testify for Hamilton and returned to California.

At the penalty phase the prosecution introduced evidence of other crimes committed by Hamilton: a 1973 escape from a Kentucky jail, a 1977 robbery in San Jose, and a September 10, 1980, liquor store robbery in Modesto. Hamilton is presently on death row in San Quentin State Prison.

testified against Allen at the 1977 murder trial: Furrow, Carrasco, Meyer, Jones, Mayfield, Doeckel, and Ray and Bryon Schletewitz. When investigators visited Kenneth's home at about the same time Kathy handed them Hamilton's mug shot.

After an article about the Fran Market murders appeared Allen asked Rainier, "Why don't you testify against me *** and see if you can help yourself or get some time off [?]" When Rainier said he could not do that Allen patted him on the back and said, "You wouldn't want to do that anyway because you do have a lovely daughter."

Shortly after the Fran Market murders Kenneth was arrested on drug charges and was interviewed about his knowledge of the murders. A week later he contacted police to offer his testimony in return for protective custody and his choice of prisons. He eventually entered a plea agreement whereby he promised to testify "truthfully and completely" in all proceedings against Hamilton, Barbo, and Allen in exchange for which he would be allowed to plead to specified charges.[55] In June 1981 a complaint was filed against Allen for the murder of Bryon Schletewitz, White, and Rocha, and conspiring to murder Bryon and Ray Schletewitz, Furrow, Carrasco, Meyer, Jones, and Mayfield.

On July 8, 1982, Allen's trial began. The jury heard 58 witnesses over 23 days. Allen took the stand in his own defense and denied any involvement in the Fran's Market murders or in the conspiracy to execute the witnesses who testified against him in his previous trial. He admitted telling Hamilton to go to Fresno, admitted writing all the

---

[55] The prosecutor later terminated the agreement after discovering Kenneth had written to Allen promising to change his testimony at trial in order to exculpate him. Nevertheless, stating he wanted to testify truthfully, and having been fully advised of his *Miranda* rights and the fact that the previous plea agreement was terminated, Kenneth testified for the prosecution at a trial conducted in Glenn County.

various letters received into evidence, and conceded that they referred to Hamilton's impending visit to Fresno. He confirmed that the letters referred to Meyer, Mayfield, and Jones and admitted that the phrase "taken care of" meant to kill. He also acknowledged that he had access to mug shots where he worked with Hamilton in Folsom Prison and admitted talking to Hamilton in the bleachers at the prison. After being confronted with a tape-recording he also admitted ordering Kathy to call the Schletewitzes to impersonate Kitts, and to pretend to be the mother of Bryon's baby in order to induce the family to call off the Kitts murder investigation.

Allen also confirmed many of the details about his former acts and convictions about which Jones, Mayfield, Furrow, Meyer, Doeckel, and Carrasco had all testified. He described how he helped transport and dispose of Kitts's body; how he executed "fool-proof" armed robberies of various K-Mart stores with his son Roger, Meyer, and Allen Robinson; his role in the Tulare K-Mart robbery; and maintained that "when a guy puts a rat jacket on himself [becomes a "snitch"], killing them would do them a favor"; he described how he brought Larry Green from Oklahoma to participate in the Visalia K-Mart robbery, and how they had planned to execute three or four additional robberies to make money for summer expenses.

Kathy tried to exculpate her father-in-law and implicate her husband as the drug-crazed, hallucinogenic mastermind of the Fran's Market murder. She recalled that Kenneth had discussed getting guns for witnesses with his father at Folsom Prison, and that Barbo had told her that she and Hamilton could not leave any witnesses. She admitted that she had previously testified for Allen, that she had tried to falsify evidence about the murders, and that she had transmitted messages to Hamilton for Allen.

After three days of jury deliberation, Allen was found guilty as charged. Allen thereafter admitted he had previously been convicted of murder. The State presented

217

evidence at the seven-day penalty trial that showed Allen masterminded several armed robberies in California.[56] Evidence also showed that while in the Fresno County jail on June 27, 1981, Allen called a "death penalty" vote for inmate Glenn Bell (an accused child molester) and directed an attack on Bell during which inmates scalded Bell with over two gallons of hot water, tied him to the cell bars and beat him about the head and face, and thereafter shot him with a zip gun and threw razor blades and excrement at him while he huddled in his blanket in the corner of the cell. The State established that Allen repeatedly threatened that anyone who "snitched" on the Allen gang would be "blown away" or killed and that Allen thwarted prosecution of the attempted robbery at Wickes Forest Products by threatening the chief prosecution witness and his family.

---

[56] Allen's robberies include: the August 12, 1974, armed robbery at the Safina Jewelry Store in Fresno in which $18,000 worth of jewelry was taken from the store safe, and the September 4, 1974, armed robbery at Don's Hillside Inn in Porterville in which $3600 was taken from the safe and hundreds of dollars in cash and credit cards were taken from patrons at the scene; the February 12, 1975, residential armed robbery of William and Ruth Cross, an elderly Fresno couple in which a coin collection valued at $100,000 was taken, the June 18, 1975, attempted robbery at Wickes Forest Products in Fresno, resulting in Allen's arrest, and the October 21, 1975, armed robbery at Skagg's Drug Store in Bakersfield in which Raoul Lopez (another stepson of Carrasco recruited by Allen) accidentally shot himself; the November 20, 1976, armed robbery at a Sacramento Lucky's market in which grocery clerk Lee McBride was shot by robber Lopez and sustained permanent damage to his nervous system; the February 10, 1977, robbery at the Tulare K-Mart in which over $16,000 in cash was taken, and March 16, 1977, Visalia K-Mart robbery in which Larry Green held a gun to the head of employee Bernice Davis and subsequently shot employee John Attebery in the chest, permanently disabling him.

Allen's prior convictions of conspiracy, first-degree murder, first-degree burglary, attempted robbery, and assault with a deadly weapon was introduced into evidence at the penalty phase. It was also stipulated that the guilt phase testimony of Ray Schletewitz, Mayfield, Jones, Furrow, and Meyer concerning the prior conspiracy to murder and the first-degree murder of Kitts in August 1974, the robbery at the Safina Jewelry Store on August 12, 1974, the burglary and robbery of the Tulare K-Mart Store on February 10, 1977, and the assault with a deadly weapon, burglary, conspiracy to commit robbery, and attempted robbery at the Visalia K-Mart Store on March 16, 1977, could be considered by the jury at the penalty phase without recalling these witnesses.

It took the jury just one day to return a verdict of death finding that Allen had a prior murder conviction (Kitts), had committed multiple-murder, and had intentionally killed Bryon Schletewitz in retaliation for his prior testimony and to prevent his future testimony. At the time of his execution Allen was legally blind and confined to a wheel chair. On January 13, 2006, Governor Arnold Schwarzenegger in rejecting Allen clemency noted: "the passage of time does not excuse Allen from the jury's punishment."

Barbo was given a life sentence for her participation in the murders. Kenneth Allen was never tried because on the eve of trial he admitted a charge of murder with special circumstances for the Fran Market murders; he is serving a life sentence without parole. Furrow was given a 5-year sentence as part of a plea bargain (*People v. Allen* (1986) 42 C3d 1222; *People v. Hamilton* (1988) 46 C3d 123).

————

Perrie Dyon Simpson, a 43-year-old black male, was executed by lethal injection at the Central Prison in Raleigh, North Carolina on January 20, 2006. Simpson was found guilty of the 1984 murder of Jean Ernest Darter, a 92-year-old white male. Simpson, who was 21-years old when he committed the capital crime, was sentenced to death on March 12, 1985, again in 1988, and again on December 20, 1993.

The Reverend Jean Darter, a retired Baptist minister, was found dead in his Reidsville, North Carolina home on the evening of August 28, 1984 by his daughter. Darter had been tied to a bedpost at the foot of his bed by a belt that was wrapped around his neck. Both of his arms had been slashed open, his head was bloated, and his face was covered with blood. There were numerous cuts and bruises on his head and his left cheek bore an imprint that matched the bottom of a broken Tab bottle lying on the bed. Blood and fragments of glass were in his eyes and a bloody razor blade lay near his right hand. Certain items were missing from the home.

Expert medical testimony showed that any of three major areas of trauma could have been life threatening but that Darter's death was due to ligature strangulation caused by the belt around his neck. His death had occurred over a period of five or six minutes or longer depending upon the amount of force used during the strangulation. Darter would have lost consciousness within three to five minutes after his breathing stopped.

Fingerprints were found in Darter's home on a hall telephone, in the bedroom, and in the kitchen. Some of the fingerprints found matched those of Simpson. Others matched the fingerprints of Simpson's girl friend, Stephanie Eury, a 16-year-old black female.

Police traced a phone call from Darter's home to a friend of Simpson who identified Simpson as the caller. On that basis Simpson was arrested on September 21 on a warrant for an unrelated assault in Greensboro. After advising Simpson of his *Miranda* rights, the arresting officers briefly questioned him about the unrelated assault. They then began to discuss Darter's murder with him. Simpson initially denied any knowledge of the murder. Officers stopped questioning him once he agreed to take a polygraph test. After the polygraph procedures were explained to him and he was told the machine would reveal any lying on his part, Simpson said that the machine would show he was lying and that there was something he needed to tell the officers.

Shortly thereafter Simpson was again advised of his *Miranda* rights. He then gave a statement in the nature of a confession indicating that he and Eury had gone to Darter's home on August 26 at her suggestion on the pretext that they were travelers who needed help. Once there the Reverend gave them food and money and allowed them to use the telephone in his home. After leaving the Darter home Simpson and Eury decided to go back and rob Darter.

Simpson said that on the evening of Monday, the 27th, he and Eury left Eury's home and began to plan the robbery and murder of Darter. Simpson stated that: "Stephanie said if we go in there and rob the man we can't let him live and I said that is the truth."

They then went to Darter's home, and after making sure that no one could see them, knocked on the door. Darter let them in. When Darter attempted to call police to help Simpson and Eury, Simpson pulled Darter away from the telephone. He told Eury to cut the phone cord, which she did. Eury ran to the living room and pulled the drapes while Simpson held Darter down on the bed in the bedroom.

Eury began to ransack the residence for valuables to steal. When she brought food to the bedroom to show to Simpson he told her to look for money. He continued to hold Darter on the bed and told Darter, "I want some money or else." Simpson stated that Darter said that he had no money and to go ahead and kill him adding that, "The preacher was smiling as he told me to kill him because he was going to heaven and this made me mad."

Simpson called to Eury to check the bedroom for money. He grabbed a belt from the footboard of the bed and looped it around Darter's neck. He held the belt tightly around Darter's neck with his right hand while he went through items on the bed with his left hand and "told the preacher that he better tell me where some more money was but the preacher could not talk as he was choking." The belt around Darter's neck broke, and Simpson grabbed a thicker leather belt from the footboard and looped it around Darter's neck, pulling it tight.

Simpson called to Eury "to bring me something in the bedroom to kill this preacher with." When the items Eury brought Simpson to kill Darter with proved unsatisfactory, he had her hold the belt and pull it tighter around Darter's neck while he went to the kitchen "and looked around for some device to beat the old preacher and finish him off."

Having found a full sixteen-ounce soft drink bottle of Tab, Simpson returned to the bedroom. He and Eury then pulled together to tighten the belt around Darter's neck. Simpson then hit Darter in the face with the bottle three times at which point it broke. Simpson tied the end of the belt to the footboard of the bed and went to the bathroom of the home and got a razor blade.

During this time Eury continued to search the house and gather up more items. Simpson cut both of Darter's arms while Eury gathered up items to be stolen and put them in a grocery bag and a plastic laundry basket. They then cut off the lights in the home and left with the items they had stolen. After Simpson confessed warrants were issued charging him with first-degree murder, robbery with a dangerous weapon, and conspiracy to commit murder.

Simpson was tried in Rockingham County Superior Court. In 1985 he was sentenced to death and then resentenced after it was ruled the trial judge's refusal to allow more than one of Simpson's attorneys to present final arguments to the jury was in error. In 1988 Simpson was again sentenced to death, but a subsequent appellate court ruled that the jury had been erroneously instructed that the finding of mitigating circumstances had to be unanimous and vacated the sentence. Ultimately, Simpson's third death sentence was confirmed. Governor Michael F. Easley denied Simpson clemency. Accomplice Eury was convicted of first-degree murder and given a life sentence (*State v. Simpson* (1987) 357 S.E.2d 332; *State v. Simpson* (1992) 415 S.E.2d 351; *State v. Simpson* (1995) 462 S.E.2d 191).

———

Marion Butler Dudley, a 33-year-old black male, was executed by lethal injection at the Texas State Penitentiary in Huntsville, Texas on January 25, 2006. Dudley was found guilty of the 1992 murder of Audrey Brown, a 19-year-old white female, Frank Farias, a 17-year-old Hispanic male, Jessica Quinonas, a 19-year-old Hispanic female, and Jose Tovar, a 32-year-old Hispanic male. Dudley, who was 20-years old when he committed the capital crime, was sentenced to death on January 10, 1995.

Dudley, who lived in Tuscaloosa, Alabama, occasionally traveled to Houston, Texas to buy drugs from Rachel and Jose Tovar. Dudley had a prior criminal record that included a felony for possession of marijuana. On June 20, 1992, Dudley and three other men drove from Tuscaloosa to Houston. After arriving, Dudley and one of the men went to the Tovar residence and asked for three kilograms of cocaine. Rachel told the men she did not have the cocaine and asked them to come back later.

Dudley and one of the other men returned to the Tovar residence a few hours later and the Tovars showed them a kilogram of cocaine. The men were told more cocaine could be obtained so the two men left. At dusk, Dudley and two other black males, Arthur "Squirt" Brown Jr., 21, and Antonia Lamone Dunson, 19, returned and tied up the Tovars and four other people in the home. All six were shot in the head. Four of the victims died: Jose Tovar, his wife's son Frank Farias, Farias's girlfriend, Jessica Quinones, who was seven-months pregnant, and Audrey

Brown, a neighbor. Rachel Tovar and Nicholas Cortez, a 22-year-old Hispanic male, survived and later identified Dudley as one of their attackers.

On August 12 Dudley and Dunson were arrested in Fayetteville, North Carolina. Returned to Texas, a Harris County jury convicted Dudley of capital murder and the court sentenced him to death. On the day of execution the Supreme Court of the United States denied a stay.

Sometime after Dudley and Dunson were arrested, Brown was arrested in Tuscaloosa, returned to Texas, and also sentenced to death for his involvement in the four murders. Dunson was sentenced to life imprisonment (*Dudley v. Dretke* (2003) 77 Fed.Appx. 741; *Dudley v. Texas* (2006) 546 U.S. 1159).

Marvin Bieghler, a 58-year-old white male, was executed by lethal injection at the Indiana State Prison in Michigan City, Indiana on January 27, 2006. Bieghler was found guilty of the 1981 murder of Kimberly Jane Miller, a 19-year-old white female, and Tommy E. Miller, a 21-year-old white male. Bieghler, who was 33-years old when he committed the capital crime, was sentenced to death on March 25, 1983.

At approximately 10:30 a.m. on December 11, 1981, Kenny Miller went to the Kokomo, Indiana trailer occupied by his brother, Tommy Miller, and his pregnant sister-in-law, Kimberly Miller, and found both of them dead. Kimberly was lying in the doorway to their bedroom and Tommy was lying at the end of the bed. The couple had been shot with nine rounds from an automatic .38-caliber pistol at point-blank range, and a dime was found near each body.

Tommy was known to have sold drugs for Bieghler and Bieghler admitted he was in the business of buying drugs in Florida and selling them in Kokomo. Bieghler's bodyguard, Harold "Scotty" Brook, testified, as did others, that someone had informed police and caused the arrest of one of Bieghler's chief operatives thereby causing the confiscation of a large amount of his marijuana. Bieghler had on many occasions warned that if he ever discovered who "dropped a dime" on him (snitching), he would "blow him away." Bieghler, who was known to carry a "super .38" automatic pistol, began to suspect that Tommy was the informer telling Brook and other people that he was going to get him.

On the evening of December 10 Brook, who cut a beneficial deal with the prosecutor on unrelated charges in exchange for his testimony, testified that he and Bieghler smoked marijuana and drank alcoholic beverages. During that evening Bieghler again spoke of getting Miller. At around 11:00 p.m. Bieghler said, "Let's go," and he and Brook went out to Bieghler's automobile.

Bieghler then drove to Miller's trailer where Brook said he tried to stop Bieghler but could not hold him back. Bieghler went to the trailer, opened the door, and walked to the bedroom door with his pistol in his hand. At one time Brook told police that he did hear shots, but at trial he said he did not hear any shots.

Bieghler ran out of the trailer and back to the car. Bieghler and Brook then proceeded to Kokomo where they picked up Bieghler's girlfriend, Thelma McVety, from work at around 11:15 p.m. After dropping McVety off at her house, Brook, his brother, and Bieghler went to the Dolphin Tavern arriving at 11:30 p.m. Brook and Bieghler then went back to McVety's where Bieghler tearfully told her that he had to go to Florida, and then left for Florida alone.

Bieghler's "super .38" was never introduced at trial, but nine shell casings found at the murder scene matched casings found at a remote rural location where Bieghler fired his gun for target practice. An expert for the State testified that the two sets of casings were fired from the same gun, which had to have been one of only three types

225

of automatic .38-caliber pistols, one of which was the "super .38."

A Howard County Superior Court jury found Bieghler guilty of two counts of murder and one of burglary, and recommended the death penalty. The jury did not believe Bieghler's trial counsel argument that Bieghler could not have committed the crimes during the time Brook testified the two men went to' the Millers' trailer, or the several witnesses who testified about the extremely hazardous, icy road conditions around the trailer that night which would have prevented a round trip from Galveston to the trailer, and then to McVety's workplace in 45 minutes, or the several witnesses who claimed talking with Tommy on the telephone that evening after 11 p.m.

The trial judge sentenced Bieghler to death for the murders, but did not sentence him for the burglary. The Indiana Parole Board unanimously recommended against clemency afterwhich Governor Mitch Daniels denied clemency. Less than a half hour before Bieghler's execution the Supreme Court of the United States denied a stay by a vote of 6-3 (*Bieghler v. State* (1985) 481 N.E.2d 78; *Bieghler v. State* (1997) 690 N.E.2d 188).

———

Jaime Elizalde Jr., a 34-year-old Hispanic male, was executed by lethal injection at the Texas State Penitentiary in Huntsville, Texas on January 31, 2006. Elizalde was found guilty of the 1994 murder of two Hispanic males: Juan Saenz Guajado, 29, and Marcos Sanchez Vasquez, 33. Elizalde, who was 22-years old when he committed the capital crime, was sentenced to death on April 2, 1997.

On the night of November 5, 1994, Marcos Vasquez and Juan Guajado were shot and killed outside the El Lugar bar in Houston, Texas. At trial Juan Millan, the manager of the bar, testified that while standing outside his establishment he saw Elizalde, accompanied by his father Jaime Elizalde Sr., first shoot Guajado and then shoot a fleeing Vasquez. Robert Garcia testified that from the bar he saw Guajado as he was shot, noting that although he did not see the killer shoot Guajado, when he exited the bar, he saw Elizalde flee with a gun.

Several days after the shooting, Millan gave a statement to police wherein he stated that he was playing pool inside the bar with Fidel Razo at the time of the shooting and did not go outside until after he heard the gunshots. At trial Razo testified that he was playing pool with Millan when the shots were fired. Millan disavowed the statement and testified that he was not initially truthful with police because "he did not want to have any problems." He also admitted that police pressured him including threatening jail time after he gave his initial statement.

On February 10, 1997, Elizalde was indicted for capital murder. On March 26 he was found guilty and six days later the jury determined that he posed a risk of future danger, and the trial court sentenced him to death. During the punishment phase the State introduced evidence of Elizalde's criminal history noting his membership in the Mexican Mafia and his involvement in prison assaults including one in which he stabbed another prisoner with a shank (a crude-sharpened weapon). On June 9, 1999, the Texas Court of Criminal Appeals affirmed Elizalde's conviction and sentence on direct appeal. On the day of execution the Supreme Court of the United States denied a stay (*Elizalde v. Dretke* (2004) 362 F.3d 323; *Elizalde v. Livingston* (2006) 546 U.S. 1160).

———

Glenn Lee Benner II, a 43-year-old white male, was executed by lethal injection at the Southern Ohio Correctional Facility in Lucasville, Ohio on February 7, 2006. Benner was found guilty of the 1985 murder of Cynthia Sedgwick, a 26-year-old white female, and the 1986 murder of Trina Bowser, a 21-year-old white female.

Benner, who was 22-years old when he committed the capital crime, was sentenced to death on May 14, 1986.

On August 6, 1985, Cynthia Sedgwick and three friends attended a rock concert at the Blossom Music Center in Cuyahoga Falls, Ohio. Sedgwick had had a few drinks and was "tipsy". She strayed from her friends several times and at the end of the concert was nowhere to be found. After waiting for Sedgwick quite a while at the conclusion of the concert, her friends left.

Benner had come to the same concert that with a group of friends and coworkers of his employer, Michael's Construction Company. Benner's foreman and another coworker testified that they had seen Benner with Sedgwick and had in fact seen him carry her into the woods adjacent to the parking lot. Benner's party was unable to find him and left the music center without him. On August 12 a parking attendant in the woods adjacent to the parking lot discovered Sedgwick's nude and partially decomposed body.

On the evening of September 26 Nancy Hale was hanging pictures in her Goodyear Heights home when without warning, she was grabbed from behind, slapped repeatedly, and thrown to the floor. Her clothes were stripped from her body afterwhich she was orally, anally, and vaginally raped. The assailant then placed his hands around Hale's throat and began choking her. While this was happening a second individual kept asking Hale where her money was. The second subject pulled the rapist off of her. Hall later reported the attack to police.

On the evening of November 19 Shelli Powell, a 19-year-old University of Akron student, was jogging along Howe Road in Tallmadge when abruptly and without any warning, she was tackled and ended up lying face down on an embankment parallel to the sidewalk. The assailant then lay on her back and repeatedly instructed her to "shut up". He then began wrapping masking tape around her head, covering her eyes.

Powell's attacker moved her down the embankment and into a marshy area where he removed her long-sleeved T-shirt and her bra. At this point Powell asked him to remove the masking tape because it was hurting her eyes. He removed the tape and Powell caught a glance of her assailant in the moonlight and was able to touch his face. The attacker fondled Powell. His attention was then diverted by something and Powell tried to escape but as soon as she rose to run, he pounced on her. The last thing Powell remembered about the attack was her assailant's hands around her neck and her inability to breathe.

When Powell regained consciousness she still had tremendous difficulty breathing. Something was bound tightly around her neck. She ran naked to a house across the street from the marshy area. The owner of the home let her in and called police. The officer who answered the call found Powell with her knotted bra tied tightly around her neck. It was tied so tightly that he was afraid to cut it with a knife. With great difficulty he untied the knot and removed it. Powell was taken to the hospital and later released.

On the evening of January 1, 1986, Trina Bowser, a childhood friend of Benner who lived just two houses away in the same neighborhood and often played together with Benner, was visiting with her friend Cheryl Leek in Akron. At approximately 9:45 p.m. Bowser left Leek's house, and the following morning at 12:15 a.m. an AT&T employee coming home from work spotted Bowser's car burning on Interstate 76. He flagged down a trucker requesting help and a fire extinguisher. The trucker stopped and both men put out the fire. There was a purse on the floor of the front passenger compartment, and there was no one inside the car. The men found the number of the Bowser residence on a bank check. They then called police and Bowser's parents. Upon arrival Bowser's parents opened the trunk of the car to find their daughter's body. Her jeans were wrapped around her head and eyes and her ankles were bound. Her knotted bra and panties were bound tightly around her neck.

Shortly after Bowser's murder Robert L. Tyson, a schoolmate and coworker of Benner, called the Tallmadge police. Apparently motivated by a reward offered by Sedgwick's parents, he told police that he knew the identity of the perpetrator of the Sedgwick, Powell, and Bowser crimes. Tyson identified Benner as the culprit and, in a series of subsequent interviews with police, told them of Benner's confession to him of the Sedgwick and Powell crimes. He also informed police of his and Benner's involvement in the crimes against Hale.

On January 10, 1986, Benner and Tyson were arrested. Benner confessed later that day to raping Hale. On the 21st the grand jury returned a 23-count indictment against Benner, charging, among other things, the aggravated murders of Sedgwick and Bowser. Each count contained death penalty specifications.

Benner elected to proceed with a three-judge panel instead of a jury. The State presented the testimony of 30 witnesses and admitted over 100 exhibits. Benner was represented by two court appointed attorneys and was convicted of 20 counts, including three counts of aggravated murder—one count for killing Sedgwick and two counts for killing Bowser.

After a penalty phase in which Benner testified but was not cross-examined, the three judges unanimously concluded that the aggravating circumstances outweighed the mitigating factors and imposed the death penalty. Benner did not seek clemency and the eight-member Ohio Parole Board unanimously denied clemency as did Governor Bob Taft.

Benner's last words: "I just need you to give me two seconds. I have been going over and over in my head trying to think of the words I can say to you that would ease the unimaginable pain that you have been going through for 20 years because of my actions. I'm sorry. Trina and

Cynthia were beautiful girls who didn't deserve what I did to them. They are in a better place. Words seem so futile. All I can say is I'm sorry. May God give you peace." Tyson, who was sentenced to 5-to-25 years for his involvment in Hale's rape, was paroled on September 27, 1990 (*State v. Benner* (1987) WL 15078).

———

Robert James Neville Jr., a 31-year-old white male, was executed by lethal injection at the Texas State Penitentiary in Huntsville, Texas on February 8, 2006. Neville was found guilty of the 1998 murder of Amy Robinson, a 19-year-old white and Native American female. Neville, who was 23-years old when he committed the capital crime, was sentenced to death on December 9, 1998.

Amy Robinson suffered from Turner syndrome.[57] On February 15, 1998, Robinson failed to report to work at 1:00 p.m. at the Kroger grocery store in Arlington, Texas and was reported missing. Robinson was last seen leaving her house on her bicycle to ride to work. In the course of the investigation of Robinson's disappearance, police contacted the six foot tall Neville and his six foot two inch tall friend, Michael Wayne Hall, an 18-year-old white male. Both men were former coworkers of Robinson. Neville told the police that he was acquainted with Robinson personally and professionally, but that he did not have any information about her disappearance.

---

[57] Turner Syndrome is a genetic disorder found only in women characterized by short stature, widely spaced nipples, low-set ears, reproductive sterility, and often accompanied by mild retardation. Robinson was four-foot five-inches tall and had the mental capacity of a third or fourth grader.

On February 28 Hall's mother[58] alerted police that Hall had been missing for several days. Hall's stepbrother[59] told police that Hall had confided that he and Neville had abducted and killed Robinson. A warrant for their arrest was subsequently issued.

On March 3 the U.S. Customs Service in Eagle Pass arrested Hall and Neville near the Mexican border. Neville admitted that he saw Robinson while driving with Hall around Arlington around 12:00 p.m. on February 15, that he and Hall asked her if she wanted a ride to work, and that she accepted the ride. Neville confessed that pretending to have a flat tire they stopped in a remote field in the Moslier Valley around 12:45 p.m.

At some point Hall persuaded Robinson to get out of the car telling her she needed to go talk to Neville near a tree. As Robinson walked toward Neville, Neville fired a crossbow at her several times. Neville missed each shot and Robinson became angry. When the last arrow grazed her hair, Robinson started walking back to the car. Hall then shot her in the back of her leg with his pellet gun.

------

[58] Karen Hall testified that her son had always been slower than other children. At age five he could not stack blocks. Hall was in special education classes from the 1st through the 8th grade, was placed in regular classes in 9th grade but could not handle them, and did not advance beyond the 10th grade. Hall's mother further testified that Hall played like an 8-year-old and associates with children who are 8, 9, and 10 years old.

[59] Damon Lee Hall testified that, at age 14 to 15, Hall associated with children ages 8 to 9, adding that his stepbrother had trouble explaining things and took a long time to do so. Hall could understand directions only when they were given slowly. Hall's brother testified that Hall had difficulty understanding how to play pool, had trouble reading analogue clocks, and also had trouble counting money often not knowing when he was shortchanged.

Neville returned to the car and got his .22-caliber rifle. Meanwhile Hall managed to maneuver Robinson back into the field where Neville shot her in the chest. Hall then shot her in the chest "three or four or six times" with the pellet gun. Robinson fell to the ground making loud noises and shaking. Hall then stood over her and stared for five to ten minutes. The two men worried that someone would hear Robinson so Neville shot her in the head killing her instantly. Hall and Neville then left Robinson and her bicycle in an area where she and the bicycle would not be easily discovered.

A few days later Neville and Hall returned to the scene. Neville fired shots into Robinson's dead body, and Hall took keys and money from her pocket. Neville later revealed the location of Robinson's body on a map where in fact it was found.

On March 24, 1998, a Tarrant County grand jury indicted Neville for capital murder. On December 4 he was found guilty and five days later he was sentenced to death. During the trial Dr. Randall Price testified that Neville was not mentally ill but had a severe psychopathic personality, adding that Neville expressed enjoyment and excitement during Robinson's murder. On December 1, 1999, the Texas Court of Criminal Appeals affirmed his conviction and sentence. In 2000 accomplice Hall was convicted of capital murder and sentenced to death (*Hall v. Texas* (2002) 67 S.W.3d 870; *Hall v. Texas* (2002) 160 S.W.3d 24; *Neville v. Dretke* (2005) 423 F.3d 474).

———

Clyde Smith Jr., a 32-year-old black male, was executed by lethal injection at the Texas State Penitentiary in Huntsville, Texas on February 15, 2006. Smith was found guilty of the 1992 murder of David E. Jacobs, a 45-year-old white male. Smith, who was 18-years old when he committed the capital crime, was sentenced to death on December 6, 1993.

On February 7, 1992, David Jacobs's body was found in his cab in the parking lot of a Houston, Texas apartment complex. An autopsy revealed Jacobs died after being shot three times in the back of his neck with a .38-caliber pistol. Jacobs's wallet and $110 was missing.

Smith was charged in Jacobs's death after an April 5 incident in which Smith shot himself in the leg at another apartment complex in Houston. While police were investigating they found a .38-caliber pistol, which ballistic tests linked to the fatal shootings of Jacobs and another cab driver, 51-year-old Victor Bilton, who was shot three times during a March 22 robbery.

In 1993 a Harris County jury convicted Smith of capital murder. Smith confessed to shooting Jacobs and gave a tape-recorded statement introduced into evidence at the punishment phase wherein he also confessed to shooting Bilton and taking $120 and a watch from the cabbie. In April 1996 the Texas Court of Criminal Appeals affirmed Smith's conviction and sentence. The Texas Board of Pardons and Paroles later denied clemency, and on the day of execution the Supreme Court of the United States denied a stay (*Smith v. Dretke* (2005) 134 Fed.Appx. 674; *Smith v. Livingston* (2006) 546 U.S. 1162).

———

Tommie Collins Hughes, a 31-year-old black male, was executed by lethal injection at the Texas State Penitentiary in Huntsville, Texas on March 15, 2006. Hughes was found guilty of the 1997 murder of Foluke G. Erinkitola, a 25-year-old black female. Hughes, who was 22-years old when he committed the capital crime, was sentenced to death on May 7, 1998.

The AMC Grand 24 movie theater in northwest Dallas, Texas had experienced a rash of robberies and burglaries in the recent past causing law enforcement officers to stake out the area in the hope of catching those responsible. During the evening of August 13, 1997, undercover officers noticed Hughes and his cousin, Derric Dewayne English, a 19-year-old black male, as the two walked through the parking lot toward the theater building.

Approximately ten minutes later both men were observed walking quickly back toward their car, a Mercury Tracer. Hughes was 20 to 30 feet behind English. English appeared to be hunched over concealing what was described as a "large bulge" beneath his shirt; the "bulge" had not been observed earlier.

After both men entered the car, Alicia Lavone Henry, the driver of the Tracer who had never left the vehicle, quickly accelerated, exiting the parking lot at a high rate of speed, and continued onto the highway reaching speeds of 90 miles an hour. To the undercover officers these actions indicated that the two men might have just burglarized a parked motor vehicle.

One officer, in an unmarked vehicle, began a clandestine pursuit of the Tracer maintaining a safe distance so as not to arouse suspicion. The officers remaining at the theater searched the parking lot for signs of a possible burglary. Within minutes theater patrons came upon Foluke Erinkitola, a University of Illinois student, and Roxanne Andrea Mendoza, a 29-year-old Hispanic female, both apparently dead of gunshot wounds. The two women worked at GTE in Irving where Erinkitola was an intern and Mendoza was an account manager. Authorities were notified of the murders and the occupants of the Tracer then became capital murder suspects.

Information of the crime and its possible suspects was immediately dispatched over police radio. The undercover officer kept the speeding Tracer within his sight until a marked police unit intervened and occupied a position directly behind and within obvious view of the fleeing vehicle. The officer did not, however, activate the unit's emergency lights at this time.

The Tracer eventually exited the highway and pulled into a gas station in south Dallas. Hughes exited and appeared as though he was preparing to activate the gas pump. The pursuing police car pulled in behind the Tracer activating its emergency lights as other marked units converged on the scene. Hughes was ordered onto the ground and arrested. English and Henry were ordered to exit the vehicle and placed under arrest. Inside the Tracer and on the suspects themselves were found the murder weapon, ammunition, bloodstained clothes, and stolen property.

On October 1, 1997, a Dallas County grand jury indicted Hughes for capital murder. Hughes, who received a bad conduct discharge from the Marine Corps and earned a lengthy criminal record, was found guilty on May 1, 1998. Six days later the court sentenced him to death. On April 12, 2000, the Texas Court of Criminal Appeals affirmed his conviction and sentence. Hughes requested and received six pieces of fried chicken with hot sauce, six jalapeno peppers, French fries, four buttered rolls, two large sodas, and two menthol cigarettes for his last meal.

At a separate trial English was convicted of capital murder, and on August 28, 1998, he was sentenced to life imprisonment. Henry pleaded to a lesser charge of aggravated robbery in exchange for her testimony against both Hughes and English. She was sentenced to 11 years' imprisonment (*Hughes v. State* (2000) 24 S.W.3d 833).

———

Patrick Lane Moody, a 39-year-old white male, was executed by lethal injection at the Central Prison in Raleigh, North Carolina on March 17, 2006. Moody was found guilty of the 1994 murder of Donnie Ray Robbins, a 34-year-old white male. Moody, who was 28-years old when he committed the capital crime, was sentenced to death on July 20, 1995.

In July 1994 Moody started having an affair with Donnie Robbins's wife, Wanda Kaye B. Robbins, a 30-year-old white female. Over the course of their affair

Moody and Wanda discussed various plans to murder her husband and share the insurance proceeds.

On September 16 Moody went to Loman's Trailer Park in Thomasville, North Carolina, where Donnie and Wanda lived. Moody identified himself as Darryl Thompson and pretended to be interested in buying Donnie's old Chevrolet automobile. He and Donnie went to a field near the trailer park where the automobile was located. Moody asked Donnie to measure the automobile, purportedly to determine whether it would fit on a "roll-back" truck. As Donnie leaned over the hood of the automobile to measure it, Moody shot him in the back of the head with a .32-caliber semiautomatic pistol he had stolen the previous day from a house near the trailer park.

Moody and Wanda had agreed to meet at the hospital following the murder. While at the hospital Moody identified himself as Darryl Thompson to investigating officers and consented to taking a gunshot residue test afterwhich Moody then left the hospital. Early the next morning Moody was apprehended and taken into custody. Later that morning, following Moody's directions, police found the murder weapon, the black jacket Moody had been wearing, and other items of evidence. After being arrested Moody waived his *Miranda* rights and made a statement.

At trial, after the State had begun its case-in-chief and had presented evidence from seven witnesses, Moody withdrew his plea of not guilty and entered a first-degree murder plea. The court found that there was a factual basis for the plea, in that Moody was competent to stand trial, that he was satisfied with his attorney, and that the plea was made freely and voluntarily.

In the capital sentencing proceeding a life insurance agent testified that Wanda had called her at 5:30 a.m. the morning after the murder to complete the paperwork necessary for Wanda's claim for the insurance benefits payable upon Donnie's death. The jury learned of Moody's prior convictions in Florida for attempted first-degree murder and conspiracy to commit first-degree murder.

Moody's half-brother, Carl Jacobs, testified in mitigation that Moody's father abused Moody when he was a young child, beating him with a board, breaking plates over his head, and locking him in his room without meals for up to 18 hours. Dr. Jerry Noble, a clinical psychologist, said that Moody had borderline intellectual functioning with an I.Q. no greater than 82, adding that he suffered from attention deficit hyperactivity disorder, alcohol dependence, mixed personality disorder, child abuse syndrome, and psychologically caused physical problems.

A Davidson County Superior Court sentenced Moody to death. On March 16, 2006, the Supreme Court of the United States denied a stay of execution, afterwhich Governor Michael F. Easley declined a request to commute Moody's sentence to life in prison. Wanda was tried separately for her part in the crime. On September 25, 1999, she was convicted of second-degree murder and sentenced to life imprisonment (*Moody v. Beck* (2005) 547 U.S. 1015; *Moody v. Polk* (2005) 408 F.3d 141; *State v. Moody* (1997) 481 S.E.2d 629).

———

Robert Madrid Salazar Jr., a 27-year-old Hispanic male, was executed by lethal injection at the Texas State Penitentiary in Huntsville, Texas on March 22, 2006. Salazar was found guilty of the 1997 murder of Adriana Gomez, a 2-year-old Hispanic female. Salazar, who was 18-years old when he committed the capital crime, was sentenced to death on March 12, 1999.

Salazar began dating a Lubbock, Texas woman named Raylene Blakeburn in the fall of 1996. On April 23, 1997, Blakeburn went to work in the morning leaving her daughter Adriana Gomez in Salazar's care as she often did. When Blakeburn came home from work at around 5:00 p.m. Salazar was not there. Blakeburn discovered

Adriana in her bed, unconscious, breathing abnormally, and with blood in her mouth. With the assistance of a neighbor, Blakeburn called for an ambulance.

When the paramedics arrived they found Blakeburn standing outside of her house holding Adriana in a blanket. The paramedics, unable to bring Adriana back to consciousness, placed her on a ventilator. As they did one paramedic noticed that the back of Adriana's head had been caved in and that it felt like "Jello." The paramedics also observed that one of Adriana's arms was twisted and deformed and that she had marks and bruises covering her neck, ankles, and chest. Suspecting child abuse the paramedics contacted police. Adriana died at roughly 7:45 p.m.

Roger Torres, one of Salazar's friends, testified that at around 4:00 p.m. that day he was walking home when Salazar drove up to him and asked if he could take a look at Salazar's fan belt. According to Torres, Adriana was not with Salazar at the time. Shortly thereafter Torres examined the fan belt, and just after 5:00 p.m. the two men drove to a nearby store and purchased some beer. At around this time Torres noticed that Salazar's shirt had on it a number of small stains, which appeared to be blood. When the two men returned from the store they saw the ambulance outside of Blakeburn's residence. They did not stop and instead drove by and continued on to Salazar's mother's house.

Once at his mother's house Salazar changed his shirt and the two men drank some beer. At this time Blakeburn called Salazar at his mother's house and told him that Adriana was injured. Salazar told Blakeburn not to tell police that he had been watching Adriana that day. He also told Torres to be quiet and that the matter was none of his business.

Salazar later gave a written statement to police in which he admitted that he had been watching Adriana while her mother was at work on the day in question. He stated that he and Adriana were taking a shower together and that he became angry because she would not stop crying, adding that Adriana generally did not like to take a shower with him when her mother was not there. Salazar also stated that in order to stop her crying he pushed her with the back of his hand causing her to fall down in the bathtub and hit her head. Salazar stated that he became scared because Adriana was unconscious and bleeding, so he abandoned the child and left the scene. A subsequent lab analysis of a bloodstain on Salazar's pants revealed that the stain was consistent with Adriana's DNA.

The pathologist who performed the autopsy testified that Adriana's death was caused by trauma from multiple blunt force injuries, and he ruled the manner of death a homicide. The pathologist stated that the injuries sustained by Adriana were inconsistent with Salazar's contention that she had fallen down and hit her head in the tub. Adriana's injuries indicated the infliction of repeated blows of severe force to her head, chest, and abdomen.

The autopsy revealed that the child had suffered at least three life-threatening injuries all of which had been inflicted within 48-hours of her death. A blow to her head resulted in a posterior basal skull fracture consistent with her skull having been slammed into a hard surface. The location of several other smaller skull fractures was consistent with her being struck multiple times, and the injuries to her eyes were consistent with being shaken or struck so hard that she would have been blind had she survived. A major blow to the chest bruised Adriana's lungs, diaphragm, and heart.

The pathologist testified that the injuries to the child's chest surpassed anything he had seen previously in cases of automobile accidents. More than one of Adriana's ribs had been broken and her heart was so severely damaged that it would have ruptured had she lived much longer. The blow to her stomach had pushed her abdomen against her backbone crushing the tissues in between. The injuries to her tongue and mouth were indicative of a blow to her face and the injury to her vagina was consistent with sexual penetration. The State also showed that in January 1997 Adriana suffered either a broken collarbone or a dislocated shoulder. When asked about the injury by a neighbor, Adriana replied that Salazar had done it.

On April 30, 1997, a Lubbock County grand jury indicted Salazar for intentionally or knowingly causing the death of a two-year-old child. On March 9, 1999, a jury found Salazar guilty of capital murder and three days later he was sentenced to death. On January 17, 2001, the Texas Court of Criminal Appeals affirmed his conviction and sentence.

Salazar's last meal: a dozen tamales, six brownies, refried beans with chorizo, two rollo candies, six hard shell tacos with lettuce, three big red sodas, ketchup, hot sauce, six jalapeno peppers, tomatoes, cheese, and extra ground beef; and last words: "To everybody on both sides of that wall, I want you to know that I love you both. I am sorry that the child had to lose her life, but I should not have to be here. Tell my family I love them all and I will see them in heaven" (*Salazar v. Dretke* (2005) 419 F.3d 384; *Salazar v. State* (2001) 38 S.W.3d 141).

———

Kevin Christopher Kincy, a 38-year-old black male, was executed by lethal injection at the Texas State Penitentiary in Huntsville, Texas on March 29, 2006. Kincy was found guilty of the 1993 murder of Jerome Samuel Harville, a 31-year-old black male. Kincy, who was 25-years old when he committed the capital crime, was sentenced to death on November 2, 1995.

In March 1993 Kincy and his cousin, Charlotte Marie Kincy, a 33-year-old black female, made plans to rob Jerome Harville and steal his car and possessions. The plan was for Charlotte, who had been romantically involved with Harville and had been accepting money from him, to seduce Harville in his Jacinto City, Texas home. Kincy would then enter the home and kill Harville.

After Harville was murdered Kincy and Charlotte brought Byron Brown, Kincy's coworker, to Harville's house. When Brown entered a bedroom he observed a man lying on the floor, realized he was dead, became frightened, and left the house.

On March 26 Harville's coworkers became concerned because of his absence from work and eventually notified the sheriff's department. A deputy discovered Harville in his home having been fatally shot in the head and stabbed several times. Although there was no sign of forced entry Harville's home had been ransacked and his Honda Accord, among other items, had been stolen. Police uncovered prints in the home consistent with a person wearing gloves.

Terkisha Dawson testified that Kincy explained to her how he surprised Harville in his home and shot him in the head. Dawson said that Charlotte admitted to stabbing Harville several times. Keenan Mosley, another of Kincy's cousins, also testified that Kincy displayed a gun he had stolen from Harville, made a list of pros and cons concerning his chances of getting caught, and mentioned having worn gloves. Mosley also testified that she observed Kincy with a Honda Accord and a large amount of home appliances and equipment.

On April 6 an FBI agent spotted Kincy driving Harville's Honda on Interstate 10 in Texas near the Louisiana border. Police apprehended Kincy in Louisiana after a lengthy high-speed chase. Police linked Kincy to the crime after recovering the murder weapon, a .25-caliber pistol, in the Honda and finding Harville's stolen 9-millimeter Ruger in a pawnshop.

In 1993 Kincy and Charlotte were both charged with capital murder. Kincy had prior convictions for possession of marijuana, theft, delivery of cocaine, burglary of a motor vehicle, and attempted murder. The State agreed to reduce Charlotte's charge to first-degree aggravated robbery for which she was sentenced to 40 years' imprisonment in exchange for her guilty plea and her promise to testify against Kincy at trial. However, when Charlotte was called as a witness in the penalty phase of the 1995 trial she refused to testify. The Harris County jury nonetheless found Kincy guilty of capital murder, and the court sentenced him to death. On January 21, 1998, the Texas Court of Criminal Appeals affirmed his conviction and sentence. On the day of execution the Supreme Court of the United States denied a stay (*Kincy v. Dretke* (5th Cir. 2004) No. 03-20656; *Kincy v. Livingston* (2006) 547 U.S. 1053).

————

Richard Alford Thornburg Jr., a 40-year-old white male, was executed by lethal injection at the Oklahoma State Penitentiary in McAlester, Oklahoma on April 18, 2006. Thornburg was found guilty of the 1996 murder of three white males: James Donald Poteet, 51, Terry Lynn Shepard, 39, and Keith Alan Smith, 24. Thornburg, who was 24-years old when he committed the capital crime, was sentenced to death on May 12, 1997.

Between 3:00 a.m. and 4:00 a.m. on September 28, 1996, the six foot four inch tall Thornburg, and two other white males, Glenn Anderson, 38, and Roger D. Embry, 32, went to Marvin Matheson's trailer in Grady County OKlahoma. All three men were armed. As they hovered over Matheson, Thornburg accused him of being responsible for shooting Thornburg the month before.[60]

---

[60] Julie Maxon, a long-time friend of Thornburg, testified that he had attempted to borrow her police scanner the night of September 27, some six hours before the murders, and that he was unusually high that evening. She also testified to a prior incident in which Thornburg had been shot. The shooting
(*continued*)

Also suspecting James Poteet of a role in the shooting, they drove Matheson to Poteet's house telling him on the way not to worry about locking his trailer because he was not coming back. When the four men arrived at Poteet's house Thornburg and Embry went inside while Matheson and Anderson remained in the car.

After hearing gunshots from the house Anderson took Matheson inside. As Matheson entered he saw Terry Shepard sitting on a chair outside the bathroom door and Poteet sitting on the bed in the back bedroom. Poteet, held at gunpoint by Thornburg, had been shot in the foot and his forehead was bruised and bloody. Matheson saw Thornburg shoot again at Poteet's feet as he attempted to get Poteet to tell him who had shot him. Anderson then instructed Thornburg to take Matheson to Poteet's rental unit near the house and get Jimmy Scott.

Thornburg escorted Matheson to the rental unit with a gun to his back, but he was interrupted when Keith Smith arrived at Jimmy's house to retrieve his girlfriend's purse.[61] Thornburg instructed Smith to knock on Jimmy's door.

(*continued*)
occurred a few minutes after Thornburg had asked Jimmy Scott to pay him back $60 that he owed. Thornburg had told her that he thought Poteet had something to do with the shooting. Terry Alexander, a deputy sheriff who had investigated the September 23 shooting of Thornburg, testified that when asked about the shooting, Thornburg had told him "not to worry about it, he'd take care of it."

[61] Jatone Kennedy, Smith's girlfriend at the time, testified that on September 27 she and Scott had been out drinking. She passed out at Scott's residence. Smith, angry because she had not come home, came and woke her around 2:00 a.m. the next day. They fought as they walked back to their house and after reconciling she told him that she had left her purse with his marijuana in it at Scott's. At about 4 a.m. Smith left to go to Scott's to get the purse but he never returned.

Donnie Scott answered the door as his brother Jimmy was not home. Thornburg then forced Donny, Smith, and Matheson to go to Poteet's house.

Once they were inside Poteet's house, Anderson held the men at gunpoint in the kitchen while Thornburg went to the back bedroom. Matheson could hear Thornburg and Poteet arguing about drugs and money. Anderson then instructed Embry to bring everyone back to the bedroom where the men injected Matheson and Poteet with drugs, as Anderson commented that he intended to "OD" them.

Anderson and Thornburg also injected themselves as Thornburg continued arguing with Poteet about whether Poteet had shot him. He told Poteet that he was going to shoot him, but then said "better yet, I ain't gonna shoot you," and instructed Matheson to shoot Poteet. Embry and Anderson pointed their guns at Matheson, threatening to shoot him if he did not shoot Poteet. When Matheson refused to shoot, Thornburg shot Poteet in the side.

Thornburg then told Matheson that Matheson was "going to shoot somebody and that it had a lot to do with if [Matheson left] the house or not." Matheson was told to shoot one of the men in the bathroom and so he attempted to shoot Scott in the head, but the gun did not have a bullet. Anderson then took the gun into the hallway, presumably to put a bullet in it, and returned insisting that Matheson shoot Scott or he would kill Matheson who then shot Scott in the chest.

Embry then gave his gun to Anderson, telling him that he did not want to be involved in shooting anyone afterwhich he escorted Matheson back to the car. Matheson heard three or four more shots coming from the house. As he was sitting in the car Embry opened the trunk and Matheson could smell gas as if Embry was siphoning gasoline. The men removed a sack of "Longneck Budweiser" bottles from the back seat. Matheson then heard someone throw something through a window and saw that Poteet's bedroom window was broken.   After setting the house on fire the men drove away.[62]

Thornburg dropped Anderson and Embry off by the side of the road so that they could stash their guns. After driving further Thornburg told Matheson to get out of the car, hide for a bit, and keep his mouth shut or the others would blame him for killing everyone.

Scott, still alive in the burning house, attempted to help Poteet crawl out but he was unsuccessful.[63] Scott made it out himself and lay down in the grass. A man and his son drove past the burning house shortly after 5 a.m. and took Scott to a convenience store where they called police.

_____

[62] Elvin Barnhill, an investigator with the State Fire Marshal's office, described how on the morning of September 28 he found Shepard in the northeast bedroom, Poteet in the hallway leading to the two bedrooms, and Smith on the bed in the southeast bedroom. Barnhill detected evidence of the use of accelerants (flammable substances) to promote the fire in four spots in the northeast bedroom, and he discovered burn patterns indicating a flammable substance near Smith and between his legs. Although no accelerants were detected in material samples from the bedroom, Barnhill explained that it was not uncommon for such substances to "leach out" during a fire. He also testified that the charring of the victims' bodies and their surroundings indicated an intense heat suggesting that accelerants were used in both bedrooms. The pattern of charring indicated that the fire started in the bedrooms and headed west down the hallway. Barnhill further explained how one could start a fire by breaking a bottle containing gasoline and a lit wick adding that the fire was likely set intentionally between 4:45 a.m. and 5:15 a.m.

[63] Fred Jordan, Oklahoma's Chief Medical Examiner, testified that each victim had been shot and some showed signs of burning while still alive. He said that Poteet's fatal gunshot wound would not have caused instantaneous death, but he would have died from loss of blood and collapsing of the lungs. Likewise, the gunshots wounds to Shepard and Smith would not likely have caused instantaneous death.

Scott survived, but Smith, Poteet, and Shepard perished in the fire.

When Matheson heard that police wanted to arrest him in connection with the murders, he turned himself in and gave the above account of his activities to officers, but not until he learned that his family was under police protection.

Thornburg was convicted of three counts of first-degree murder, shooting with intent to kill, first-degree arson, and two counts of kidnapping in the District Court of Grady County. Thornburg did not seek clemency. Anderson was convicted of first-degree murder, shooting with intent to kill, first-degree arson, and kidnapping. He was sentenced to death for first-degree murder, life imprisonment for shooting with intent to kill, 35-years for first-degree arson, and 10-years for each kidnapping. Embry was convicted of first-degree murder, first-degree arson, and kidnapping. He was sentenced to life imprisonment without the possibility of parole, 35 years' imprisonment, and 10 years' imprisonment (*Anderson v. State* (1999) 992 P.2d 409; *Thornburg v. Mullin* (2005) 422 F.3d 1113).

———

Willie Brown Jr., a 61-year-old black male, was executed by lethal injection at the Central Prison in Raleigh, North Carolina on April 20, 2006. Brown was found guilty of the 1983 murder of Vallerie Ann Roberson Dixon, a black female, age unknown. Brown, who was 38-years old when he committed the capital crime, was sentenced to death on November 15, 1983.

At approximately 5:47 a.m. on the morning of March 6, 1983, a Zip Mart convenience store on Main Street in Williamston, North Carolina, was reported empty and the store clerk Vallerie Dixon was missing. A patrolling police officer had seen Dixon in the store less than 30 minutes prior to the report. Money from the cash register and a store safe had been taken along with Dixon's automobile, and so a search for Dixon was immediately begun.

At about 6:20 a.m. a police officer spotted Dixon's automobile traveling on a nearby road. The automobile was stopped by police officers, and Brown, who was driving alone in the vehicle, was immediately placed under arrest and advised of his *Miranda* rights. A .32-caliber six-shot revolver, a paper bag containing approximately $90 in cash and change, and a change purse containing Dixon's driver license and social security card were found in the automobile. A pair of ski gloves and a toboggan cap with eyeholes cut out of it were found on Brown's person. The exterior of the car was partly covered with fresh mud.

According to police officers Brown admitted that he robbed the Zip Mart and fled in Dixon's car, but claimed that Dixon was unharmed when he left the store. When questioned about Dixon, Brown had an intense emotional reaction—crying and shaking.

At approximately 4:00 p.m. that afternoon Dixon's body was found on a muddy logging road in a rural area outside Williamston. Forensic pathology and firearm tests revealed that Dixon had been shot six times with the same .32-caliber revolver that police had found in Dixon's car.

Brown testified at his Martin County Superior Court trial disputing the police officers' version of the events on the day of the murder. According to Brown, he was jogging near the Zip Mart when a man ran past him and away from a parked car with an opened door. Brown said that he saw a gun and bag of money on the seat of the car, sat down in the vehicle, and was arrested by police before he could get out of the vehicle. Brown denied robbing or killing Dixon, and denied making any admissions to police. He admitted to a lengthy criminal record but denied he was guilty of committing any crimes.[64]

---

[64] Brown had been convicted in 1963 in North Carolina of six counts of felonious larceny and six counts of breaking or entering. In 1965 Brown was convicted in Virginia of five counts of armed robbery and one count of felonious assault. The victim

The jury convicted Brown of first-degree murder and robbery with a dangerous weapon, found no mitigating circumstances, and recommended that he be sentenced to death, which the trial court imposed. On April 20, 2006, the Supreme Court of the United States denied a stay of execution, and Governor Michael F. Easley denied clemency (*Brown v. Lee* (2003) 319 F.3d 162; *Brown v. North Carolina* (2006) 547 U.S. 1096; *State v. Brown* (1985) 337 S.E.2d 808).

———

Daryl Linnie Mack, a 57-year-old black male, was voluntarily executed by lethal injection at the Nevada State Prison in Carson City, Nevada on April 26, 2006. Mack was found guilty of the 1988 murder of Betty Jane May, a 55-year-old white female. Mack, who was 52-years old when he committed the capital crime, was sentenced to death on May 15, 2002.

Betty May lived in a basement room at a boarding house in Reno, Nevada. Steven Floyd lived in the house next door with the managers of the boarding house, Jim and Kelly Bassett. On the night of October 28, 1988, Floyd, who had been drinking at a nearby bar that night, was returning home to try to borrow some money. He knew May and saw that her light was on, so he went to her room to ask for money. Floyd knocked on her door, which was slightly open, but there was no response. He opened the door and saw May kneeling by her bed with her upper body facedown on the bed. He then turned her over and realized that she was dead. Floyd immediately went home and told the Bassetts, and police were called.

An autopsy was performed the next morning. Fingernail scrapings and evidentiary swabs from May's

---

of the assault was a Virginia police officer, who testified at the sentencing hearing that he was shot and paralyzed when Brown shot him three times in an attempt to avoid arrest.

vagina and left foot were collected. The swabs tested positive for semen. There were abrasions on May's neck, bruises on her inner thighs, lacerations of her fingertips, lips, and nose, blood in her vagina, and a hemorrhage within her cervix. May was wearing a blue blouse that was bloodstained. The medical experts at trial all agreed that she had been manually strangled to death. An expert for the State testified that May had suffered forceful traumatic sexual penetration not long before her death.

In April 1994 Mack strangled a woman, Kim Parks, to death for which he was convicted of first-degree murder and sentenced to life in prison without possibility of parole. At that time of his arrest police had taken a blood sample from Mack. Some 12 years later, with DNA forensic testing more fully established, Detective David Jenkins took over the May investigation and requested DNA testing of the samples taken from May in 1988. Jenkins also obtained a saliva sample from Mack pursuant to a seizure order.

A criminalist for the Washoe County Sheriff testified that semen taken from May's body and that blood stains on May's blouse matched Mack's DNA profile. Blood and tissue found under May's fingertips were also consistent with Mack's DNA.

The State charged Mack with the first-degree murder with deliberation and premeditation and/or during the perpetration or attempted perpetration of a sexual assault. The State sought the death penalty, alleging two aggravating circumstances: the six foot three inch tall Mack committed the murder while under sentence of imprisonment, and he committed the murder while committing or fleeing after committing a sexual assault. Mack denied any involvement in killing May.

Before trial Mack personally informed the Second Judicial District Court of Washoe County that he would "like to waive the jury trial and have a judge trial alone." After carefully reviewing the matter, the court granted Mack's request afterwhich one judge, James W. Hardesty, found him guilty.

During the penalty phase the State argued for the death penalty showing that Mack was under sentence of imprisonment for a burglary conviction in California in June 1988. Mack offered condolences, spoke to May's family, and apologized to his own family. He said that he could not find words to express his shame and he asked the panel for the opportunity to continue his rehabilitation in prison. The three-judge panel sentenced him to death. Mack did not pursue any federal appeals. His last words were, "Allah is great, Allah is great" (*Mack v. State* (2003) 75 P.3d 803).

Dexter Lee Vinson, a 42-year-old black male, was executed by lethal injection at the Greensville Correctional Facility in Jarratt, Virginia on April 27, 2006. Vinson was found guilty of the 1997 murder of Angela Felton, a 25-year-old white female. Vinson, who was 34-years old when he committed the capital crime, was sentenced to death on February 11, 1999.

On May 19, 1997, Angela Felton and her three children resided with Nethie Pierce and her children in Portsmouth, Virginia. The family previously had lived with Vinson in Portsmouth for about "about a year and a half," afterwhich the unmarried couple had been living apart about three weeks.

At about 9:00 a.m. on the 19th Felton borrowed Pierce's "1988 red [Chevrolet] Beretta" automobile to take her children to school. In a hurry to get the kids to school, Felton wore only a "shift-type" robe and underwear. Pierce's 14-year-old daughter, Willisa Joyner, rode with Felton.

About 6:30 a.m. on the same day Faye Wilson was completing a weekend stay with Vinson in a Suffolk motel. Wilson owned a 1988 blue Mercury Tracer automobile that she let Vinson use that morning. After Felton delivered her children to school, she drove with Joyner to the home she had shared with Vinson in order to "get the mail." Upon arrival Joyner got out of the car at which time Felton saw Vinson driving a blue automobile. Joyner reentered the red vehicle when Felton said, "Get back in the car." As Felton "started driving" Vinson twice rammed the rear of the Beretta with the front of the Tracer.

Felton stopped the Beretta and Vinson walked to the driver's side window where she was sitting. He then "punched" out the window. Vinson next "grabbed" Felton, hit her in the face and chest with his hand, and "took her out of the car." Vinson held Felton by the arm and, in the presence of bystanders, "snatched" off her robe leaving her standing in her "underclothes," screaming and bleeding from her nose and mouth. Vinson next took Felton to the Tracer and "made her get in" the car. When the Tracer "wouldn't start up," Vinson "put her" in the Beretta and "they drove away."

Police officers arrived on the scene after Vinson had abducted Felton. There they obtained a description of Vinson and the Beretta. Shortly afterwards Vertley Hunter noticed from her home a red Beretta, "wrecked in the back" that was "pulled off the street and parked behind" a vacant house in her neighborhood. Boards were nailed over the windows of the house. Hunter observed a young "white female" and a young "black man" sitting in the vehicle with the female sitting in the driver's seat with "her hand outside the window to duck off a cigarette that she was smoking."

According to Hunter the man "got out on the passenger side of the car and went to the back *** and got a piece of rope out" and "leaned back into the car" holding the rope. Hunter heard the woman tell the man "to leave her alone so she could go on with her life," and heard her "ask the Lord to spare her life because he was going to kill her." At that time the man was "choking her with the rope."

The man then "grabbed her by the hair from the back seat of the car and pulled her over the seat and he pulled

252

the rope from around her neck at the same time." He "pulled her down in the floor" and "told her that he was going to kill her." While the woman was still inside the car, the man "slammed the door on her head twice."

Hunter next saw the man kick dirt beside the car to cover blood that was on the ground. He pulled off "a board" covering a window of the house, raised the window, and climbed inside through the window. Hunter saw the man enter the house twice and wipe blood off himself with a towel. Hunter watched the events for a period of several hours until the man drove the Beretta into the woods behind the house and left the area around 11:00 a.m. Hunter later identified Vinson as the man she observed committing these acts.

Janice Green, who also lived near the vacant house, testified that during the morning of the 19th she observed a man "messing around" with a red Beretta in the yard behind the house. She saw the man pull "boards off the house" and enter the home twice. The second time the man "was dragging" into the house from the car "something heavy"; she "thought it was a rug he was pulling." Green also identified Vinson as the man she observed at the vacant house.

On May 20 Portsmouth detective Jan Westerbeck went to the vacant house and discovered Felton's body inside what she described as a recently "busted wall" in one of the bedrooms. The body was nude and partially covered with a brown blanket and feces were found on and under her neck.

Forensic evidence connected Vinson with the crimes. His fingerprints were found on the abandoned Beretta, on the kitchen sink of the vacant house, and on a pane of glass from the house's kitchen window. Felton's DNA was matched to a bloodstain found on a pair of blue shorts belonging to Vinson. According to Hunter, Vinson was wearing a sky blue short set when she observed him. An expert placed the odds of the DNA on Vinson's shorts being that of someone other than Felton at one in 5,500,000,000.

An autopsy performed on Felton's body showed that she bled to death from deep cuts to both forearms, either of which would have been sufficient to cause death. The cut to the right forearm was two inches deep and severed two main arteries; the left forearm bore a similar wound that cut one artery. According to the medical examiner Felton did not die instantaneously—it "probably would have taken her a few minutes, several minutes to die" as Felton had sustained numerous other injuries including additional knife wounds on her shoulders, neck, and cheek, scratches on her buttocks, and cuts on her torso and on one of her legs, and a "blunt force trauma" to her head.

The medical examiner noted that Felton had sustained significant vaginal injuries inflicted while she was alive, including a laceration of her inner vaginal lip, massive bruising over her vulva area, and a "massive laceration," which tore the tissue separating the vagina from the anus and which tore around her anal opening. In the medical examiner's opinion, the vaginal injuries "would have been done by an object [not an erect penis] being penetrated in Miss Felton."

A Circuit Court, City of Portsmouth jury convicted Vinson of capital murder. During the eight day trial the prosecution presented evidence that in 1987 Vinson had assaulted a police officer who was attempting to arrest him; in 1988 had assaulted a correctional officer who was attempting to move him to a cell; and in 1997 had resisted arrest near a Suffolk convenience store so violently that it took eight police officers to subdue him.

Dr. Paul Mansheim expressed the opinion for the State "that there is at least a fifty percent chance" that Vinson would commit "another violent offense in the next five years." On April 27, 2006, the Supreme Court of the United Stated voted 7-2 against a stay of execution, and Governor Timothy M. Kaine rejected a plea for clemency. Vinson had no last words and requested that his last meal not be released to the public (*Vinson v. Commonwealth* (1999) 522 S.E.2d 170; *Vinson v. Kelly* (2006) 547 U.S. 1109).

———

Joseph Lewis Clark, a 57-year-old black male, was executed by lethal injection at the Southern Ohio Correctional Facility in Lucasville, Ohio on May 2, 2006. Clark was found guilty of the 1984 murder of David A. Manning, a 23-year-old white male. Clark, who was 34-years old when he committed the capital crime, was sentenced to death on March 4, 1985.

On January 8, 1984, Clark robbed Kim Reno at gunpoint. Four-days later Clark killed 21-year-old Donald Harris during a robbery of the Lawson Store at 4401 Hill Avenue in Toledo, Ohio.[65] The following day Clark shot and killed David Manning during a robbery of the Clark Gas Station at 3070 Airport Highway in Toledo.

According to a statement made by Clark to Toledo police Detective Sergeant Larry Przeslawski, at approximately 9:00 p.m. Clark entered the Clark Gas Station armed with a drawn .32-caliber revolver. Manning was working alone and Clark demanded money. Manning told Clark that there was no money, but Clark repeated his demand for money. Manning then walked to the back room

---

[65] Clark entered the Lawson Store and proceeded to jump up onto the counter and then over it, whereupon he removed the cash drawer and money from the safe. Clark then shot Harris in the back of the head. Two witnesses who later entered the store to make purchases discovered Harris in a pool of blood behind the counter. Harris was admitted to the hospital in critical condition and died later from the gunshot wound. An investigation revealed that two black males had been observed waiting in an automobile outside the store, and that a black male was observed inside the store looking around prior to the robbery and shooting.

of the service station, returned to the counter, handed Clark approximately $60 from the cash drawer, and told him that was all of the money on the premises. Clark "told him it wasn't all of it." Manning responded that there was no more money, but reached down and produced an envelope containing more cash. According to Clark's statement, Manning then tried to "force his way on me" whereupon Clark shot Manning once in the right upper chest.

Clark then ran out the service station door to his car and drove home. Shortly thereafter two Toledo police officers arrived on the scene in response to a silent alarm. One of the officers walked through the service station without seeing anyone, but looking further he found Manning slouched behind the service counter.

On January 16 Clark was arrested after allegedly committing an assault and robbery at the Ohio Citizens Bank. Robert Roloff was seriously wounded during the incident. The arresting officer found a .32-caliber revolver in Clark's coat pocket. Clark, with the assistance of an appointed public defender, was arraigned the next day in the Toledo Municipal Court for the assault and robbery at the bank. The public defender was aware that Clark was a suspect in the Manning murder and advised Clark not to discuss it with anyone but him. Later that day Clark tried to hang himself in his jail cell afterwhich he was taken to St. Vincent's Medical Center for examination.

On January 23 Clark was released from the hospital and taken to the Toledo Police Detective Bureau where he was questioned by Przeslawski and Detective James Lagger. The detectives asked Clark if he was under the influence of alcohol or drugs and Clark responded that he was not. The detectives then gave Clark a standard form containing his *Miranda* rights. After each paragraph was read the detectives asked Clark if he understood what he had read and each time Clark responded that he understood what he had read and thereupon initialed each paragraph.

After reading his *Miranda* rights Clark recited and signed the portion of the form waiving his rights. Clark was subsequently interrogated by the detectives for one and three-quarter hours, and then moved to another room where his statements were tape-recorded. Przeslawski then again read Clark his rights whereupon Clark made a statement about the Harris murder.

After making this statement Clark was given another chance to hear his rights recited when the tape was replayed for him. Eventually he made a tape-recorded statement confessing to the murder of Manning after his rights were again recited to him. The detectives gave Clark an opportunity to make any corrections in his statement upon replaying the tape for him. Clark offered no corrections, additions, or changes to his tape-recorded statements as they related to the Manning murder.

On February 2, 1984, Clark was indicted by a Lucas County grand jury on six criminal counts, two of which alleged aggravated murder. Clark, whose criminal activity began at the age of 11, entered a plea of not guilty to the Manning murder and the case proceeded to trial.

On November 6 the jury returned a verdict finding Clark guilty of the aggravated murder of Manning while committing aggravated robbery. A mitigation hearing was held seven days later, and the same jury recommended the death penalty. The trial court agreed with the jury and on November 28 Clark was sentenced to death by electrocution.[66] Clark was tried again and on February 21, 1985, another jury found him guilty of the Harris murder for which he was sentenced to life imprisonment on March 4.

---

[66] In 1993 the State passed a bill signed into law by Governor George V. Voinovich allowing death row inmates to choose between death by electrocution or lethal injection up to seven days before the scheduled execution. The default method was then electrocution, which Governor Bob Taft eliminated as an option in 2001.

On April 17, 2006, the nine member Ohio Parole Board unanimously recommended that Governor Bob Taft deny clemency, which the governor did, noting that he found "no justifiable basis for mercy." It took 86 minutes instead of an expected 10 minutes for the State to execute Clark because of the difficulty in finding a suitable vein (*State v. Clark* (1986) WL 15254).

——

Jackie Barron Wilson, a 39-year-old Hispanic male, was executed by lethal injection at the Texas State Penitentiary in Huntsville, Texas on May 4, 2006. Wilson was found guilty of the 1988 murder of Lottie Margaret "Maggie" Rhodes, a 5-year-old white female. Wilson, who was 21-years old when he committed the capital crime, was sentenced to death on November 25, 1989, and again on June 14, 1994.

On the morning of November 30, 1988, the body of Maggie Rhodes was found face down on the side of a road in a secluded area of Grand Prairie, Texas. The child's shorts had been pulled down, exposing her buttocks. It was immediately apparent that she had been run over by a car. A further examination revealed that she had been both vaginally and anally raped, strangled, and suffocated. There were tire marks on her body that reflected two distinct tire patterns and a pair of semen-stained panties was found near the body.

Investigators discovered that Maggie, who lived in the Arlington Village Apartments in Arlington with her mother, brother, and a live-in babysitter,[67] had been abducted from

---

[67] Wilson was acquainted with the family because he was a friend of the live-in babysitter. Evidence showed that Wilson had visited Maggie's apartment before and, in at least one instance Wilson "exhibited undue interest in Maggie at a birthday party prior to the murder." Evidence was also admitted showing that Wilson was familiar with the apartment complex because he had

her bedroom at night. The window in her bedroom had been broken from the outside and several pieces of glass recovered from inside and outside Maggie's bedroom had Wilson's fingerprints on them.

Several witnesses testified that they saw Wilson driving a red spray-painted Mercury Cougar on the night of the murder, and in a statement he gave police, Wilson admitted to driving the car that evening. The two types of tire tracks found on Maggie's body were consistent with the two types of tires on the Cougar,[68] and 38 human hairs that were found to be microscopically consistent with Maggie's hair were recovered from the undercarriage of the Cougar, and fibers mixed in with those hairs were consistent with the Cougar's carpet fibers. An additional 19 hairs were recovered from inside the Cougar that were found to be consistent with Maggie's hair, and a chest or pubic hair recovered from Maggie's genitalia was consistent with a racial group that includes Hispanics—Wilson is Hispanic.

The State also provided evidence of a similar crime committed by Wilson the same evening that Maggie was murdered. In that crime another resident of the Arlington Village Apartments testified that Wilson broke into her apartment and sexually assaulted her as she slept on the couch. When she awoke she ordered Wison to leave whereupon he offered her drugs in exchange for sex.

---

resided there sometime before the murder. The live-in babysitter testified that he had never allowed Wilson into the children's bedrooms and so he was eliminated as a suspect based on hair, blood, and fingerprint samples he voluntarily submitted to investigators prior to trial.

[68] Evidence at trial showed that there was one Nitto brand tire and three Goodyear brand Eagle GT tires on the Cougar. There were 15 points of comparison between the Nitto tire and the tread print on Maggie's leg, and 6 points of comparison between the tread print on Maggie's back and the Goodyear tires.

Declining the offer she again ordered Wilson to leave, which he did. It appeared that Wilson had entered through a window.

Several witnesses who saw Wilson drive toward the Arlington Village Apartments instead of heading home in the other direction just before midnight the evening of Maggie's murder, also testified that Wilson had been drinking heavily and using cocaine before he departed. When investigators were given Wilson's name by another child living in the apartment complex a police officer went to Wilson's residence to question him. Upon the officer's arrival Wilson fled.

Wilson was indicted in Dallas County. In 1989 he was convicted of capital murder and sentenced to death. On direct appeal the Texas Court of Criminal Appeals of Texas reversed the judgment based on an error in jury selection. The case was remanded to the trial court and on June 8, 1994, Wilson was again convicted and sentenced to death six days later. On February 12, 1997, the Texas Court of Criminal Appeals affirmed his conviction and sentence (*Wilson v. State* (1993) 863 S.W.2d 59; *Wilson v. State* (2006) (Tex.Crim.App. No. 75,062).

———

Jermaine Herron, a 27-year-old black male, was executed by lethal injection at the Texas State Penitentiary in Huntsville, Texas on May 17, 2006. Herron was found guilty of the 1997 murder of Betsy Nutt, a 41-year-old white female, and Cody Nutt, a 15-year-old white male. Herron, who was 18-years old when he committed the capital crime, was sentenced to death on April 28, 1999.

Ron Lucich and his family lived in a trailer home on their cattle ranch some 10 miles north of Refugio, Texas. Living in a second trailer on the property were Betsy Nutt and her son, Cody. Herron was familiar with the Lucichs and their ranch, because he and his father had lived on the property many years earlier when his father had been Ron's ranch foreman.

At approximately 11 a.m. on June 25, 1997, Herron and Derrick Wayne Frazier, a 20-year-old black male, paid a visit to the Lucich residence to see about getting work. Ron was out and only his three children were home. Herron and Frazier decided to "hang out" for a while and sometime during the visit, Ron's wife came home. She became concerned and called Ron who told her to "get them out of there" which she did by taking everyone out for lunch.

After lunch Ron's wife dropped Herron and Fraizer off at the house of one of Herron's friends. During the visit Herron and Frazier observed a number of guns that were kept in plain view around the Lucich house. They also learned that the Lucichs were planning an out-of-town day trip the next day.

Later that afternoon Herron, Frazier, and Michael Brown made plans to burglarize the Lucich residence, steal their guns, and take the Nutt's truck. At around 4 p.m. they drove to a roadside park from which the ranch could be viewed so they could discuss details. At one point Herron pointed to the Nutt's truck and said, "That's my truck."

Around 9:00 p.m. that evening Crystal Mascorro drove Herron, Frazier, and Brown to Trey Johnson's house where Herron picked up a .22-caliber rifle. Mascorro then drove Herron, Frazier, and Brown to the entrance of the Lucich's ranch and dropped them off so that they could carry out their plans. The three men were wearing bandanas on their face and Herron was carrying the rifle. Mascorro briefly tried to talk them into abandoning their plans but ultimately left believing that they would make their way back to town by stealing the Nutt's truck.

Both Mascorro and Brown were under the impression that the rifle Herron had picked up from Johnson's house was broken and could not be used. Brown was also under the impression that no one was to be at the Lucich home. Once there Herron started talking about killing someone.

261

At that point Brown felt that it was time to turn back and when the porch light came on at the Lucich house, he ran. Herron and Frazier subsequently joined him and they all left the ranch.

A few hours later in the early morning hours of June 26 Herron and Frazier convinced Brown to drive them back to the Lucich ranch in order to complete the burglary. Brown left after dropping Herron and Frazier off. The pair then hid and waited for the Lucichs to leave. At around 7:30 a.m. the Lucichs left and Herron and Frazier entered the trailer.

After burglarizing the home, finding the guns, and gathering up everything they wanted to steal, Herron telephoned Brown and told him that he and Frazier had found some alcohol. They then positioned some chairs in front of the living room window so that they could observe the road leading up to the residence spending the next four to five hours sitting around, drinking, and waiting.

At around 2 p.m. Betsy pulled up to her trailer in her truck. Herron and Frazier, who had observed Betsy pull up, walked over to her trailer house and asked to use the phone. They told Betsy that their car had broken down. Once inside they forced Betsy and her son to get on their knees and Herron shot each of them in the head twice. Shortly thereafter Herron called Brown again and told him that he had killed a woman and a little boy.

On June 29 after a warrant was issued for Herron's arrest Herron contacted his uncle, Captain Willie Brown of the Refugio County Sheriff's Office and surrendered himself to Brown at Brown's home. Brown read Herron his *Miranda* rights and informed him that if he had anything to say that he needed to say it to the investigating officer and not to him. After being transported to the county jail Herron quickly initiated contact and made a videotaped statement confessing to the crimes.

On July 1 Herron inititiated a second videotaped interview that was introduced at trial, and on August 8 Herron and Frazier were indicted for capital murder. The two men were tried separately—Frazier in October 1998 and Herron in April 1999—and both found guilty of the same crime. On October 9, 2002, the Texas Court of Criminal Appeals affirmed Herron's conviction and sentence, and on August 31, 2006, the State of Texas executed Frazier (*Frazier v. Dretke* (2005) 145 Fed.Appx. 866; *Herron v. State* (2002) 86 S.W.3d 621).

———

Jesus Ledesma Aguilar, a 42-year-old Hispanic male, was executed by lethal injection at the Texas State Penitentiary in Huntsville, Texas on May 24, 2006. Aguilar was found guilty of the 1995 murder of Leonardo Chavez Sr., a 33-year-old Hispanic male and Annette Esparza Chavez, a 31-year-old Hispanic female. Aguilar, who was 31-years old when he committed both murders, was sentenced to death on May 7, 1996.

Aguilar and Rick Esparza were longtime friends, who worked together selling marijuana. Esparza initially worked for Aguilar beginning in November 1994 by transporting marijuana in Esparza's vehicle from each of their homes in Texas to Mississippi. Shortly thereafter another supplier asked Esperaza to transport marijuana to Mississippi and he began dealing without Aguilar. Aguilar felt that Esparza was stealing his business and this caused friction between the two men.

Aguilar began stopping by Esparza's trailer in Harlingen, Texas and accusing him of running drugs without him. Esparza testified that Aguilar threatened his life on a number of occasions adding that he was afraid of Aguilar because he had seen "the way [Aguilar] hurts people." In spite of Aguilar's threats Esparza continued to maintain his own drug courier business.

Esparza's sister, Annette Chavez, was also known to make frequent trips to Mississippi returning to Texas with large amounts of cash. Esparza often asked Annette and her family to stay at his home during out-of-town trips, and on June 8, 1995, Esparza and his wife took a load of drugs to Mississippi while Annette, her husband Leonardo Chavez, and their two children, 9-year-old Leonardo Jr. ("Leo") and 2-year-old Lincoln, stayed at his home.

Aguilar spent much of the afternoon and evening of June 9 drinking with friends. At approximately 9:00 p.m. Aguilar was at a friend's house with David Quiroz, and Aguilar's 17-year-old nephew, Christopher Quiroz. As David left the house he saw Aguilar and Christopher leave together.

At approximately 5:00 a.m. Leo was awakened from his bed in Esparza's trailer by the sound of a gunshot. Leo got out of bed and entered the kitchen. Because there was no wall between the rooms Leo could see into the living room that was illuminated by a small lamp. Leo saw his parents on the floor with two men standing over them. Leo testified that the "American" man told his father to "get your fat ass up," and then saw the man shoot his father. The "Mexican" man then took the gun and shot his mother afterwhich Leo ran to the neighbors for help. A pathologist later testified that the couple had been shot "execution style" and that before they were shot markings on the bodies showed they were both severly beaten.

That afternoon Daniel Pena was driving around with Aguilar and Christopher when Aguilar asked Pena to go to Rafael Flores Jr.'s residence where Aguilar offered to sell a .22-caliber revolver to Flores. Flores bought the revolver and gave it to his brother who in turn gave it to their father. Police later received a tip that they could recover the murder weapon from the Flores's residence, which they did. After recovering the weapon the police lab compared bullets from .22-caliber revolver with the .22-caliber bullets recovered from the Chavez's bodies but could not decide if it were the murder weapon.

Approximately two weeks after the murders Leo's grandmother was reading the newspaper when Leo saw a picture and told her that two of the men in the picture were the men who "hurt" his parents. His grandfather took Leo to the police station where the boy identified Chris Quiroz as the "American" who shot his father and Aguilar as the "Mexican" who shot his mother. Leo was unable to identify Aguilar in a police lineup but an investigator for the Cameron County Sheriff's office testified that Leo became visibly upset when Aguilar entered the lineup room.

On August 8, 1995, a Cameron County grand jury indicted Aguilar for capital murder. On April 30, 1996, Aguilar was convicted, and two days later the jury recommended a death sentence for which he was sentenced to death five days later. On June 18, 1997, the Texas Court of Criminal Appeals affirmed his conviction and sentence. Accomplice Christopher Quiroz was convicted of capital murder and sentenced to life imprisonment (*Aguilar v. Dretke* (2005) 428 F.3d 526).

———

John Albert Boltz, a 74-year-old white male, was executed by lethal injection at the Oklahoma State Penitentiary in McAlester, Oklahoma on June 1, 2006. Boltz was found guilty of the 1984 murder of Doug Kirby, a 23-year-old white male. Boltz, who was 52-years old when he committed the capital crime, was sentenced to death on November 21, 1984.

At approximately 9:30 p.m. on April 18, 1984, the Shawnee Police Department received a call from Boltz's wife, Pat Kirby. Pat informed police that she was at her mother's house and that Boltz, who had been drinking, had forced his way into the house and had made accusations about her to her mother. She further stated that when she threatened to call police Boltz left afterwhich she gave the dispatcher Boltz's license number and his home address.

Sometime later Pat Kirby called the police department and inquired as to whether Boltz had been taken into custody. When she was informed that he had not been arrested she went to her son Doug's house. After they had been there for a short time Boltz called and talked to Doug. The conversation lasted only a few minutes and a short time later Boltz called back and again talked to Doug. After this call Doug left to go to Boltz's trailer house in Pottawatomie County Oklahoma.

Immediately thereafter Boltz called a third time and Pat answered the phone. Boltz told her, "I'm going to cut your loving little boy's head off." He also threatened Pat who immediately called police and reported the threats. She told the dispatcher where Boltz lived and stated that she was going over there.

Vita Witt, who lived next door to Boltz, testified that on the evening of the 18th she heard the screeching of brakes, a car door slam, and loud and angry voices. When she heard a sound like someone getting the wind knocked out of him she looked out the window and observed a man later identified as Doug Kirby laying on the ground on his back and not moving. Witt testified that Boltz was standing over Doug screaming obscenities and beating him. She told her son to call police.

Witt testified that she observed Boltz pull something shiny from his belt and point the object at the man, adding that when Boltz looked up and saw her watching, she turned away out of fear. Doug had been stabbed repeatedly while retreating from the trailer house in an attempt to escape. During the struggle with Boltz he was finally overcome and collapsed in the yard.

Dr. Fred Jordan testified that Doug's autopsy revealed a total of eleven wounds including eight stab wounds to the neck, chest and abdomen, and three cutting wounds to the neck. One of the wounds to the neck was so deep that it had cut into the spinal column. The carotid arteries on both sides of the neck were cut in half and the major arteries in the heart were also cut.

Boltz, a Pentecostal minister, was arrested in Midwest City, Oklahoma at the American Legion Hall after a friend informed police of his location. Boltz had informed the friend that he had killed his stepson and had probably cut his head off. Boltz surrendered to police upon their arrival. Subsequently he did not follow his attorney's advice and accept a pretrial plea bargain for first-degree manslaughter for which a death sentence would not have been imposed and for which the court called "a lack of knowledge as to what was a good deal."

The six foot two inch tall Boltz testified at trial that Doug had called him in the evening and threatened to kill him claiming that when Doug arrived at his house he kicked in the front door and as he went for a gun Boltz stabbed him twice adding that he did not remember anything after that point. A .22-caliber revolver was recovered from the passenger seat of Doug's car and although the seat was splattered with blood the gun had no blood on it.

The Pottawatomie County jury convicted Boltz of first-degree murder, and notwithstanding the fact that he had no prior criminal record, imposed the death penalty. The five member state Pardon and Parole Board unanimously denied clemency, and on the day of execution the Supreme Court of the United States denied a stay (*Boltz v. Mullin* (2005) 415 F.3d 1215; *Boltz v. Sirmons* (2006) 126 S.Ct. 2350; *Boltz v. State* (1991) 806 P.2d 1117).

———

Timothy Tyler Titsworth, a 34-year-old white male, was executed by lethal injection at the Texas State Penitentiary in Huntsville, Texas on June 6, 2006. Titsworth was found guilty of the 1993 murder of Christine Marie Sossaman, a 26-year-old white female. Titsworth, who was 21-years old when he committed the capital crime, was sentenced to death on October 28, 1993.

Titsworth and Christine Sossaman had been living together in Amarillo, Texas, for approximately two months, when on July 22, 1993, Sossaman was murdered. A friend of Sossaman testified that the day before the murder Sossaman told her she intended to ask Titsworth to move

267

out of the house because she believed that he was stealing from her.

After initially denying the murder Titsworth confessed to killing Sossaman and taking her property. In his confession Titsworth claimed he and Sossaman had an argument after she accused him of "messing around." After slapping Titsworth around Sossaman went to bed. Titsworth left the house and bought some crack cocaine and a pill he thought was LSD. Titsworth ingested the drugs, went back to the house, and retrieved a dull two-bladed ax from a closet while Sossaman was asleep in bed. Claiming he had blacked out Titsworth remembered hitting Sossaman with the ax four or five times.

An autopsy showed that Sossaman had been struck with a dull two-bladed ax approximately sixteen times excluding the defensive wounds to her hands and legs. Sossaman probably was asleep in bed when she was axed. At some point during the attack Sossaman "was either taken off or came off the bed." Sossaman suffered at least seven blows from the ax while she was on the floor. After the attack Titsworth left Sossaman on the floor. The medical examiner testified Sossaman could have lived anywhere from 20 minutes to "a number of hours" after the attack. After she died Sossaman suffered at least one more blow from the ax.

Titsworth claimed that when he realized what he had done, he did not know what to do so he sold some of Sossaman's property and bought more crack cocaine. On his first trip back to Sossaman's home Titsworth claimed Sossaman "was still breathing and it looked like she had tried to crawl into the bathroom." Titsworth left the house with more of Sossaman's property that Titsworth sold to buy more crack cocaine. Titsworth claimed he was taking a friend home when police arrested him.

John Ballard was with Titsworth on the day he was arrested and confessed. Ballard told the jury that he accompanied Titsworth on two trips to the trailer where

Sossaman's body lay although he apparently did not know then of the killing or see her body.

On the first trip Ballard helped Titsworth remove and sell an expensive television. They then purchased and smoked crack with the $100 they had received. After exhausting these funds they returned and removed an expensive stereo set and sold it to purchase more crack cocaine. When the money was finally gone and the dope was smoked, they slept for 11 hours. On awakening they left the house they were in and were quickly arrested—the body having been found by the Sossaman's mother in the meantime. The trial court found that Ballard "gave uncontradicted testimony that Titsworth had slept from 10 to 11 hours immediately prior to his arrest and that during this time neither Ballard nor Titsworth consumed any drugs or alcohol."

A Randall County jury convicted Titsworth of capital murder for which the court sentenced him to death.[69] On

---

[69] Titsworth's theory at trial was that he was not guilty of capital murder because the evidence showed only that he killed Sossaman under the influence of drugs as a result of a "lover's spat" and not with the intent to take her property. Titsworth later claimed his confession was involuntary and should have been suppressed because he was intoxicated.

Cindy Risley, the deputy responsible for booking Titsworth into the Randall County Jail, testified that Titsworth was under the influence of drugs or alcohol during the hour or so it took to book him into the jail. Risley also stated that she had told fellow officers of Titsworth's condition at the time of booking, but was told not to say such things.

Risley testified that Titsworth was "grinning and laughing" and that he "didn't seem to be aware of the seriousness at the time." According to Risley: "He would laugh, he'd nod off. I had to wake him up a couple of times during the booking process. He didn't seem to understand at the time what he was being brought in for." She recalled that he answered questions as if the
(continued)

November 22, 1995, the Texas Court of Criminal Appeals, in a split decision, affirmed his conviction on appeal (*Titsworth v. Dretke* (2005) 401 F.3d 301).

———

Lamont Reese, a 28-year-old black male, was executed by lethal injection at the Texas State Penitentiary in Huntsville, Texas on June 20, 2006. Reese was found guilty of the 1999 murder of three black males: Riki Jackson, 17, Alonzo Stewart, 25, and Anthony Roney, 26. Reese, who was 21-years old when he committed the capital crime, was sentenced to death on January 18, 2001.

On March 1, 1999, Riki Jackson, Alonzo Stewart, and Anthoney Roney flirted with Reese's 18-year-old black girlfriend, Kareema S. Kimbrough, outside a Fort Worth, Texas convenience store. After an exchange of words, Kimbrough, Reese, and three black males, Brian Kenson Johnson, 19, Steven Lamont Kindred, 16, and Jason Montel Leadley, 14, left the store. Kimbrough drove them back to the store armed where Reese shot and fatally

---

(*continued*)
victim were still alive.

Jean Roper, Titsworth's longtime probation officer, when shown a picture of Titsworth taken while he was being booked and having recounted his long difficulties with addiction and repeated failure in treatment, observed that he was probably still high. Roper's opinion was however contradicted by both Sergeant B.J. White's and John Ballard's testimony that Titsworth had just slept 11 hours prior to being arrested.

The prosecution offered evidence that Titsworth admitted the crime both to Roper when she visited him in jail and to Risley when she was making jail rounds. A report from a Dr. Shaw found that Titsworth was competent and that his behavior at the time of the offense was consistent with someone under the influence of alcohol and drugs.

wounded Jackson, Stewart, and Roney injuring an unidentified 13 and 24 year-old.

After the murders Reese and his friends returned to Kimbrough's home where they bragged about their crime. One of the men told another man who had not participated in the shooting that Reese had shot three people with an assault rifle, and Reese did not dispute this statement. Reese boasted that he got the men who were at the pay phone at the store.

On the heels of his arrest police impounded Reese's vehicle and found five live cartridges in the glove compartment that were identical to several live rounds of ammunition discovered at the crime scene. After his arrest Reese approached the jailer and asked if he was classified as a "celebrity inmate." The jailer responded that Tarrant County had no such classification but instead classified appropriate inmates as "high profile." When he assured Reese that he would check on his classification Reese announced, "Hell, I killed three people."

On May 25, 1999, Reese was indicted in Tarrant County. On November 30, 2000, he was convicted of capital murder. On November 6, 2002, the Texas Court of Criminal Appeals affirmed his conviction and sentence. Accomplices, Kimbrough, Johnson, Kindred, and Leadley, were also convicted of capital murder, and sentenced to life, 50 years, 45 years, and 30 years, respectively (*Reese v. Dretke* (2004) 99 Fed.Appx. 503).

———

Angel Maturino Reséndiz, a 45-year-old Hispanic (Mexican) male, was executed by lethal injection at the Texas State Penitentiary in Huntsville, Texas on June 27, 2006. Reséndiz was found guilty of the 1998 murder of Claudia Gabriella Benton, a 39-year-old Hispanic female. Reséndiz, who was 38-years old when he committed the capital crime, was sentenced to death on May 15, 2000.

Dr. Claudia Benton, M.D., a native of Lima, Peru and a clinical geneticist at the Baylor College of Medicine lived with her husband George and their twin daughters in West University Place, an affluent suburb of Houston, Texas. On December 16, 1998, Benton was home alone while her husband and their girls were visiting relatives in Arizona.

Some time after midnight the five foot six inch tall Reséndiz slipped in through an unlocked door in the Benton house and went upstairs where Benton was sleeping. Reséndiz sexually assaulted Benton, stabbed her to death, and subsequently beat her with a two-foot tall bronze statuette he picked up in the house. Reséndiz then stole money, ivory figurines, jewelry, electronic gear, and a meat cleaver before fleeing away in Benton's jeep.

Police found Benton, Reséndiz's third victim, face down on the floor, her head partially enclosed in a plastic bag, and her torso covered with blankets. Her right arm was broken and bones in her face were shattered. Fingerprints, DNA, and stolen items recovered from Reséndiz's home in Mexico tied him to the killing.

On July 13, 1999, Reséndiz aka the *Railroad Killer* voluntarily surrendered to Texas Ranger Drew Carter. Prior to his arrest Reséndiz had been deported from the United States to Mexico on at least 17 occasions. He had a long criminal record that included a prior conviction in Florida for burglary, vehicle theft, and aggravated assault, for which he was sentenced to 20 years' imprisonment and paroled in August 1985, and a prior burglary conviction in New Mexico for which he was sentenced to 18 months' imprisonment and paroled in April 1993.

Reséndiz, a serial killer[70] believed to have killed more than two-dozen people since 1986 was tried in Harris

---

[70] FBI Special Agent Alan Brantley formed the opinion that Reséndiz was a "geographically mobile" - "organized sexual serial killer" (an offender who committed "well-planned, well-orchestrated" multiple murders with a sexual element) by

County in spring 2000. After being found guilty of the Benton murder, the jury heard evidence of numerous other murders committed by Reséndiz over a period of several years[71] and recommended the death penalty. On May 21,

---

committing murders at night, using rear locations to enter homes, committing murders near railroad tracks, and selecting random victims by traveling nationally and internationally.

[71] Holly Dunn, a white female, testified that in August 1997 Reséndiz approached her and Christopher Maier, a 21-year old white male college student near some railroad tracks in Lexington, Kentucky. Reséndiz robbed both of them afterwhich he gagged Maier and bound his hands and feet. Reséndiz then picked up a large object and beat him in the head with it crushing his skull and killing Maier. Reséndiz then sexually assaulted Dunn hitting her in the head with a large object before leaving the scene. Dunn survived but suffered multiple facial fractures and the trauma of the sexual assault.

In October 1998 Reséndiz unlawfully entered the home of 87-year-old Leafie Mason in Hughes Springs, Texas. Reséndiz killed Mason by hitting her in the head with an iron.

In May 1999 Reséndiz traveled to Weimar, Texas where he beat Skip Sirnic, 46, and Karen Sirnic, 47, to death with a sledgehammer while they slept in their home. He also sexually assaulted Sirnic.

In June 1999 Reséndiz unlawfully entered Noemi Dominguez's home in Houston, Texas. The 26-year old schoolteacher was sexually assaulted and killed with a pickax. Reséndiz stole Dominguez's car and traveled to Schulenberg, Texas where later that day he killed 73-year-old Josephine Konvicka, a white female, with the same pickax used on Dominiguez. Reséndiz left the pickax embedded in Konvicka's head.

Also in June 1999 Reséndiz unlawfully entered the home of 80-year-old George Morber in Gorham, Illinois. Morber's 52-year old daughter, Carolyn Frederick, was with him when Reséndiz broke in. Reséndiz tied Morber to a chair, shot him in the back

(continued)

273

2003, the Texas Court of Criminal Appeals affirmed his conviction and sentence (*Reséndiz v. State* (2003) 112 S.W.3d 541).

———

Sedley Alley, 50-year-old white male, was executed by lethal injection at the Riverbend Maximum Security Institution in Nashville, Tennessee on June 28, 2006. Alley was found guilty of the 1985 murder of Suzanne Marie Collins, a 19-year-old white female. Alley, who was 29-years-old when he committed the capital crime, was sentenced to death on March 18, 1987.

In the late evening of July 11, 1985, Alley, a civilian married to a military person, abducted Lance Corporal Suzanne Collins while she was jogging near Millington Naval Base in Millington, Tennessee. Two marines jogging near where Collins was abducted heard her scream and ran toward the sound, but before they reached the scene they saw Alley's car drive off. They reported to base security and accompanied officers on a tour of the base, looking for the car they had seen. Unsuccessful, they returned to their barracks.

Soon after returning to their quarters the two marines were called back to the security office where they identified Alley's car, which had been stopped by officers. Alley and his wife gave statements to the base security personnel accounting for their whereabouts. The security personnel were satisfied with Alley's story, and Alley and his wife returned to their on-base housing.

Collins's body was found a few hours later and Alley was immediately arrested by military police. Alley

---

(*continued*)
of the head with a shotgun, and then sexually assaulted Frederick and struck her in the head with the shotgun with such force that the shotgun broke into two pieces. Neither Morber nor Frederick survived.

voluntarily gave a statement to police admitting to having killed Collins while drunk and led officers back to the scene where the murder took place. Alley also confessed to having mutilated her with a long, broken-off tree branch, consistent with the grave internal injuries that Collins suffered, and led police to the place where the tree limb had been broken off. Alley contended that he did this in order to simulate a sexual assault and thereby (in his thinking) deflect suspicion from himself. He gave police some other purported details of the killing that were inconsistent with the forensic evidence.

Alley's defense at trial was that he was insane at the time of the murder because he suffered from multiple personality disorder and had committed the murder while under the control of an abnormal personality. Alley sought to offer into evidence videotapes of interview sessions conducted while he was under the influence of hypnosis and/or sodium amytal (truth serum).[72]

---

[72] The trial judge viewed the tapes finding them to be sensational, unreliable, and likely to confuse the jury. He also found that the tapes elicited no facts about what happened on the night of the murder. He weighed the probative value of their use against the risk that the tapes might confuse or mislead the jury and granted the State's motion to exclude them. Specifically, the judge ruled that the tapes could not be shown to the jury, and that "statements or words and actions of the defendant while under hypnosis [could not] be related to the jury by a witness." However, the judge held that witnesses could testify that the interviews were conducted, and they could express their opinions as to whether multiple personalities were present during the interviews.

Dr. Allen Battle, a psychologist, had videotaped these interviews, and based his conclusion on a viewing of the tapes. Battle testified that he had treated more than a dozen cases of multiple personality disorder throughout his career explaining that he had hypnotized Alley on several occasions and that
(*continued*)

(*continued*)
based on those interviews it was his opinion that Alley suffered from the condition.

Battle talked about two alternate personalities explaining that Alley was aware of the existence of *Billie*, an alternate personality that stemmed from Alley's troubled childhood. Battle testified at greater length regarding the second alternate personality—*Power*. Battle testified to having had contact with *Power* through the hypnosis sessions and that *Power* was psychotic. He explained that *Power* claimed not to be bound by the rule of law and recognized no limitations on his behavior. Battle opined that Alley suffered from the disorder at the time of the murder. Battle further testified that there was evidence tending to suggest that *Power* was in control at the time of the murder including the fact that the nature of the crime fit more with *Power's* personality than it did with Alley's. Battle said that he could not be sure that an alternate personality was in control during the murder and for this reason Battle admitted that he could not support an insanity defense.

Dr. Willis Marshall, a psychiatrist who was not present during the interviews based his conclusion on viewing the tapes, testifying that Alley suffered from multiple personality disorder, and that Alley exhibited at least two alternate personalities, *Power* or *Death*, and a female named *Billie*. Marshall opined that *Power* was legally insane. Marshall further testified, both on the basis of the videotaped interviews and other interviews he had conducted with Alley that there was evidence that *Power* was in control at the time of the murder. Marshall described to the jury a portion of one of the hypnosis interviews during which Alley struggled with himself, spoke in a whisper, and repeatedly tried to choke himself. Marshall explained that Alley says he feels one of the others choking him whenever he tries to speak about his alternate personality, *Billie*.

In addition to discussing the videotapes Marshall described the ways in which his alternate personality diagnosis was consistent with various aspects of Alley's case. Marshall first explained that during both an initial interview and the sodium amytal interviews Marshall had conducted, Alley spoke of both *Death* and *Billie* being in the car with him the night of the murder.

The jury convicted Alley of kidnapping, aggravated rape, and premeditated first-degree murder. The jury then imposed a sentence of death for the murder, and the trial court imposed consecutive 40-year sentences for the remaining two counts. The jury found two aggravating circumstances to justify the punishment of death: the murder was especially heinous, atrocious, or cruel; and Alley committed it during a kidnapping or rape.

Alley was originally scheduled to die by electrocution on May 2, 1990, but his execution was stayed by the state Court of Criminal Appeals.[73] Two additional reprieves followed, and on June 28, 1986, the Supreme Court of the United States denied a stay and Governor Phil Bredesen denied clemency (*Alley v. Bell* (2002) 307 F.3d 380; *Alley v. Bell* (2004) 392 F.3d 822; Alley v. Bell (2006) 126 S.Ct. 2975; *In re Sedley Alley* (2006) 126 S.Ct. 2976).

———

Sean Derrick O'Brien, a 31-year-old black male, was executed by lethal injection at the Texas State Penitentiary in Huntsville, Texas on July 11, 2006. O'Brien had been

---

Marshall also testified about Alley's childhood and adult life explaining how both were consistent with having a multiple personality disorder noting that Alley's brother observed Alley's strange actions and character and had come to the conclusion several years earlier that Alley had multiple personalities. Marshall detailed how Alley had suffered from memory lapses and distortions throughout most of his life and explained that this "is probably the most common sign of multiple personality."

[73] The Court granted a reprieve in order to assign a new trial judge ruling that the original trial judge, W. Fred Axley, should have been recused for making such prejudicial statements as: "[A]s I said when I spoke to the Rotary Club some few months ago, the best way to give them bed space-I can give them fifty-seven beds tomorrow, if they'll just execute some of these people that are already in line for it."

found guilty of the 1993 murder of Jennifer Ertman, a 15-year-old white female. O'Brien, who was 18-years old when he committed the capital crime, was sentenced to death on April 7, 1994.

On the night of June 24, 1993, in downtown Houston, Texas, a five foot eight inch tall O'Brien participated in the initiation of Raul Omar Villarreal, a 17-year-old Hispanic male, into a gang called the Blacks and Whites. Four other Hispanic gang members, Peter Anthony Cantu, 18, Jose Ernesto Medellin, 18, Efrain Perez, 17, and Roman Sandoval, were present at the initiation, as were Frank Sandoval and Vernancio Medellin, brothers of two of the gang members. The initiation consisted of Villarreal fighting each of the other gang members for several minutes. Following this ritual the gang members drank beer.

At about 11:30 p.m. Jennifer Ertman and her friend, Elizabeth Pena, 16, were returning to their homes after visiting a friend. They took a shortcut through Houston's T.C. Jester Park and as they passed Jose Medellin, he grabbed Pena and dragged her down a hill while she screamed for help. Ertman ran back to help Pena but Medellin grabbed her and dragged her down the hill as well. Cantu forced Ertman to perform fellatio on him and O'Brien raped both girls.

The gang rape continued for more than an hour. O'Brien and other members of the gang later boasted that they gang-raped both girls. Four days later the girls' bodies were found close to each other and in an advanced state of decomposition.

Joe Cantu, Peter Cantu's brother, testified that he received a call from O'Brien after the murders. O'Brien admitted raping and killing the girls and he also expressed concern that the girls might still be alive and that the gang left evidence including beer bottles with fingerprints at the crime scene. Both Roman Sandoval and Vernancio Medellin testified that the gang had no formal leader and

O'Brien acted voluntarily throughout the rape and murders of the two girls.

On June 29 O'Brien, Perez, Villarreal, Peter Cantu, and the Medellin brothers, Jose and Vernancio, were arrested. When police knocked on O'Brien's door and announced their presence O'Brien attempted to flee out the back door where he was arrested.

Officer Todd Miller of the Houston Police Department read O'Brien his *Miranda* rights and advised him that he was under arrest for capital murder. O'Brien replied that he knew it was about the two girls who were killed adding that he wanted to make a statement. Police then took O'Brien to the police station where he was again informed of his rights and was brought before a magistrate who again informed O'Brien of his rights.

O'Brien informed police that he gave his belt to Jose Medellin who used it to strangle one of the girls. At Medellin's instruction O'Brien grabbed one end of the belt and helped strangle the victim. They pulled so hard that one end of the belt broke off. O'Brien consented to a search of his apartment where police found the belt.

Dr. Marilyn Murr of the Harris County Medical Examiner's Office testified that the girls' bodies were badly decomposed and covered with maggots. Most of the soft tissue on Ertman's head and the external portion of her vagina were eaten by maggots indicating that there was trauma, hemorrhaging, and bleeding. Autopsy photographs showed the differences in decomposition between those areas that suffered trauma and those that did not such as Ertman's legs, chest, and abdomen.

Murr explained that maggots and bacteria are attracted to blood and these cause decomposition. Strangulation would cause blood to accumulate in the head area and cause hemorrhaging in the eyes and mouth because the pressure on the blood vessels in the neck prevents blood from draining from the head. Murr concluded that Ertman died from trauma to the neck such as strangulation. Due to the state of decomposition Murr could not tell what was used to strangle Ertman but the evidence was consistent with a belt or hands being used—she also had three fractured ribs.

Pena's body was similarly decomposed. Several teeth were missing and one tooth was fractured. Murr concluded from this that she was punched or kicked in the mouth. Murr concluded that Pena also died of trauma to the neck consistent with strangulation.

On February 4, 1994, O'Brien, Perez, Villarreal, Peter Cantu, and Jose Medellin were charged with the Ertman murder.[74] O'brien's trial began on April 5 and two days later the jury found him guilty of capital murder. Several witnesses testified during the penalty phase of the trial.[75]

---

[74] All five received the death penalty: Cantu was sentenced on February 3, 1994; Villarreal was sentenced on September 21, 1994; and Medellin and Perez were sentenced on October 11, 1994. On June 22, 2005, Governor Rick Perry commuted Perez's and Villarreal's death sentences to life in prison when in March 2005 the Supreme Court of the United States barred executions for those who were 17 at the time of their crimes (see Roper v. Simmons (2005) 543 U.S. 551). In April 2007 the Court agreed to review whether Jose Medellin, a Mexican national, had been denied legal help available to him under the 1963 Vienna Convention on Consular Relations. Medellin's brother, Vernancio, was 14 at the time of the murders and was tried as a juvenile. He was convicted and sentenced to 40 years in prison.

[75] Joyce Jones, a teacher at a Houston school for children with behavioral problems, testified that she taught O'Brien in 1987-1988. According to Jones, O'Brien fought with other children and sometimes had to be restrained. Jones described O'Brien as "very aggressive." On one occasion O'Brien broke another child's jaw and Jones was not surprised when she heard about O'Brien's involvement in these murders.

Raymond Earl Ray testified that he worked as a security guard at K-Mart in 1989. Ray arrested O'Brien for shoplifting a pellet pistol. Another security guard at a Houston public school testified that she once saw O'Brien brandish a handgun at another school security guard. O'Brien threatened to kill the other guard and fired the gun into the air. O'brien also brought a toy gun to school, and on another occasion security guards received a report that O'Brien had a gun but no gun was found. O'Brien also bragged about stealing cars, consumed alcohol on the school bus, and once jumped out the bus emergency door with six other students when there was no emergency.

Houston Police Office Timothy Sutton testified that he witnessed O'Brien and Peter Cantu punch, kick, and drag another man at Burger King restaurant about three months before the murder. O'Brien and Cantu were charged with simple assault.

Gregory Ristivo testified that he engaged in criminal activity with O'Brien including stealing cars and stealing jackets and shoes from people. Ristivo estimated that he and O'Brien stole between 25 and 50 cars. They would then drive the cars, vandalize them, and sometimes play bumper cars with two stolen cars. O'Brien once tried to steal a gun from a car. O'Brien also used a gun to shoot at lights and stop signs while joy riding with Ristivo. Sometimes O'Brien and Cantu would start fights with random people. O'Brien once grabbed a person at a mall in mid-day, threw him against a wall, and stole his shoes. O'Brien intimidated another student at his school into giving him his Nike shoes. Ristivo also saw O'Brien hit a teacher with a piece of wood, and O'Brien bragged about stabbing someone with a screwdriver while breaking into a car. Ristivo and O'Brien burglarized Ristivo's father's house.

Others testified as well. Houston Police Officer Jones testified that he arrested O'Brien for stealing a car. When Jones came upon the scene O'Brien was fighting with two wrecker drivers. O'Brien continued to yell at the wrecker drivers threatening to kill them after Jones arrested him and placed him in the police car. Christopher Rodriguez, who knew O'Brien from his neighborhood, testified that O'Brien bragged about being a member of the Crips gang and wore Crips colors, and that O'Brien often bragged about robbing people. Dr. Stanley Smoote, a psychologist with the Houston Independent School

(continued)

Sentencing proceedings took place on April 9 and based on the jury's answers to special issues O'Brien was sentenced to death. On May 15, 1996, the Texas Court of Criminal Appeals affirmed O'Brien's conviction and sentence. O'Brien's last words: "I am sorry. I have always

---

(*continued*)

District, testified that, based on O'Brien's records, O'Brien had conduct disorder that includes physical aggression toward others. Officer Mike Knox of the Houston Police West Side Gang Unit testified that O'Brien had tattoos that suggested O'Brien was a member of the Folk Nation, a group espousing "the promotion of the black race" and engaging in criminal activity. Leslie William Morgan, who was housed on the same floor as O'Brien at the Harris County Jail, testified that O'Brien denied involvement in the Ertman and Pena murders for the first six months he was in jail but changed his story when other inmates began taunting him after some news stories came out about the case. According to Morgan, O'Brien then said, "That they were nothing but just whores anyway and that [the] pussy was real good."

O'Brien was also implicated in another murder. On January 4, 1993, Houston Police found the dead body of Patricia Lopez in a park. Lopez was nude from the waist down. Police found a broken belt a few feet from the body, and five empty beer cans, cigarette butts, and other items in the area. Lopez's shirt was unbuttoned and heavily blood stained; it had three holes in the back. Her jacket also had three holes in it and her bra was cut. There was a stab wound and a cutting wound on her neck, a stab wound on the abdomen, and three stab wounds on the back. Several of the stab wounds could have been fatal. There was no evidence of strangulation, and no evidence of sexual intercourse. No one was charged with this homicide but one of the fingerprints lifted from the crime scene evidence belonged to O'Brien. Jose Martin Medellin, the brother of Jose and Vemancio Medellin, testified that Peter Cantu told him that O'Brien admitted trying to rape the victim. He was unable to do so and killed her. O'Brien was present when Cantu made his statement, and O'Brien agreed with the statement.

been sorry ***. It is the worst mistake that I ever made in my whole life" (*O'Brien v. Dretke* (5th Cir. 2005) No. 05-70006; *Medellin v. Dretke* (5th Cir. 2005) No. 03-20687.)

———

Rocky Barton, a 49-year-old white male, was voluntarily executed by lethal injection at the Southern Ohio Correctional Facility in Lucasville, Ohio on July 12, 2006. Barton was found guilty of the 2003 murder of Kimbirli Jo Barton, a 44-year-old white female. Barton, who was 46-years old when he committed the capital crime, was sentenced to death on October 10, 2003.

Barton and Kimbirli Barton married on June 23, 2001, during Barton's incarceration for attempted murder in Kentucky. It was Barton's fourth marriage. Following his release from prison in 2002 Barton lived with Kimbirli and Jamie, her 17-year-old daughter from a prior marriage, in a Warren County Ohio farmhouse in Waynesville on Bellbrook Road. Barton's father, Donald, lived in Florida and owned the house. Barton and Kimbirli generally had an amicable relationship and had planned to renew their wedding vows in May or June 2003.[76]

At 7:20 a.m. on January 16, 2003, Barton awakened Jamie and told her to get her things together: "You're going

———

[76] Tiffany, Kimbirli's 22-year-old daughter from a prior marriage, described her mother's relationship with Barton as "sometimes good, sometimes bad, the highs were very high, the lows were really low." Julie, Kimbirli's 27-year-old daughter from a prior relationship, also described Kim and Barton's relationship as "up and down ***. Really good [or] really bad."

Tiffany described Barton as "very moody, possessive *** controlling *** just very manipulative." Julie also thought Barton could be at times "very jealous, very controlling, very manipulative, always accusing [Kimbirli] of things, causing fights." Jamie agreed that Barton acted "controlling and possessive," although she felt close to him and described him as the only father figure that she could depend upon.

to Tiff's house. The wedding's off. Your mom's a psycho bitch." Barton then drove Jamie to Tiffany's home and told Tiffany that her mother "had gone off the deep end and that she was crazy and she was leaving him." Jamie described Barton as acting "really strange" and "aggravated."

Ten minutes later Kimbirli arrived at Lasik Plus where she worked as a technical assistant. Karla Reiber and Molly Wolfer, her coworkers, recalled that Barton had called more than six times that morning. He insisted on being placed on hold while Kimbirli tended to patients, often for as long as 10 or 15 minutes, until she became available. Reiber described Barton as "very angry," and Wolfer described him as "very agitated, very angry," and "very irate."

After speaking with Barton on the phone around 10:30 a.m. Kimbirli related to coworkers that she had heard shots fired. She told others that she had heard a "bang" over the phone. Police later recovered a spent shotgun shell in a bedroom at Barton's home, which supported her suspicion that Barton had fired a shotgun while talking with her on the telephone.

Wolfer described Kimbirli as crying, "very frantic," and "very scared" when she left work just after 10:30 a.m. Before leaving Kimbirli called Tiffany and asked whether she and Jamie could live with her temporarily. Tiffany described her mother as hysterical, frantic, and scared and agreed to have her mother and sister move in with her.

Barton also talked on the telephone with several others that day. Around 7:45 a.m. he left a message with his employer saying that he would not be at work that day because of a family emergency. Around 10:45 a.m. Barton spoke with his supervisor, Carol Williamson, and informed her that Kimbirli had been "acting strange" due to her medication and that Kimbirli intended to leave him.

Barton also called Randy Hacker, Julie's former husband, and complained about Kimbirli and Julie. Barton seemed "edgy" and "irritated," according to Hacker, and left

Hacker a message, saying, "Before I go on to my demise, I should call you." In a later call, Barton informed Hacker that Kimbirli intended to move out and that he would be going back to jail.

Barton also spoke on the telephone several times that day with Glen Barker, an insurance agent. Barker has a background in counseling and he offered to serve as a mediator between Barton and Kimbirli. Barton visited Barker at his office around 9:30 a.m. and seemed calm and quiet but Barton was anxious to speak with his father. Barker called Kimbirli at work on Barton's behalf but Kimbirli would not discuss the matter. Barker testified that Barton adamantly refused to allow Kimbirli to collect her possessions from their house.

That morning Barton's father talked with Barton and Kimbirli in an effort to defuse the situation. He told Barton not to worry because anything that Kimbirli might take from the farmhouse could be replaced, and he informed Kimbirli that she could keep his car, which she currently drove. Larry Barton, Barton's uncle, also spoke with Barton several times by telephone offering assistance. Barton told Larry that he thought police would be called, and he vowed,"he wouldn't go back to jail."

Around 11:00 a.m. Kimbirli arrived at Tiffany's home. Barton called 25 or 30 times; Jamie and Tiffany overheard Barton cursing and yelling on the telephone and described his voice as "scary." Jamie overheard him tell Kimbirli, "I'm going to kill you, you fucking bitch," causing Kimbirli to become "really nervous and scared" while "crying and shaking."

Around 3:00 p.m. Kimbirli and Jamie made plans to return to their Bellbrook Road home to retrieve some clothing and personal effects. When Larry arrived at Tiffany's house, however, he strongly advised Kimbirli not to go home. She agreed to stay away but gave Larry a list of things that she and Jamie wanted him to retrieve.

Immediately after Larry left to retrieve the items, Barton called again and persuaded Kimbirli and Jamie to come to Bellbrook Road to obtain their things. When Larry arrived at Bellbrook Road, Barton had locked the gate, something he rarely did. Larry asked Barton to open the gate, but Barton absolutely refused to allow him onto the property. He kept saying, "I've lost it." Barton stood near his own truck behind the locked gate while Larry's truck remained parked on the road.

When Kimbirli and Jamie arrived, however, Barton unlocked the gate and instructed Larry to lock it after they entered because he did not want "the police *** coming in." Then Barton got in his truck, backed up "real fast" into the garage, and closed the garage door. Larry and Kimbirli separately drove onto the property.

As Kimbirli got out of the car and turned to shut her door Barton came out the side door of the garage with a shotgun. As he ran toward Kimbirli he yelled, "You aren't going anywhere, you fucking bitch," and he then fired the shotgun while four to six feet from her and struck her in her side. Feeling the impact Kimbirli fell but moved toward her daughter yelling, "Oh, Jamie, Oh Jamie." As Jamie reached for her mother, Barton shot Kimbirli in the back from a distance of one to two feet. Kimbirli fell to the ground while Jamie screamed, "Mom, can you hear me? Can you hear me? Please stay with me, mommy, please stay with me." Barton then aimed the gun at Jamie's head and at Larry. Barton next walked to the side of Larry's truck and said, "I told you I was insane," dropped to his knees, and shot himself in the face. Barton then walked into the house.

Jamie and Larry called 9-1-1. Emergency Medical Services (EMS) personnel arrived and upon examining Kimbirli found her ashen in color, not breathing, and with fixed and dilated pupils and no pulse. Following an autopsy Dr. Karen Powell, a forensic pathologist, determined that Kimbirli had died from "shotgun wounds of the left shoulder and right back regions" that caused injuries to her lungs, heart, and liver.

In response to the emergency call police arrived and located Barton who was alert and cooperative inside the house. An EMS technician described him as suffering from a gunshot wound with non-life-threatening injuries to his chin, mouth, and nose. Upon investigation, police confiscated the murder weapon, a .410 gauge pump-style shotgun, and four spent shotgun shells. Police also recovered six live shotgun shells from Barton at the hospital.

On February 10, 2003, the Warren County grand jury returned an indictment against Barton charging him with aggravated murder of Kimbirli with prior calculation and design, a gun specification, and a death-penalty specification for his prior conviction for attempted murder and unlawful possession of a firearm while under a disability from a prior conviction (namely, that Barton had the firearm "within five years of the date of [his] release from imprisonment" for attempted murder). Barton pleaded guilty to the weapon-under-disability charge but elected a jury trial on the aggravated-murder charge.

The death-penalty specification was separately tried to the court during which Barton made the following unsworn statement to the jury: "At this time my attorneys advised me to beg for my life. I can't do that. I strongly believe in the death penalty. And for the ruthless, cold-blooded act that I committed, if I was sitting over there, I'd hold out for the death penalty ***.

"I've recently done 10 years in prison. Life in prison would be a burden to all the citizens of Ohio. It would be at their cost. I wouldn't have nothing to worry about. I'd get fed every day, have a roof over my head, free medical, you people pay for it, I'd have a stress-free life. That's not much of a punishment. Punishment would be to wake up every day and have a date with death. That's the only punishment for this crime. That's all I've got to say." The jury convicted Barton on both counts and the trial court found Barton guilty of the death-penalty specification. Barton did not seek clemency and did not want his attorney to represent him at the clemency hearing (*State v. Barton* (2006) 844 N.E.2d 307).

———

William E. Downs Jr., a 39-year-old white male, was voluntarily executed by lethal injection at the Broad River Capital Punishment Facility in Columbia, South Carolina on July 14, 2006. Downs was found guilty of the 1999 murder of Keenan O'Mailia, a 6-year-old black child. Downs, who was 31-years old when he committed the capital crime, was sentenced to death on June 27, 2002.

On or about April 17, 1999, Downs said he stopped Keenan O'Mailia as the boy rode his bicycle along a dirt path in North Augusta. Downs, just having relocated to South Carolina, said that he asked O'Mailia his name, threw him to the ground, and strangled him to death. Downs took then O'Mailia into a wooded area of a park where he was raped.

After newspapers reported the murder Downs told his sister that he had committed the crime. Down's sister reported this to police and disclosed Down's location. Police found and detained Downs who subsequently confessed and was indicted for killing O'Mailia with malice aforethought by means of asphyxia due to manual strangulation.

Downs was charged in Aiken County with murder, kidnapping, and first-degree criminal sexual conduct with a minor. At the plea hearing Downs expressed the desire to plead guilty but was uncertain whether he wanted to later present evidence that he was mentally ill at the time of the crime. Downs repeatedly stated that he knew he wanted to admit guilt. When the judge asked if Downs wanted to impanel a jury, admit guilt, and ask the jury to decide the sentence, Downs answered in the negative.[77] The court accepted Downs's guilty plea as voluntarily, knowingly, and intelligently entered. Before he was sentenced Downs told the judge, "I think it would be disrespectful to the family and disrespectful to the whole world if you did not give me the death penalty." In 2003 Downs also pleaded guilty to

---

[77] A hearing was then held to determine whether Downs was guilty but mentally ill. During the competency hearing Downs was able to relate that it was possible that existence stops when you die and said that would be preferable to living in prison. Downs stated he hoped for better things after death and that he preferred lethal injection because it was peaceful.

Dr. Schwartz-Watts, a forensic psychiatrist, opined that Downs was competent. Schwartz-Watts testified that Downs met the cognitive prong because he understood the proceedings and his punishment, and that he was able to communicate that he desired lethal injection. She stated that he wanted to be free but otherwise that he wanted to be executed instead of being imprisoned. She testified that he did not suffer from delusions and that he hoped for something better in the afterlife. Schwartz-Watts testified that Downs had depression, not otherwise specified; Post-Traumatic Stress Disorder (a controversial and relatively recent diagnosis of serious anxiety brought on by experiencing a traumatic event, often years later), paraphilia (strong sexual fantasies), pedophila (sexual attraction to a child), and substance abuse. She testified that he had a mild form of depression that did not prevent him from doing the things he needed to do and that he could have had depression and still be competent.

James Whittle, the attorney who represented Downs for his plea, stated that Downs forbade him from offering mitigation evidence but that he was able to seek a guilty but mentally ill finding by telling Downs his case could help others. Whittle felt Downs had significant mental health issues and that he was depressed. Whittle testified that he felt Downs was competent to stand trial and had the ability to rationally communicate with him. After considering the evidence the court ruled that Downs failed to prove he was guilty but mentally ill.

kidnapping, raping, and killing in 1991, a 10-year-old boy, James Porter, in Augusta, Georgia. Therafter Downs pursued no appeals.

Downs's last meal consisted of salted cashew nuts, instant French roast coffee, chocolate chip cookie dough, moose tracks ice cream and three Mr. Goodbar candy bars (*State v. Downs* (2004) 604 S.E.2d 377; *State v. Downs* (2006) 631 S.E.2d 79).

———

Maurecio Mashawn Brown, a 31-year-old black male, was executed by lethal injection at the Texas State Penitentiary in Huntsville, Texas on July 19, 2006. Brown was found guilty of the 1996 murder of Michael T. LaHood Jr., a 25-year-old black male. Brown, who was 21-years old when he committed the capital crime, was sentenced to death on May 15, 1997.

In the early morning hours of August 15, 1996, Brown, and three other black males, Kenneth Foster, 19, DWayne Dillard, 20, and Julius Steen, 19, had been together smoking marijuana and driving around San Antonio, Texas in a vehicle driven by Foster. Brown suggested, and the others agreed, to look for individuals to rob. After they robbed four individuals in two separate incidents Foster began following a pair of vehicles that ultimately stopped at the residence of Michael LaHood Jr., a St. Mary's University law student. Foster had begun to turn the car around to exit the unfamiliar neighborhood when Mary Patrick exited one of the two vehicles Foster had been following and confronted the occupants of the vehicle that had been following her.

After the brief confrontation Patrick and LaHood, who had been driving the second followed vehicle, began walking toward the entrance to the LaHood residence. Brown subsequently exited the car and walked up to LaHood with a gun in hand. According to Patrick, Brown demanded LaHood's keys, pointed a .44-caliber pistol at LaHood's face, and shot. LaHood died as a result.

In May 1997 a jury convicted Brown and Foster of capital murder and the court imposed the death penalty on both men. On February 17, 1999, the Texas Court of Criminal Appeals affirmed Brown's conviction and sentence. On August 30, 2007, the day of Foster's execution, Governor Rick Perry accepted the Texas Board of Pardons and Paroles' 6-1 recommendation and commuted Foster's death sentence to life without parole. Accomplices Dillard and Steen were given a life sentence for capital murder and aggravated robbery, respectively (*Brown v. Dretke* (5th Cir. 2005) No. 04-70054).

Robert James Anderson, a 40-year-old white male, was voluntarily executed by lethal injection at the Texas State Penitentiary in Huntsville, Texas on July 20, 2006. Anderson was found guilty of the 1992 murder of Audra Reeves, a 5-year-old white female. Anderson, who was 21-years old when he committed the capital crime, was sentenced to death on November 15, 1993.

On June 9, 1992, Audra Reeves of Amarillo, Texas went outside to play. As the child was passing Anderson's residence the six foot two inch tall Anderson abducted her and took her inside where he attempted to rape her. Anderson then choked, stabbed, beat, and ultimately drowned Reeves.

In the early afternoon of the same day several witnesses reported seeing Anderson pushing a grocery cart up the street with a white ice chest inside. One witness reported seeing Anderson near a dumpster in an alley, and another witnesses who found the ice chest containing Reeve's body in the dumpster gave a description of Anderson to police.

Anderson, who had no prior convictions, was arrested later in the day after he was identified as the individual who pushed the grocery cart. Anderson gave police a written statement in which he admitted to killing Reeves and stuffing her body in a white ice chest and dumping the chest in a dumpster.

A Potter County grand jury indicted Anderson for capital murder. On November 10, 1993, a jury found him guilty and five days later he was sentenced to death. On September 11, 1996, the Texas Court of Criminal Appeals affirmed his conviction and sentence. In February 2005 Anderson dismissed his appeal with the Fifth Circuit Court of Appeals, saying "I don't want to hurt anybody any longer, and I want to be executed" (*Anderson v. State* (1996) 932 S.W.2d 502).

————

Brandon Wayne Hedrick, a 27-year-old white male, was executed by electrocution at the Greensville Correctional Center in Jarratt, Virginia on July 20, 2006. Hedrick was found guilty of the 1997 murder of Lisa Yvonne Alexander Crider, a 23-year-old black female. Hedrick, who was 18-years old when he committed the capital crime, was sentenced to death on July 22, 1998.

On May 10, 1997, Hedrick and Trevor Andrew Jones, an 18-year-old white male, spent the evening consuming alcohol, smoking crack cocaine and marijuana, and employing the services of four prostitutes. After driving the last two prostitutes back to downtown Lynchburg, Virginia, Hedrick and Jones saw Lisa Crider. Jones knew that Crider's boyfriend was a crack cocaine dealer and the two decided to pick Crider up, have sexual relations with her, and rob her of any crack cocaine in her possession. Crider voluntarily traveled with Hedrick and Jones back to Jones's apartment where Jones paid Crider $50 to have sexual intercourse with him.

Afterwards Hedrick retrieved a shotgun from Jones's car at Jones's direction and robbed Crider of the $50 at gunpoint. Hedrick and Jones handcuffed Crider, duct-taped her eyes and mouth, and led her out to Jones's truck leaving the apartment around 1:00 a.m. After driving for some time Jones stopped the truck because Hedrick wanted to have sexual intercourse with Crider. Hedrick raped Crider after telling her not to "try anything" because he had a gun.

Afterwards the two men decided to kill Crider fearing retaliation from Crider's boyfriend for the rape. As they drove in search of a suitable location Crider, pleading for her life, asked if there was anything she could do to keep them from killing her. Hedrick told Crider, "If you suck my dick, I'll think about it," at which point Crider performed fellatio on Hedrick.

They continued driving until daybreak when Jones stopped the truck near the James River. Jones led Crider to the riverbank, told Hedrick to "do what you got to do," and walked back to the truck. Hedrick shot Crider and left with Jones. The two men fled Virginia in Jones's truck the next day. That evening Crider's body was discovered at the James River with a shotgun wound to the face. About one week later the authorities arrested Hedrick and Jones in Lincoln, Nebraska.

Hedrick was convicted of capital murder in the commission of robbery, rape, and forcible sodomy, and use of a firearm in the commission of murder.in the Circuit Court, Appomattox County. Hedrick testified on his own behalf discussing his extensive drug and alcohol use the day of the crime and in the months leading up to it, denying sexual contact with Crider after her abduction, and claiming that the shooting was accidental. Jones testified for the prosecution that Hedrick had raped Crider.

At the sentencing phase prosecutors called a number of witnesses regarding Hedrick's past robberies and behavior in jail including his escape attempts and destruction of property. In mitigation Hedrick presented evidence that he was significantly immature for his age, and that he had a problem with drugs and alcohol that accelerated in the months leading up to the crimes. Dr. Gary Hawk, Hedrick's court-appointed clinical psychologist, testified that Hedrick's low I.Q. score of 76 was "far below average" although "not so low as to suggest mental retardation." Hawk testified that Hedrick's lack of intelligence, immaturity, and intense drug abuse diminished his ability to reflect and deliberate at the time of the murder.

Finding that Hedrick posed a "continuing serious threat to society" and that his conduct in committing the offenses was "outrageously or wantonly vile, horrible or inhuman in that it involved torture, depravity of mind, aggravated battery to the victim beyond the minimum necessary to accomplish the act of murder," the jury recommended a sentence of death. The Circuit Court followed the jury's recommendation.

Hedrick chose to be electrocuted when given the alternative of lethal injection. On the day of execution the Supreme Court of the United States denied a stay by a vote of 7-2 afterwhich Governor Timothy M. Kaine denied clemency. Accomplice Jones was sentenced to life in prison (*Hedrick v. Commonwealth* (1999) 513 S.E.2d 634; *Hedrick v. Kelly* (2006) 127 S.Ct. 10; *Hedrick v. True* (2006) 443 F.3d 342).

———

Michael William Lenz, a 42-year-old white male, was executed by lethal injection at the Greensville Correctional Facility in Jarratt, Virginia on July 27, 2006. Lenz was found guilty of the 2000 murder of Brent Henry Parker, a 41-year-old white male. Lenz, who was 35-years old when he committed the capital crime, was sentenced to death on October 20, 2000.

Lenz was serving a 29-year-90-day sentence in Augusta Correctional Center in Craigsville, Virginia for the 1993 conviction of burglary and illegal firearm possession. Brent Parker, a fellow inmate, was serving a 50-year sentence for the 1985 murder of Ralph "Jimmy" Jenkins in a Virginia trailer park.

On the evening of January 16, 2000, Lenz joined Parker, Jeffrey Remington,[78] an inmate who had previously been convicted for robbery, abduction, rape, and use of a firearm during the commission of robbery, and three other inmates at Augusta for a meeting of a group known as the "Ironwood Kindred." Lenz intended to lead an Asatru[79] ceremony at the meeting. Lenz and Parker had a history of conflict relating to the practice of Asatru.

According to Lenz, Parker and others had thwarted his efforts to form an official group devoted to Asatru within the prison and Parker had threatened his life on two separate occasions. Lenz admitted he planned to kill Parker that evening.

The Asatru ceremony began with Lenz performing some ritual incantations, reciting poetry, and calling upon

---

[78] Remington was later tried on an indictment charging him with the capital murder of Parker for "the willful, deliberate, and premeditated killing of any person by a prisoner confined in a state or local correctional facility." The jury found Remington guilty of capital murder. In the penalty phase the jury fixed Remington's punishment at death, finding that he represented a continuing serious threat to society and that his conduct in committing the offense was outrageously or wantonly vile, horrible, or inhuman in that it involved torture, depravity of mind, or aggravated battery to the victim. In 2004 Remington committed suicide while on death row.

[79] Asatru is a polytheistic religion that worships Norse gods and has a high regard for family, rejecting discrimination on race, gender, or any other diverse criteria. Hitler's National Socialist Party attempted to adopt Asatru beliefs into racist doctrines of the Nazi party and some neo-Nazi's today continue with this practice. The Asatru faith supports that when good people die, they go to Hell, a place of calm and peace. The Christian place of torment, Hell, is derived from the Asatru word.

an Asatru deity whereupon Lenz then called Parker to the altar. Lenz felt Parker was "disrespecting the gods" and "saying that he was teaching Asatru but what he was teaching was not Asatru." Lenz stated, "I asked - and I said to him, 'It's been a long, hard path between us.' And he said, 'Yes, it is.' And I pulled the knife out of my pocket. And I said, 'Are you trying to take it to the next step?' And he said, 'Yes, I am.' And so I stabbed him." Lenz further testified that when he started stabbing Parker, "Jeffery attacked him ***. Jeffery [Remington] attacked him as well. And [Parker] wasn't ready for it. [Parker] was surprised. He - he was probably just as surprised as the people were at Pearl Harbor in 1941, though he shouldn't have been. And then the other guys jumped up and—and tried to—to jump on Jeffery Remington."

The only correctional officer present was stationed outside the meeting room and saw a commotion in the room. As the office walked to the door three of the inmates ran out and said: "They're stabbing him." Through a window in the door, the officer observed Lenz and Remington repeatedly stabbing Parker while Parker lay face-up on the floor between them "making a feeble attempt to defend himself" with his hands. As Parker would put his hands up Remington and Lenz pushed Parker's hand aside and continued to stab him. The officer did not enter the room because he was unarmed but opened the door and told Remington and Lenz to stop stabbing Parker. They simply looked at the officer and went back to stabbing

While the officer awaited assistance, Lenz and Remington continued their assault. The next officer to arrive observed Parker in a fetal position, making no attempt to defend himself, while Lenz stabbed him "over and over and over." This second officer also ordered Lenz and Remington to stop, but to no avail. Once sufficient additional personnel arrived, correctional officers entered the room and apprehended Lenz and Remington.

A prison nurse called to the scene found Parker alive but in very critical condition. Despite her best efforts Parker continued to bleed profusely and he died at the Augusta Medical Center. An autopsy revealed that he had sustained sixty-eight stab wounds, all inflicted while he was still alive. These included seven stab wounds each to Parker's left lung and liver, either set of which would have been fatal even without his numerous additional injuries.

Lenz was tried before a jury in Virginia state court and convicted of murder. The jury fixed his punishment at death after finding each of two possible statutory aggravating factors: that his future violent acts "would constitute a continuing serious threat to society" and that his offense conduct "was outrageously or wantonly vile, horrible or inhuman." On the day of execution the Supreme Court of the United States denied a stay by a vote of 7-2 afterwhich Governor Timothy M. Kaine denied clemency (*Lenz v. Kelly* (2006) 127 S.Ct. 10; *Lenz v. Washington* (2006) 444 F.3d 295; *Remington v. Commonwealth* (2001) 551 S.E.2d 620).

————

William E. Wyatt Jr., a 41-year-old black male, was executed by lethal injection at the Texas State Penitentiary in Huntsville, Texas on August 3, 2006. Wyatt had been found guilty of the 1997 murder of Damien Willis, a 3-year-old black male. Wyatt, who was 32-years old when he committed the capital crime, was sentenced to death on February 13, 1998.

On February 4, 1997, Damien Willis, the son of Wyatt's then-girlfriend, Renee Porter with whom Wyatt lived in Texarkana, Texas was left in Wyatt's care while Porter was at work. At approximately 6:00 p.m. the six foot one inch, 250 pound Wyatt called 9-1-1, reporting that the child had accidentally drowned in the bathtub. When emergency personnel arrived the child had no pulse, was not breathing, and was cold to the touch.

Paramedics attempted CPR and transported the child to the hospital where he was pronounced dead at 7:24 p.m. The attending physician noted the child was unusually cold (his temperature was 84 degrees, when approximately 96 would have been expected) and had bruising on his forehead and thighs and both fresh and healed injuries to his rectum; and opined that the child had been sexually assaulted prior to his death. The medical examiner who performed an autopsy on the child stated that the cause of death was homicidal violence, including smothering.

Wyatt was taken to the police station where he signed three statements over three days. His first statement made on February 4 provided: he was in the laundry room while the child was bathing; Wyatt returned to the bathroom to find the child underwater; and, after attempting CPR, he called 9-1-1.

On the 5th Wyatt gave a similar statement, acknowledging he had not told the entire truth previously, and confessed to sodomizing the child before he took a bath. The following day Wyatt again acknowledged he had not been completely truthful previously because he was scared, and stated: while Porter was at work, the child wanted to take a bath; after the child began running the bath water, Wyatt saw something on the television that "made [him] feel like having sex"; Wyatt sodomized the child; Wyatt left the room and returned; believing the child had lodged something in the light socket, he hit the child with a belt five or six times; the child began screaming; to stop him, Wyatt held a plastic bag over his mouth; when the child tried to jerk away from Wyatt, the child hit his head on the tub; Wyatt left to get ice for the child's forehead; when Wyatt returned, the child was not breathing; and after attempting CPR, Wyatt called 9-1-1.

On March 5, 1997, Wyatt, who had no prior criminal history, was indicted for capital murder of a child under the age of six in Bowie County. On February 13, 1998, he was found guilty and sentenced to death the same day. The

Texas Court of Criminal Appeals affirmed his conviction and sentence. The former jailer's last words were, "I would like to say to Damien's family I did not murder your son. I did not do it. I just want you to know that - I did not murder Damien and would ask for all of your forgiveness and I will see all of you soon. I love you guys. I love you guys. That's it" (*Wyatt v. Dretke* (5th Cir. 2006) No. 04-70051; *Wyatt v. State* (2000) 23 S.W.3d 18).

———

Darrell Wayne Ferguson, a 28-year-old white male, was voluntarily executed by lethal injection at the Southern Ohio Correctional Facility in Lucasville, Ohio on August 8, 2006. Ferguson was found guilty of the 2001 murder of Thomas King, a 61-year-old white male, Arlie Fugate, a 68-year-old white male, and Mae Fugate, a 69-year-old white female. Ferguson, who was 23-years old when he committed the capital crime, was sentenced to death on September 12, 2003.

In July 1999 Ferguson, a 230 pound former high school wrestler, was convicted of burglary and sentenced to two years in prison. On November 8, 2001, Ferguson was ordered to complete a substance-abuse treatment program at the Talbert House in Cincinnati, Ohio while on post-release control.[80] On December 20 Ferguson was granted a two-day pass to visit his mother at her home in Dayton. The pass was effective from 9:00 a.m. on the 21st until 12:00 p.m. on the 23rd when he was required to return to Talbert House. Ferguson went to his mother's Dayton home but he did not return to Talbert House when his pass expired.

Around 4:00 a.m. on the 23rd Ferguson broke into the Dayton apartment of William Ferrell and James Nicholson,

---

[80] Ferguson said at age 9 that he began huffing—inhaling chemical vapors to achieve a feeling of euphoria. He started drinking at 15 and using crack cocaine at 18.

a double amputee in a wheelchair. Once inside their apartment Ferguson knocked Nicholson to the ground, removed his wallet from his pants pocket, and took cash from the wallet. As he left Ferguson warned Nicholson and Ferrell that if they called police he would return and kill them.

On Christmas Day Ferguson went to Thomas King's home in East Dayton. Ferguson knew King because Ferguson's mother had been married to King's brother. King was disabled and could walk only with crutches. Ferguson knocked on the door, and King, who was alone, let Ferguson into the house. After Ferguson and King talked for a time Ferguson attacked King, repeatedly stabbing him with a kitchen knife, and kicked and stomped him with his steel-toed boots. Ferguson then took a 13-inch television, a 19-inch television, and a stereo "boom box" and fled.

According to his later confession Ferguson went to a Meijer's store and purchased some gold spray paint to "huff." Ferguson then went to an area underneath a bridge and "tried to put a bread bag over [his] face to go ahead and just do [himself] in because [he] knew what [he] did was wrong."

On the evening of December 26 Ferguson went to the Fugate home in East Dayton. Ferguson knew Arlie and Mae Fugate because Ferguson's family had once lived nearby. Ferguson knocked on the Fugates's door and asked to use their bathroom. The Fugates let Ferguson inside their house. After Ferguson came out of the bathroom, he took a knife from the kitchen and attacked the Fugates. Ferguson repeatedly stabbed, stomped, and kicked both of them with his boots.

Following the attack Ferguson stole Mae's wedding ring and other jewelry, Arlie's wedding band, and loose change that was kept in jars and jugs in the house. Ferguson then left the Fugate home to walk to Sid's Towing Service. Around 1:00 a.m. or 1:30 a.m. on the 27th

Ferguson approached Jeffrey Fleming Jr., an acquaintance who worked at Sid's Towing. Ferguson asked Fleming for a ride to another location in Dayton and Fleming drove him there. Fleming noticed blood on Ferguson's jeans but Ferguson told Fleming that the blood was from a fight.

Ferguson traded several of the stolen items to Vicki Miller for crack cocaine. Miller identified Ferguson from a photo array as the man who had made the trade. Police recovered this property from Miller's residence in Dayton, from Miller's father, and from a Dayton pawnshop; the 13-inch television was never recovered.

Around noon on December 27 Ferguson went to the Dayton home of Ricky Webb, another acquaintance. Webb, Dwayne Abney, and Willie Townsend were at the house when Ferguson arrived. Ferguson said that he wanted to watch the noon headlines on television. The group then watched news coverage of the three murders with Ferguson stating he had killed the victims at both locations.

While watching the news Ferguson asked how to get blood out of clothes. Townsend told him to soak the clothes in cold water. Abney noticed that there were darkish brown stains on the bottom of Ferguson's jeans and that Ferguson was wearing black, steel-toed boots.

Later on the 27th Ferguson went to the Dayton home of Irma Hess where he washed his pants to get the blood out. Ferguson remained at the Hess home until he was arrested the next day. At the station Detective Burke advised Ferguson of his *Miranda* rights which he waived. Ferguson then provided police with a detailed account of the murders and also gave a videotaped confession.

Dr. Russell Uptegrove, Deputy Coroner for Montgomery County, performed or supervised autopsies of all three victims observed that Mae suffered numerous stab wounds and blunt-force injuries to the head and face. She died as the result of "multiple stab wounds of the back." Arlie suffered numerous blunt-force facial injuries that were consistent with being kicked or stomped. Arlie died from "multiple stab wounds of the chest." King also suffered numerous blunt-force injuries to the head consistent with being kicked or stomped with steel-toed boots. He suffered six stab wounds in the chest caused by a single-edge knife. King died as the result of multiple sharp and blunt-force injuries.

A three-judge panel in Montgomery County tried Ferguson. Before sentencing and against the advice of counsel Ferguson, who had an I.Q. of 77, read a letter to the court: "I, Darrell W. AKA Gator Ferguson, does not care if you're here to get justice served to you or not. I, Darrell W. AKA Gator Ferguson, does not care what you don't like about what I did to your loved ones. And I, Darrell W. AKA Gator Ferguson, does not care what you think about me, because who I am and what I am and * * * will always remain that way.

"When I killed Thomas S. King, Sr., and Arlie Fugate and Mae Fugate, I did it intentionally, and the killings * * * were malicious and hideous acts just as I intended them to be. I took the satisfaction, Brenda King and James Cornett, of killing your loved ones with pleasure. And I enjoyed it ***.

"I, Darrell W. Gator Ferguson, does not have no remorse for either side of the victim's family nor do I have no remorse for their slaughtered loved ones. I hate you and I hate you and I hate you. I pray that Thomas S. King, Sr., Arlie Fugate, and Mae Fugate are in hell right now in agonizing pain and torment. They shall never rest, only burn for eternity.

"Brenda King and James Cornett, if I had the power to bring your loved ones back, I, Darrell W. Gator Ferguson, would not bring them back. I will never show any remorse even on that day that I die. The only thing I want for Thomas S. King, Sr., Arlie Fugate, Mae Fugate, is to suffer, burn, and have agonizing pain in hell." Ferguson did not seek clemency, which Governor Bob Taft said he would not grant (*State v. Ferguson* (2006) 844 N.E.2d 806).

David Thomas Dawson, a 48-year-old white male, was voluntarily executed by lethal injection at the Montana State Prison in Deer Lodge valley, Montana on August 11, 2006. Dawson was found guilty of the 1986 murder of David Rodstein, a 39-year-old white male, Monica Rodstein, a 39-year-old white female, and Andrew Rodstein, an 11-year-old white male. Dawson, who was 28-years old when he committed the capital crime, was sentenced to death on April 15, 1987.

The Rodstein family was staying at the Airport Metra Inn in Billings, Montana, preceding a family move from Billings to Atlanta, Georgia. Dawson checked into the room next to theirs at approximately 4:45 a.m. on Friday, April 18, 1986. At about 5:00 a.m., Amy, the teenage daughter of the Rodsteins, went outside to load the family car. Dawson carrying a duffel bag from which a gun protruded, followed her back to her room.

Dawson then took all members of the family to his own room where he bound and gagged all of them but Amy. He directed her to help him move the family's belongings into his room. Then he bound and gagged Amy and went through the family's belongings taking out credit cards, cash, and jewelry.

Dawson injected David and Monica Rodstein with an unknown substance that he said would make them sleep. Sometime shortly thereafter they were strangled to death with a telephone cord. The bodies were placed under the sink in the rear of the motel room and were covered by a bedspread. Amy, who lay bound and gagged on the floor in another part of the room, did not see her parents being strangled or their bodies being moved.

Later that day Dawson gave Andrew Rodstein a liquid to drink that caused him to sleep. Andrew was strangled to death and his body was placed with those of his parents. Amy did not see the murder or her brother's body being moved. Dawson had Amy help him move the Rodsteins'

303

vehicles from the motel parking lot to an area behind a nearby gas station. Dawson also gave Amy a liquid to drink but while he was not looking she dumped it on the bedspread and covered the wet area with a pillow.

On Saturday, Dawson and Amy left the motel room several times. During these trips Dawson made several phone calls, went to the bank, went to a fast food store, and stopped at his own apartment and a friend's house. Amy did not attempt to get away because she believed her family was still alive and that an escape attempt might jeopardize their lives.

Later that evening the Billings police conducted an investigation at the motel after receiving reports that the Rodsteins were missing. During the investigation Dawson came out into the parking lot and talked with police. Detective Hatfield went to Dawson's motel room door and asked permission to look through his room. When Dawson changed his position and opened the door slightly Hatfield entered the room and noticed the bedspreads in the back of the room. Dawson said, "Amy, they're here to help you," or words to that effect. Hatfield found the bodies of the Rodsteins and summoned other officers for assistance. Hatfield found Amy in the bathroom where Dawson had instructed her to stay after he observed police outside.

An autopsy revealed that David died of asphyxiation. He had been strangled with "a great deal of force." He also had several bruises on his scalp. Although needle marks were present in his arms the substance with which he had been injected could not be identified. Monica had also died of asphyxiation. Her blouse, brassiere, and jeans had been opened prior to her death but no evidence of sexual assault was found. She had bruises on her head and needle marks on her arm. Andrew had also died of asphyxiation by strangulation. On his chest were a number of bruises "as if the skin were pinched very hard, very firmly, either by a finger or perhaps some object, some instrument."

Dawson did not testify at trial but he had made prior statements to other trial witnesses about a third party being involved. The Yellowstone County jury found Dawson guilty on three counts of deliberate homicide, four counts of aggravated kidnapping, and one count of robbery afterwhich he spent 18 years on death row before dropping his final appeals (*State v. Dawson* (1988) 761 P.2d 352).

Richard Hinojosa, a 44-year-old Hispanic male, was executed by lethal injection at the Texas State Penitentiary in Huntsville, Texas on August 17, 2006. Hinojosa was found guilty of the 1994 murder of Terry Wright, a 29-year-old white female. Hinojosa, who was 32-years old when he committed the capital crime, was sentenced to death on July 25, 1997.

On May 9, 1994, Terry Wright, the manager of a dentist office, had made a date to see her boyfriend, Charles Miller, after work. They were unable to meet because Miller had to work late and she had a late meeting. Around 11 p.m. Miller called Wright at her home in San Antonio, Texas. She had just returned from work and sounded tired from working all day. That was the last time they spoke.

Wright did not show up for work the following morning. Upon hearing this news Wright's father went to her house to investigate. The front of Wright's house was completely caged by burglar bars. Wright's father unlocked the gate and the front door with a spare key. The house was in disarray, particularly Wright's bedroom. Wright's nightgown, torn at the straps, lay on the floor. The cord to an oscillating fan was cut. Numerous items had been thrown around the room and it appeared that a jewelry box had been rummaged through.

Outside, police discovered that the phone lines on the side of the house had been severed. The perpetrator had apparently gained entry by climbing up the burglar bars onto the roof, lowering himself into an enclosed garden atrium that was not visible to the street, and throwing a flower pot through the atrium window into the dining room. Police found mud on the burglar bars, a footprint in the mud inside the atrium, and muddy footprints inside the house leading from the dining room into Wright's bedroom.

At 8 a.m. that same morning police found Wright's abandoned black Beretta car about one and one-half miles from her home. A trail of transmission fluid guided police from the car to a dirt road off the freeway where a metal pipe protruding through the mud apparently severed the car's transmission line. With the assistance of a K-9 unit police found Wright's nude body, which had been covered with grass in a nearby field. She had been stabbed 11 times in the chest and back. Blood splattered on vegetation indicated that Wright was still alive when she arrived at the field.

Vincent DiMaio, the medical examiner, testified that the presence of sperm on vaginal swabs taken from Wright's body indicated that she had sexual intercourse within 24 hours of her death. According to the State's DNA expert only 1 in 19,900,000 randomly selected people of Hinojosa's racial classification group would match the DNA profile of the sperm collected on the vaginal swab and Hinojosa possessed a DNA profile that matched the sperm taken from Wright's body.

Police found a footprint identical to the one found in the atrium near Wright's body. According to a Fila brand shoe representative the prints were made by a leather Fila "Slant Shot" tennis shoe, style number 1-T32-0517. The Slant Shot was first distributed in January 1994 and was a "low seller," comprising only 1 percent of Fila shoe sales in North America. Hinojosa's wife, Rebecca Alfaro, purchased a pair of size 10 or 11 white Fila tennis shoes for him and a couple of months later bought the same style of shoes for herself at a different store. She stated at trial that the soles of Hinojosa's shoes were the same as the soles of her shoes.

The soles of Alfaro's shoes were identical to the prints found at the crime scenes except that the prints were the size of a man's shoe. When police began asking about Hinojosa's shoes Alfaro looked for the shoes but could not find them. Hinojosa offered his wife several excuses for why the shoes were missing: maybe his father accidently threw them away, maybe a dog carried them away, or maybe somebody stole them.

On May 9, the day of the murder, Hinojosa was serving parole on a prior murder conviction. Hinojosa, his father, wife, sister, brother-in-law, and sister's children all lived next door to Wright in Hinojosa's father's house. On the 9th Hinojosa returned home from work around 11 p.m. close to the same time as Wright. According to family members Hinojosa had developed a persistent, hacking cough from years of heavy smoking. Lisa Pecina, Hinojosa's sister, awoke around 1 a.m. and could hear him coughing until about 2:30 a.m. or 3:00 a.m. Two dogs in the backyard of Hinojosa's father's house normally barked at everybody, including Hinojosa, but not that night.

Laurie Lowry, who lived directly behind Wright, was awake feeding her newborn baby between 2:00 a.m. and 3:00 a.m. on the night of the murder. Through the closed blinds in Wright's bedroom Lowry could see the silhouettes of a woman, a big muscular man with a bushy ponytail, and a shorter man with spiked hair. Lowry saw a lot of movement in the room and it appeared that the three were dancing.

Hinojosa's father woke Hinojosa between 5:30 a.m. and 6:00 a.m. on the 10th to get ready for work. Because Hinojosa did not have a car his brother-in-law drove him to his sister Irene Hernandez's house so that she could drive him to the Brooks Club at Brooks Air Force Base where Hinojosa had worked for several years as a custodian. Hinojosa clocked in at 8:04 a.m. He also worked the following day but skipped work on the 12th.

After working a half-day on the 13th Hinojosa never returned to work again. Hinojosa moved out of his father's house on the day Wright's body was found and stayed with Hernandez for two weeks before moving back in with his father. Soon after the murder Hinojosa called the manager of the Brooks Club attempting to use the club bartender and a retired tech sergeant as *alibis*, neither of who testified at trial.

Two of Hinojosa's former coworkers identified Wright as a woman that Hinojosa had brought to the Brooks Club about six months before the murder suggesting that she and Hinojosa were somehow involved. Two other coworkers testified that when they heard news that Wright's body had been found they asked Hinojosa if he had known her to which he confirmed that Wright had been his next-door neighbor, but adding, "I don't know the bitch." A couple of weeks later Hinojosa visited the club and another former coworker asked him where he had been lately. He replied jokingly that he had been a "fugitive on the run."

In March of 1995 Alfaro and Hinojosa moved out of Hinojosa's father's house and into apartments. When Hinojosa was arrested shortly thereafter Alfaro went to live with her mother, boxed up Hinojosa's personal things, and took them with her. On October 16 she gave the boxes to his nephew, who gave them to Hinojosa's sister, Hernandez.

A few days before trial investigators working for Hinojosa's counsel requested clothes for him to wear during the trial. While looking through the clothing Hernandez found a pair of men's size 10 Fila athletic shoes. Like Rebecca Alfaro's shoes these shoes were leather Filas. The defense submitted these shoes into evidence, and although the shoes submitted by the defense were similar in appearance to Alfaro's shoes, Hinojosa's shoes were a different style (1-J17-0517) and had wholly dissimilar soles.

On August 15, 1995, a Bexar County grand jury indicted Hinojosa for capital murder. Convicted and sentenced to death in 1997, the Texas Court of Criminal Appeals affirmed his conviction and sentence on October 27, 1999 (*Hinojosa v. State* (1999) 4 S.W.3d 240).

———

Samuel Russell Flippen, a 36-year-old white male, was executed by lethal injection at the Central Prison in Raleigh, North Carolina on August 18, 2006. Flippen was found guilty of the 1994 murder of Britnie Nichole Hutton, a 28-month-old white female. Flippen, who was 24-years old when he committed the capital crime, was sentenced to death on March 7, 1995, and again on May 23, 1997.

At approximately 9:15 a.m. on February 12, 1994, Tina Flippen left her home in Forsyth County, North Carolina for work leaving her daughter Britnie in the care of Flippen, her husband. Britnie, Flippen's stepdaughter, was emotionally close enough to Flippen that she called him "daddy" even though Tina and Flippen had been married for just five months.

At 10:11 a.m. on the 12th Flippen called 9-1-1 to report that Britnie had fallen and was having difficulty breathing. Five emergency medical personnel from both the Clemmons Rescue Squad and the Forsyth County Emergency Medical Services arrived at Flippen's trailer. Several members of the rescue teams testified that when they arrived Britnie was pale, her lips were ash gray, her pupils were fixed and dilated, and she was making gasping-type respirations. Despite rescue efforts Britnie was pronounced dead at the North Carolina Baptist Hospital in Winston-Salem at 10:51 a.m.

Dr. Donald Jason, a forensic pathologist who performed an autopsy on Britnie, testified that he observed six injuries to her head, at least three injuries to her chest, injuries to her pelvis, hip bone, eye, and forehead, and bruises on her arms and right thigh. Jason testified that

Britnie died as a result of internal bleeding due to severe tearing of her liver and pancreas. He opined that these injuries could not have been caused by an accident such as a single fall but rather that the injuries were consistent with one or more very powerful punches or blows to Britnie's abdomen.

In 1995 Flippen was first tried by a Forsyth County jury, convicted of capital murder and sentenced to death. On appeal the sentence was overturned based on the fact that the judge had failed to instruct the jury that a mitigating circumstance existed. The prosection and Flippen had previously agreed that one of Flippen's mitigating factors was that he had had no prior criminal history. Two years later another Forsyth County jury recommended a death sentence. One day before his execution Governor Michael F. Easley declined to grant Flippen clemency (*State v. Flippen* (1996) 477 S.E.2d 158; *State v. Flippen* (1998) 506 S.E.2d 702).

———

Justin Chaz Fuller, a 27-year-old black male, was executed by lethal injection at the Texas State Penitentiary in Huntsville, Texas on August 24, 2006. Fuller was found guilty of the 1997 murder of Donald Whittington III, a 21-year-old male. Fuller, who was 18-years old when he committed the capital crime, was sentenced to death on March 4, 1998.

On April 21, 1997, Fuller, Samhermendre Raemune Wideman, a 22-year-old black male, and two other friends, Elaine Kay Hays, a 25-year-old white female, and Brent Bates Chandler, a 19-year-old white male, kidnapped Donald Whittington from his Tyler, Texas apartment, forced him to withdraw approximately $300 from an ATM, and then drove him to a wooded area where they shot him once in the arm and twice in the head with a .22-caliber pistol, killing him.

That evening Fuller took two Chapel Hill High School students to see Whittington's body and told them what had happened. Those two students invited Kevin Ballard, Kevin's brother, and three other youths to view the body the next day. Ballard later saw on a television broadcast that Whittington's body had been discovered and he contacted police and led them to the body four days after the murder.

Police interviewed the youths and were told what Fuller had said about killing Whittington. After searching Fuller's dwelling police found Whittington's ATM card in Fuller's wallet and Whittington's watch in Fuller's living room. After being arrested Fuller confessed to being involved in the crime but denied being the triggerman.[81]

A Smith County jury convicted Fuller, who had no prior criminal record, of capital murder and sentenced him to death. On the day of execution the Supreme Court of the United States denied a stay by a vote of 7-2. Accomplices' Hays and Wideman were also convicted of capital murder and given life sentences. Chandler, who testified against Fuller at trial, was convicted of aggravated robbery, aggravated kidnapping, and arson, and sentenced to 25 years, 25 years, and 10 years, respectively (*Fuller v. Dretke* (5th Cir. 2006) No. 05-70004; *Fuller v. Quarterman* (2006) 127 S. Ct. 28).

---

[81] During the trial and the punishment phase Fuller's counsel attempted to introduce evidence of the moral culpability of separately tried Wideman wanting to demonstrate Wideman's propensity to violence and that Wideman was the organizer of the crime, thereby diminishing Fuller's role in the murder. The trial court excluded the evidence because it had no probative value. After Fuller's conviction Hays, another codefendant, asserted that following the shooting, Wideman said that it felt good to shoot somebody. Under Texas law, even if the jury believed that Fuller was not the triggerman, the jury could have still sentenced him to death as guilty of capital murder.

Eric Allen Patton, a 49-year-old black male, was executed by lethal injection at the Oklahoma State Penitentiary in McAlester, Oklahoma on August 29, 2006. Patton was found guilty of the 1994 murder of Charlene Kauer, a 56-year-old white female. Patton, who was 37-years old when he committed the capital crime, was sentenced to death on December 2, 1996.

On the morning of December 16, 1994, Patton, employed as a brick mason, left the job site in Edmond, Oklahoma, ostensibly to purchase electrical connection boxes at a local hardware store. Patton drove coworker Chris Williams's car and was gone four hours. When he returned he did not have the electrical boxes and was wearing clothes belonging to Williams, which were clothes different than he had worn earlier in the day.

During the time Patton was gone he went to the home of Les and Charlene Kauer in northeast Oklahoma City. Patton had some painting work for the Kauers and worked with them at Dial American Marketing.

Patton knocked at the front door, was surprised when Charlene answered, and asked to borrow money. Charlene gave him $10. Not satisfied, Patton forced his way into the home, grabbed Charlene by the throat, and dragged her through the house looking for money and valuables. He took her to the bedroom where he forced her to undress and then struggled with her. He stabbed her numerous times and dragged her down the hallway into the kitchen.

The struggle between Patton and Charlene continued and he stabbed her several more times with a variety of knives. As the fierceness of the attack broke a succession of knives, Patton resorted to a barbecue fork. Unsure if the severely wounded Charlene was dead, he plunged a pair of scissors into her chest.[82] Patton left the scene, cleaned up, and traded his bloody clothes for a pair of coveralls found in Williams's car. The bloody clothes were dropped in a field in northwest Oklahoma City.

Patton, initially not a suspect, was asked on December 29 to come to the police station because of his association with the Kauers. He initially denied any involvement in the murder stating he had seen a suspicious vehicle at the Kauer residence and suggested that Les was involved. When asked about a scratch on his lip and cuts on his hands he explained that he was changing a tire and the jack slipped and hit him. Patton gave police body samples, answered questions, and was subsequently arrested when fingerprint comparison revealed his prints at the murder scene.

The following day Patton took the officers to a field in northwest Oklahoma City where he had disposed of his bloody clothes and showed the officers several convenience stores which he admitted robbing.

Patton was interviewed again on January 7, 9, and 13, 1995, and each time he waived his *Miranda* rights. In one interview Patton inculpated Williams in the murder. He told police he had a lot of information to give them but he was protecting someone. He said he was guilty just because he was at the Kauer home but that the other person committed the murder. Patton went on to say that Charlene was not

---

[82] Although the exact order in which the wounds were inflicted could not be determined by the medical examiner she did state that Charlene was alive when she received certain wounds, particularly the stab wounds to the throat and chest, adding that while none of the wounds individually were fatal, it was the totality of the wounds that caused her death. This evidence combined with the evidence of the defensive wounds and that of a struggle clearly established that Charlene was conscious and aware of the attack and supported a finding of torture as an aggravating circumstance.

supposed to be home the day he had gone over to steal some items from the house and discovered her there by accident. Patton said the other person assaulted Charlene and tore her clothes off and that he intervened because he was afraid Charlene was going to be raped and that was when he was cut on the hand and scratched on the lip. He added that they "had only gotten a lousy $14 and the woman didn't even put up a fight."

In another interview Patton admitted that Williams was not involved in the murder but there had been a woman with him at the Kauer home. This woman, called a "strawberry" by Patton, took part in the murder. Patton said the woman stabbed Kauer while he wrestled with the Kauer's dog, eventually stabbing the dog. He said the cuts on his hand and the scratch on his lip came from Kauer's dog that bit him. At the end of this interview Patton admitted there had been no "strawberry" with him.

In yet another interview Patton admitted seeing himself at the murder and stabbing Charlene but said there were demonic forces present and that Charlene was a demon. Patton also said that he had ingested cocaine before the murder and believed the drug was "laced" with another drug.[83] He said he was "tripping" from the effects of the drugs. Patton described in detail his activities immediately before the murder, during the murder, and afterwards.

Patton was convicted of first-degree murder and first-degree burglary in the District Court, Oklahoma County

---

[83] Patton had the presence of mind to clean himself up and exchange his bloody clothes for those of Williams. Witnesses who talked with Patton shortly after the murder testified he was not under the influence of cocaine. Williams testified that when Patton returned to the job site on the day of the murder he did not seem to be under the influence of cocaine. Sandra Moore, Patton's girlfriend, testified that she saw Patton and talked to him only a few hours after the murder and his demeanor seemed "normal."

after the jury was provided video and audiotapes of Patton's interviews and forensic evidence indicating that Patton's fingerprints were present in the Kauer home and that blood at the scene matched Patton's type. The jury found four aggravating circumstances: Patton was previously convicted of a felony involving the use or threat of violence; the murder was especially heinous, atrocious, or cruel; the murder was committed for the purpose of avoiding or preventing a lawful arrest or prosecution; and the murder was committed while he was on parole for California felony convictions (*Patton v. State* (1998) 973 P.2d 270; *Patton v. Mullin* (2005) 425 F.3d 788).

―――

James Patrick Malicoat, a 31-year-old white male, was executed by lethal injection at the Oklahoma State Penitentiary in McAlester, Oklahoma on August 31, 2006. Malicoat was found guilty of the 1997 murder of Tessa Ann Leadford, a 13-month-old white female. Malicoat, who was 21-years old when he committed the capital crime, was sentenced to death on March 2, 1998.

At about 8:25 p.m. on February 21, 1997, Malicoat and his girlfriend, Mary Ann Leadford, brought their daughter Tessa Leadford, to the county hospital emergency room. The hospital staff determined that Tessa had been dead for several hours. Her face and body were covered with bruises and she had a large mushy closed wound on her forehead and three human bite marks on her body. A post-mortem examination revealed two subdural hematomas from the head injury, and severe internal injuries including broken ribs, internal bruising and bleeding, and a torn mesentery. The medical examiner concluded the death was caused by a combination of the head injury and internal bleeding from the abdominal injuries.

On February 2 Tessa and Mary Ann began living with Malicoat in Chickasha, Oklahoma. Malicoat worked a night shift on an oilrig and was responsible for Tessa's care

315

during the day. The six foot one inch tall Malicoat admitted that he routinely poked Tessa hard in the chest area and occasionally bit her, both as a disciplinary measure and in play.

When interviewed by police officers Malicoat initially denied knowing how Tessa had received the severe head injury and suggested that she had fallen and hit the edge of a waterbed frame. Eventually he admitted that he had hit her head on the bed frame one or two days before she died. He also admitted that, at about 12:30 p.m. on February 21 while Mary Ann was at work he twice punched Tessa hard in the stomach. He stated that Tessa stopped breathing and that he gave her CPR. When Tessa began breathing again Malicoat gave her a bottle containing a soft drink and went to sleep next to her on the bed.

When he awoke around 5:30 p.m. she was dead. He put Tessa in her crib and covered her with a blanket, spoke briefly with Mary Ann, and went back to sleep in the living room. Mary Ann eventually discovered that Tessa was not moving and the couple took her to the emergency room.

Seeking to explain the events leading to Tessa's death Malicoat reported that he had worked all night, had car trouble, took Mary Ann to work, and was exhausted. He added that he had hit Tessa when she would not lie down so he could sleep. He said he sometimes intended to hurt Tessa when he disciplined her but he never meant to kill her.

Malicoat admitted biting Tessa in play and anger, hitting her head on the bed rail, and punching her twice in the stomach while she screamed in pain. Medical evidence showed these injuries, especially the head and abdominal injuries, would have been very painful with obvious physical symptoms. Malicoat said Tessa had trouble eating after the head injury and thought of taking her to a doctor but did not because he was afraid authorities would take her away. He claimed he had suffered through such extreme abuse as a child that he did not realize his actions would seriously hurt or kill Tessa.

Malicoat was tried by Grad County jury and in accordance with the jury's recommendation, sentenced to death by the Honorable Judge Joe Enos.[84] On August 1, 2006, the five-member state Pardon and Parole Board unanimously denied clemency. Mary Ann was sentenced to life imprisonment for the first-degree murder of her child (*Malicoat v. State* (2000) 992 P.2d 383; *Malicoat v. Mullin* (2005) 426 F.3d 1241).

———

Derrick Wayne Frazier, a 29-year-old black male, was executed by lethal injection at the Texas State Penitentiary in Huntsville, Texas on August 31, 2006. Frazier was found guilty of the 1997 murder of Betsy Nutt, a 41-year-old white female, and Cody Nutt, a 15-year-old white male. Frazier, who was 20-years old when he committed the capital crime, was sentenced to death on October 7, 1998.

At approximately 11 a.m on June 25, 1997, Frazier and Jermaine Herron, an 18-year-old black male, visited the Lucich ranch, located approximately 10 miles from Refugio in the country north of Corpus Christi, Texas. The two men were loking for work. Betsy Nutt and her son Cody were also living on the ranch in a mobile home.

During the visit Frazier and Herron noticed a number of guns in the Lucich residence. That afternoon Frazier, Herron, and Michael Brown made plans to burglarize the

---

[84] The courtroom had a wooden carving on the wall directly behind the judge's bench that depicted a man and a woman holding a sword bearing the inscription: "AN EYE FOR AN EYE AND A TOOTH FOR A TOOTH." On appeal it was ruled that the display did not constitute structural error because there is no evidence that the inscription caused the jurors to bring Bibles into deliberation.

Lucich residence and to steal Betsy's pickup truck. In the evening Brown drove Frazier and Herron to the ranch. Frazier and Herron knew where guns were kept having been inside the place before. In the car Frazier and Herron discussed stealing the guns. They planned to quickly retrieve the guns and kill anyone in the home but before they could enter the Lucich's home the lights came on and the three men had to drive away.

The next morning Brown drove Frazier and Herron back to the Lucich's home, dropped them off, and drove away. In his videotaped confession Frazier narrated the following set of events occurring that morning. After burglarizing the Lucich home Frazier and Herron took a 9-millimeter pistol and went to the Nutt's trailer. Hiding the pistol the two men approached Betsy and Herron conversed with her afterwhich Betsy offered to take Frazier and Herron to Refugio. The three of them entered Betsy's pickup truck but as she started the engine Betsy realized she had forgotten her mobile phone. She turned off the engine and went back inside her home to retrieve the phone.

While Betsy was in her home Herron told Frazier, "I'm going to do 'em now," which Frazier took to mean that Herron was going to kill Betsy and Cody. Frazier responded, "It's your business." When Betsy came back to her truck and started the engine Herron told her that he needed to use the bathroom. Betsy told him that he could go inside and do so and Herron entered the Nutt residence. Soon afterwards Herron returned from the residence and told Betsy that she had a telephone call. Betsy exited the truck and entered her home with Frazier following her.

Once inside the Nutt's home Herron pointed the pistol at Betsy and told her not to move. Hearing the commotion Cody came into the room occupied by Frazier, Herron, and Betsy. Herron then shot Cody with the pistol. After shooting Cody, Herron handed the gun to Frazier and told Frazier to shoot Betsy. Although he did not want to do it,

318

Frazier shot Betsy twice in the head. The first shot was from six to seven feet away while the second shot occurred when Frazier was standing over Betsy with the gun two or three feet away from her. Herron then set the house on fire afterwhich Herron and Frazier drove away in Betsy's truck.

On August 8, 1997, a Refugio County grand jury indicted Frazier and Herron for the capital murder of Betsy and Cody Nutt. The two men were tried separately some six months apart. Both were convicted and sentenced to death.[85] On March 28, 2001, the Texas Court of Criminal Appeals affirmed Frazier's conviction and sentence. On May 17, 2006, Herron was executed by lethal injection (*Frazier v. Dretke* (2005) 145 Fed.Appx. 866; *Herron v. State* (2002) 86 S.W.3d 621).

————

Farley Charles Matchett, a 43-year-old black male, was executed by lethal injection at the Texas State Penitentiary in Huntsville, Texas on September 12, 2006. Matchett was found guilty of the 1991 murder of Uries Anderson, a 52-year-old black male. Matchett, who was 28-years old when he committed the capital crime, was sentenced to death on April 30, 1993.

In 1991 Matchett was in serious need of money for his crack cocaine habit, and while attempting to cash a check stolen from his uncle, Uries Anderson, Matchett was arrested by the Houston, Texas police. Arraigned in open court in 1993, Matchett pleaded guilty to stabbing Anderson twice in the back with a knife and beating him on the head with a hammer. Anderson's body was found on July 14, 1991, two days after the murder.

---

[85] Brown testified that Herron later called Brown on the telephone. During their conversation Herron told Brown that Herron had killed a lady and a little boy. At a later date when Brown and Herron were in jail, Herron told Brown that Frazier was the one who shot both Betsy and Cody.

After pleading guilty in open court the jury was then brought in and sworn afterwhich the State read the indictment to the jury and the trial court informed the jury, without objection, that Matchett had knowingly and voluntarily pleaded guilty to the charges against him. After the State presented its evidence and rested the trial court instructed the jury to return a verdict finding Matchett guilty.

During the punishment phase the State introduced Matchett's confessions to the July 11 murder of 74-year-old Melonee Josey, a friend and neighbor in Huntsville. Matchett bludgeoned Josey to death with a meat tenderizer when she refused to give him money but offered to pay him if he mowed her lawn. Josey received 41 stab wounds to her chest, blunt force trauma to her head, lacerations to the head, and, her throat had been slashed.

The State also introduced Matchett's confession of his July 10 assault with a hammer upon 91-year-old Ola Mac Williams, a woman who refused to pay him for lawn work he had not performed at her Huntsville home. Williams was stabbed four times in the chest and further received a series of lacerations on her neck.

Matchett was sentenced to death for the Anderson murder. He also received a 99-year sentence for the Williams beating, and a life sentence for the Josey murder. In November 1996 the Texas Court of Criminal Appeals affirmed his conviction and sentence. Matchett's final meal was four olives and a bottle of wild-berry flavored water (*Matchett v. State* (1996) 941 S.W.2d 922).

―――

Clarence Edward Hill, a 48-year-old black male, was executed by lethal injection at the Florida State Prison in Starke, Florida on September 20, 2006. Hill was found guilty of the 1982 murder of Stephen Taylor, a 26-year-old white male. Hill, who was 24–years old when he committed the capital crime, was sentenced to death on May 27, 1983.

On October 19, 1982, Hill stole a pistol and an automobile in Mobile, Alabama. Later that day Hill and Cliff Jackson, an 18-year-old black male, drove to Pensacola, Florida and robbed a savings and loan association at gunpoint. Inside the bank Hill did most of the talking, demanded money, and threatened that he would "blow some brains out." Hill also physically abused a bank teller by kicking him and pulling him by the hair while he lay on the floor.

When police arrived during the robbery Hill fled out the back of the savings and loan building. Jackson exited through the front door where he was apprehended immediately. Hill approached two police officers, Stephen Taylor and Larry Bailly, from behind as they attempted to handcuff Jackson. Hill then drew his pistol and shot the officers—killing Taylor and wounding Bailly. A gun battle ensued during which Hill received five bullet wounds.

Hill was convicted in Escambia County of first-degree murder and the jury recommended the death penalty by a 10-2 vote. Hill was also convicted of attempted first-degree murder, three counts of armed robbery, and the possession of a firearm during the commission of a felony for which he received consecutive life sentences for the attempted murder and armed robbery convictions. No sentence was imposed for the possession of a firearm conviction. The trial court sentenced Hill to death for the murder conviction after finding five aggravating circumstances.[86]

On January 24, 2006, Hill was strapped to the gurney when the Supreme Court of the United States granted a

---

[86] Hill had previously been convicted of another capital offense or violent felony; Hill had knowingly created a great risk of harm or death to many persons; the murder was committed while Hill was engaged in the commission of a robbery; the murder was committed for the purpose of avoiding or preventing a lawful arrest or escaping from custody; and the murder was cold, calculated, and premeditated.

stay to evaluate Florida's lethal injection protocol; 239 days later the Court denied a stay by a vote of 5-4 and Hill was executed.

The grand jury also indicted Jackson for the same offenses. Prior to trial Jackson and the State entered into a plea agreement under which Jackson pleaded guilty to first-degree murder for which he was sentenced to prison for life (*Hill v. McDonough* (2006) 127 S.Ct. 34; *Hill v. Moore* (1999) 175 F.3d 915; *Hill v. State* (1985) 477 So.2d 553; *Hill v. State* (1987) 515 So.2d 176).

Arthur Dennis Rutherford, a 57-year-old white male, was executed by lethal injection at the Florida State Prison in Starke, Florida on October 18, 2006. Rutherford was found guilty of the 1985 murder of Stella Salamon, a 63-year-old white female. Rutherford, who was 36–years old when he committed the capital crime, was sentenced to death on February 1, 1986, and again on December 9, 1986.

During the summer of 1985 Rutherford told his friend Harold Attaway that he planned to kill a woman and place her body in her bathtub to make her death look like an accident. Rutherford also told a long-time business associate, Sherman Pittman, that he was going to get money by forcing a woman to write him a check and then putting her in the bathtub. If the woman initially refused to make out the check, Rutherford explained that he would "get her by that arm and she would sign." It was then that Rutherford bragged that he would do the crime but not the time.

About a week after making those statements Rutherford again told Attaway about his homicidal plan. Rutherford also told his uncle that they could get easy money by knocking a woman Rutherford worked for in the head.

Stella Salamon, who was born in Australia, lived alone in Milton, Florida. She had no family in the United States other than a sister-in law in Massachusetts. Rutherford, who hired out to do odd jobs, installed sliding glass doors in the doorway leading from Salamon's patio to her kitchen. Before long Salamon had the sliding glass doors replaced because they did not close and lock properly. She told her long-time friend and next-door neighbor that the unlocked doors made her nervous and that she wondered if Rutherford had intentionally made the doors so that she could not lock them. Salamon said that Rutherford kept coming to her house and acted as though he was "casing the joint."

It is unclear whether Salamon notified Rutherford about the problems with the doors but on the morning of August 21, 1985, Rutherford asked Attaway to come along with him when he went to repair the doors he had installed for her. When they got to Salamon's house she told them she had the doors replaced. Attaway left to get money to give her as a refund on the doors and Rutherford stayed behind at Salamon's house.

Around noon that day Salamon received a call from her friend Lois LaVaugh. Salamon told LaVaugh that she was nervous because Rutherford had been at her house for "quite awhile." LaVaugh drove over there and found Rutherford sitting shirtless on Salamon's porch. Rutherford left after LaVaugh arrived and Salamon told her that Rutherford "really has made me nervous" and had been sitting on her couch. Salamon never got the refund that Attaway was supposed to bring and Rutherford left the old glass doors in her garage.

At 7:00 the next morning, August 22, Rutherford and Attaway went to retrieve the old doors from Salamon's garage. When they reached the house Rutherford told Attaway that he had a gun in his van and said, "If I reach for that gun, you'll know I mean business." Attaway testified that this was the first time he really believed that Rutherford might actually hurt someone. While they were loading the doors Attaway overheard Salamon say to Rutherford, "You can just forget about the money."

Around noon on the 22nd Rutherford went to see Mary Frances Heaton. Rutherford showed her one of Salamon's checks and asked her to fill it out. Heaton, who cannot read or write other than to sign her name, called for her 14-year-old niece, Elizabeth. Rutherford promised Elizabeth money if she would fill out the check as instructed. Elizabeth filled out the check the way Rutherford told her to, making it payable to Heaton, but she did not sign anyone's name on it.

Rutherford told Heaton that he owed her money for work she had done for him and asked her to accompany him. He took Heaton to Santa Rosa State Bank, gave her the check, and sent her into the bank to cash it. Because of the blank signature line the teller refused to cash the check; Heaton returned to Rutherford's van and told him.

Rutherford responded by driving them to the nearby woods where he took out a wallet, checkbook, and credit cards wrapped in a shirt and threw the bundle into the trees. He also signed Salamon's name onto the check and then went back to the bank. Outside the bank Heaton watched as Rutherford endorsed Heaton's name on the check. Heaton re-entered the bank and this time she successfully cashed the check and left with $2000 in one hundred dollar bills. Rutherford gave Heaton $500 of those funds and she in turn gave Elizabeth $5 for filling out the check.

Around 3:00 p.m. on the 22nd Rutherford visited his friend Johnny Perritt. Rutherford told Perritt that he had "bumped the old lady off" and showed him $1500 in cash. He wanted Perritt to hold $1400 of that amount for him. Rutherford said that he had hit the "old lady" in the head with a hammer, stripped her, and put her in the bathtub. Perritt refused to take the cash and his mother later notified police of Rutherford's claim to have committed a murder.

Earlier on the 22nd Salamon had made plans to go walking that evening with Beverly Elkins and another neighbor. At 6:30 p.m. Elkins tried to contact Salamon by phone but got no answer. She went to Salamon's house, saw her car outside, and realized that she must still be at home. Elkins rang the front doorbell and after receiving no answer went around the back and through the sliding glass doors where she saw that the television was on and that the normally calm dogs were jumping around excitedly. Elkins retrieved a spare key to the house, met up with the other neighbor, and the two women let themselves into Salamon's home.

When the two women entered the kitchen through the carport door they heard water running. They followed the sound to a little-used guest bathroom where they found Salamon's naked body floating face up in the water that filled the tub to overflowing. Realizing that Salamon was dead the women went to call for help.

When the crime scene investigators arrived they found three fingerprints on the handle of the sliding door to the bathtub, one fingerprint on the tile wall of the tub, and a palm print on the windowsill inside the tub with the fingers up and over the sill as though the person had grabbed it. All of those prints were later identified as Rutherford's. Blood was spattered on the bathroom walls and floor. According to an expert the spatter pattern indicated that the blows occurred while Salamon was sitting or kneeling on the bathroom floor.

Salamon had been viciously beaten. There were bruises on her nose, chin, and mouth and a cut on the inside of her lip consistent with a hand being held forcefully over her face. Her lungs showed signs of manual asphyxiation, apparently from someone covering her nose and mouth. Her arms and knees were bruised and scraped and her left arm was broken at the elbow. Of the three large wounds on her head, two were consistent with being struck with a blunt object or having her head slammed

down. The other wound, a puncture that went all the way to the bone, appeared to be from a blow with a claw hammer or screwdriver. Her skull was fractured from one side to the other.

Early in 1986 Rutherford was tried for first-degree murder and armed robbery. During the trial Rutherford moved for a mistrial based on a discovery violation by the prosecution, but the court reserved ruling and the proceedings continued. The Santa Rosa County jury found Rutherford guilty and, by an 8-4 vote recommended a sentence of death. Rutherford then renewed his motion for a mistrial that the trial court granted.

In the fall of 1986, after a change of venue to Walton County, Rutherford was retried. During the guilt stage of the trial Rutherford, who was represented by two public defenders, took the stand and tried to explain his prints in the bathroom by claiming that Salamon had asked him to realign the shower door when he was at her house the day before she was killed because her nieces and nephews had knocked the door off its track.

Salamon did not have any nieces or nephews, and according to Elkins, no young children had visited Salamon's house in the weeks prior to her death. Rutherford denied the testimony of three witnesses that he had confided to them his plans to murder a woman. Rutherford insisted he never would have said such things "because I've got a good mother." He argued that every one of the witnesses against him was lying. At the time of trial Heaton was residing in a mental institution against her will, and that at the time of the murder she had trouble distinguishing fact from fantasy.[87]

---

[87] In an affidavit dated December 16, 2005, Heaton's former housemate Alan Gilkerson stated that in the early 1990's Heaton told him that "she once killed an old lady with a hammer and made it look like A.D. Rutherford committed the crime."

On October 2, 1986, a jury found Rutherford guilty. During the penalty phase the defense presented character evidence and testimony about Rutherford's childhood, his family, his service as a Marine during the Vietnam War, and his nervousness, nightmares, and night sweats since returning from Vietnam. The jury recommended death, this time by a 7-5 vote. The trial court imposed a death sentence based on three aggravating circumstances: the murder was especially heinous, atrocious, and cruel; it was cold, calculated, and premeditated; and it was committed in the course of a robbery and for pecuniary gain. On January 31, 2006, while strapped to the gurney, the Supreme Court of the United States stayed Rutherford's executiuon; 260 days later the Court voted 8-1 against a second stay (*Rutherford v. Crosby* (2006) 126 S.Ct. 1191; *Rutherford v. McDonough* (2006) 127 S.Ct. 465; *Rutherford v. State* (2006) 926 So. 2d 1100).

————

Bobby Glen Wilcher, a 43-year-old white male, was executed by lethal injection at the Mississippi State Penitentiary in Parchman, Mississippi on October 18, 2006. Wilcher was found guilty of the 1982 murder of Velma Odell

---

Gilkerson stated that Heaton told him that her motive for "murdering the old lady" was to get money.

In a second affidavit dated December 23, 2005, defense investigator Michael Glantz stated that in a conversation with Heaton the previous day, Heaton confirmed that she knew Gilkerson and had previously resided with him. Heaton denied having told Gilkerson that she committed the murder. Heaton stated that she knew Salamon, had been present at her home at the time of the murder, had witnessed Rutherford strike the fatal blow, and had been present when Salamon's belongings were buried. Heaton claimed that she had previously provided this information to law enforcement officers during their investigation of the crime and had also tried to lead the officers to the location where Salamon's belongings were buried.

Noblin, a 63-year-old white female, and Katie Bell Moore, a 47-year-old white female. Wilcher, who was 19-years old when he committed the capital crimes, was sentenced to death on July 31, 1982, and again on June 23, 1994, for the Noblin murder, and again on September 13, 1982, and on July 21, 1994, for the Moore murder.

On the night of March 5, 1982, Wilcher met Velma Noblin and Katie Moore at Robert's Drop-In, a Forest, Mississippi bar. The bar closed at midnight, afterwhich Wilcher persuaded the two women to take him home. Under this pretext Wilcher directed the women down a deserted service road in the Bienville National Forest where he robbed and brutally murdered them by stabbing them a total of forty-six times.

At approximately 1:40 a.m. Forest Police Officer Henry Williams Jr. stopped Wilcher, who was driving Noblin's car, for speeding. The women's purses and one of their bras were on the back seat. Wilcher was covered in blood and had a bloody knife in his back pocket that had flesh on the blade. Wilcher explained his condition by telling the policeman that he had cut his thumb while skinning a possum. The officer followed Wilcher to the hospital where Wilcher's wound was cleaned and covered with a band-aid. Another officer was called to the hospital to observe Wilcher, the knife, the car, the purses, and the bra.

The officers left the hospital on an emergency call and Wilcher went home. The next morning Wilcher abandoned Noblin's car at an apartment complex. He also threw the women's purses and the bra in a ditch. Wilcher was arrested later that day. The women's jewelry was subsequently found in Wilcher's bedroom.

On March 11, 1982, Wilcher was indicted for both murders. Later that year Wilcher was tried separately for each murder; the Noblin trial lasted three days and the Moore trial lasted just one day, and upon jury recommendations, Circuit Court Judge Marcus D. Gordon sentenced him to death. In October 1993 the U.S. Fifth

Circuit Court of Appeals vacated the sentences of Wilcher and 16 other death row inmates based on errors in jury instructions.

The following year Judge Gordon again resentenced Wilcher to death in Rankin County for the Noblin murder and in Harrison County for the Moore murder. In denying Wilcher clemency Governor Haley Barbour noted: "The real tragedy in this case is that justice was delayed for more than two decades." On the day of execution the Supreme Court of the United States denied a stay (*Wilcher v. Epps* (2006) 127 S.Ct. 466; *Wilcher v. State* (1984) 448 So.2d 927; *Wilcher v. State* (1984) 455 So.2d 727; *Wilcher v. State* (2003) 863 So.2d 776).

———

Jeffrey Don Lundgren, a 56-year-old white male, was executed by lethal injection at the Southern Ohio Correctional Facility in Lucasville, Ohio on October 24, 2006. Lundgren was found guilty of the 1989 murder of Dennis Avery, a 49-year-old white male, and four white females: Cheryl Avery, 46, Karen Diane Avery, 7, Rebecca Lynn Avery, 13, and Trina Denise Avery, 15. Lundgren, who was 38-years old when he committed the capital crime, was sentenced to death on September 21, 1990.

The Avery family moved to Kirtland, Ohio in the summer of 1987. On April 17, 1989, the Averys were invited to the Lundgren farm on Chillicothe Road in Kirtland on the pretext of having dinner and preparing to go to the wilderness. Lundgren made arrangements for the Avery family to check in at the local Red Roof Inn and had their belongings moved to the Lundgren farmhouse that was located next to the Kirtland Temple, a religious site for the Reorganized Church of Latter Day Saints (RLDS).[88]

---

[88] Lundgren was born in Missouri and raised in the RLDS. The RLDS, headquartered in Independence, Missouri, and the
(*continued*)

329

Lundgren later instructed Richard Brand, a 25-year-old church follower living with the Lundgrens, to pick up the Averys, also church followers, and bring them to the farmhouse. Upon their arrival at the farm Lundgren directed Cheryl Avery to write a letter to her mother explaining that the family would be moving to Wyoming.

After dinner, Brand, Ronald Luff, 29, a church follower not living with the Lundgrens, Lundgren's son, Damon P. Lundgren, 18, and two more church followers, Daniel D. Kraft, 24, and Gregory S. Winship, 18, had two meetings with Lundgren to discuss Lundgren's specific plan to kill the Averys whom he deemed disloyal.

The first meeting took place in Damon's bedroom where Lundgren inquired of each of the five men, "Are you with me, or not?" The second meeting took place in the barn located in the rear of Lundgren's premises. During that meeting Lundgren delegated responsibilities to each of the men. Two of the men would apply duct tape to the Averys' mouths, hands, and feet, while another would run a

---

(*continued*)
Utah-based Mormon Church both trace their origins to the prophet Joseph Smith Jr. The two groups splintered in 1844 when Smith died. Today there are several differences to the groups in that Mormons do not allow women or blacks into the priesthood whereas the RLDS do not hold such principles.

In 1984 Lundgren and his family moved from Missouri to Kirtland so that Lundgren could serve as senior temple guide, a job that had no pay but did include family lodging. Over the next three years Lundgren served as a temple guide and taught classes on the Bible and the Book of Mormon. Despite the church's direction to turn over all money received from temple visitors to the church Lundgren solicited and kept contributions received from visitors causing the church to eventually remove him as a religion teacher. In October 1987 Lundgren was fired as a temple guide and evicted him from his quarters next to the temple. By October 1988 the RLDS had excommunicated Lundgren.

chain saw, and two others would carry the bodies to a six-foot long by seven-foot wide pit that had been dug as a grave. After these meetings all six men proceeded to the barn.

Under the guise of needing help Luff told Dennis Avery that he was to go to the barn to help gather materials to take to the wilderness. There, Dennis was attacked with a stun gun, wrestled to the ground, bound with silver duct tape with his eyes left uncovered, carried over a pile of garbage, and shot twice in the back by Lundgren with a .45-caliber semiautomatic weapon. Lundgren preached that he left Dennis's eyes uncovered so that he could see his executioner. Dennis died from the gunshots.

Luff was then sent to the house to retrieve Cheryl Avery who was also led to the barn, attacked with a stun gun, wrestled to the ground, bound with duct tape, carried over the pile of garbage, dropped into the pit, and shot three times in the back by Lundgren. Cheryl also died from the gunshots.

Under the guise of playing a game, Luff returned to the house and retrieved Trina Avery who was then bound, dropped into the pit, and killed by Lundgren who shot her once in the head and twice in the body.

Using the ruse of offering to show horses, Luff returned to the house to retrieve the two remaining Avery daughters, Becky and Karen. Luff carried them to the pit, bound their hands and feet with duct tape, and dropped them into the pit. Lundgren shot and killed both of them. Becky was shot once from behind and once from the front. Karen was shot in the head and the chest.

When the entire family had been murdered, lime was spread over their bodies to enhance their decomposition. The pit was then piled with rocks and dirt and was covered with garbage and old appliances. Lundgren then proceeded to remove all of the Averys' belongings from the Red Roof Inn. Lundgren later related that this method of burial was necessary pursuant to passages in the Old

Testament books of Isaiah and Deuteronomy which stated that he "shall put people to death" by binding their hands and feet, stoning them, and casting them into "utter darkness". Lundgren believed that "darkness" meant "death" in Hebrew.

The next day the FBI visited the group to question them about a conspiracy to overthrow the temple. The members panicked, gathered their belongings, and headed for Davis, West Virginia where they camped in a rural wooded area for five and one-half months. In October 1989 the group disbanded after local authorities in Davis became suspicious of the group's connection to the Kirtland investigation whereupon some of the members then headed to Missouri.

Lundgren subsequently moved to National City, California where he and the remainder of his followers were arrested on January 7, 1990. After the arrests the Bureau of Alcohol, Tobacco and Firearms searched the motel rooms in which Lundgren had been staying and found the group's collection of weaponry along with a roll of silver duct tape. Two guns sought by the Kirtland Police Department were later discovered in West Virginia. The murder weapon, a .45-caliber automatic combat elite semiautomatic, was recovered from Charles Judy who had purchased the gun from Paxton's Sports Shop in Elkins, West Virginia. The second gun, a .45-caliber gold cup, was obtained from Steven Lester who had purchased the weapon from Mountaineer Sports Center, also in Elkins.

Two days prior to his arrest Lundgren was charged in Lake County, Ohio with five counts of aggravated murder and five counts of kidnapping. On August 23 a Lake County jury trial commenced and six days later the jury returned a verdict of guilty on all counts. On September 20 the jury recommended that the sentence of death be imposed. On September 26, 2006, the eight member Ohio Parole Board unanimously recommended that Governor Bob Taft deny clemency. On the day of execution the governor denied clemency and the Supreme Court of the United States denied a stay. Several of Lundgren's accomplices were also punished[89] (*Lundgren v. Mitchell* (2006) 440 F.3d 754; *Lundgren v. Taft* (2006) 127 S.Ct. 466; *State v. Lundgren* (1993) Not Reported in N.E.2d, 1993 WL 346444).

————   •

Daniel Harrold Rolling, a 52-year-old white male, was executed by lethal injection at the Florida State Prison in Starke, Florida on October 25, 2006. Rolling was found guilty of the 1990 murder of Christa L. Hoyt, an 18-year-old white female, Sonja Larson, a 17-year-old white female, Tracy Inez Paules, a 23-year-old white female, Christina Powell, a 17-year-old white female, and Manuel R. Taboada, a 23-year-old white male. Rolling, who was 36-years old when he committed all five murders, was sentenced to death on April 20, 1994.

In the early morning hours of August 24, 1990, Rolling, armed with both an automatic pistol and a Marine Corps K-Bar knife, broke through the rear door of a Gainseville,

---

[89] Lundgren's wife, Alice, was convicted of aggravated murder and kidnapping and sentenced to 150 years-to-life, and his son, Damon, was convicted of aggravated murder and kidnapping and sentenced to 120 years-to-life. Ronald Luff was convicted of aggravated murder and kidnapping and sentenced to 170 years-to-life. Daniel Kraft was convicted of aggravated murder and kidnapping and sentenced to 50 years-to-life. Gregory Winship was convicted of murder and sentenced to 15 years-to-life. Richard Brand was convicted of murder and sentenced to 15 years-to-life. Sharon Bluntschly, Susan Luff, and Deborah Olivarez were convicted of conspiracy to aggravated murder and sentenced to 7-to-25 years. Kathryn Johnson, Dennis Patrick, and Tonya Patrick were convicted of obstructing justice. Johnson was sentenced to one year and the Patricks were sentenced to 18 months, their sentences suspended and placed on 1-year probation.

Florida apartment shared by University of Florida college students Sonya Larson and Christina Powell. Upon entering the apartment Rolling observed Powell asleep on the downstairs couch. He stood over her briefly but did not awaken her.

Rolling then crept upstairs where he found Larson asleep in her bedroom. After pausing to decide with which young woman he desired to have sexual relations he attacked Larson as she lay in her bed stabbing her first in the upper chest area. He then placed a double strip of duct tape over her mouth to muffle her cries and continued to stab her as she unsuccessfully attempted to fend off his blows. During the attack she was stabbed on her arms and received a slashing blow to her left thigh. Larson maintained consciousness for less than a minute and died as a direct result of the stab wounds inflicted by Rolling.

After killing Larson Rolling returned to the downstairs of the apartment where Powell remained asleep. He pressed a double strip of tape over her mouth and taped her hands behind her back. Rolling cut off her clothing and undergarments with the K-Bar knife and sexually battered Powell threatening her with the knife. Rolling then forced her to lie facedown on the floor near the couch and stabbed her five times in the back causing her death. Rolling posed the bodies of the two girls and left the apartment.

Approximately 42 hours later during the evening hours of Saturday, August 25, Rolling broke into Santa Fe Community College student, Christa Hoyt's apartment, located about two miles away from the first crime scene by prying open the sliding glass door with a screwdriver. Armed with the same automatic pistol and K-Bar knife Rolling waited in the living room for the arrival of Hoyt into whose bedroom he had peeked a few days earlier.

When Hoyt eventually returned home at about 11 a.m. Rolling surprised her from behind placing her in a chokehold and subduing her after a brief struggle. Rolling taped her mouth and her hands and then led her into her bedroom where, after cutting and tearing off her clothing and undergarments, he forced her onto her bed, threatened her with his knife, and sexually battered her. Rolling subsequently turned Hoyt facedown in her bed and stabbed her through the back rupturing her aorta and killing her. Just as he had done with his first two victims, Larson and Powell, Rolling posed Hoyt's body and left the apartment.

At approximately 3 a.m. on August 27 Rolling entered a third apartment occupied by roommates and University of Florida college students, Tracy Paules and Manny Taboada. Rolling broke into the apartment by prying open the double-glass sliding door with the same screwdriver he had used to enter the Hoyt apartment. Armed with the same pistol and knife Rolling crept into one of the bedrooms where he found Taboada asleep. The six-foot one-inch, 200 pound Rolling attacked him, stabbing him in the solar plexus and penetrating his thoracic vertebra. Taboada, awakened by the blow, struggled with Rolling but after being repeatedly stabbed in the arms, hands, chest, legs, and face, soon died.

Hearing the commotion caused by the struggle Paules approached Taboada's bedroom and catching a glimpse of Rolling, fled to her room where she attempted to lock her door. Rolling, who was covered with Taboada's blood, followed Paules and broke through her bedroom door. Rolling subdued her, taped her mouth and her hands, and cut or tore off her t-shirt. He sexually battered her and threatened her with his knife before turning her over on the bed and killing her with three stabbing blows to her back. Rolling then cleaned and posed the body of Paules and left the apartment.

On September 8, 1989, Rolling was arrested for a boched robbery in Ocala, Florida. Convicted and while serving time, DNA evidence linked him to three unsolved killings in Shreveport, Louisiana. Based on that information and more DNA evidence, on November 15, 1991, the grand jury of Alachua County indicted Rolling for the serial murders he committed in Gainseville, Florida.

The so-called *Gainseville Ripper* was charged with five counts of first-degree murder, three counts of sexual battery, and three counts of armed burglary of a dwelling with a battery. On June 9, 1992, Rolling entered a plea of not guilty on all counts. On February 15, 1994, the day set for trial, Rolling changed his plea to guilty on all counts. His last meal included a lobster tail (*Rolling v. State* (1997) 695 So.2d 278).

———

Gregory Lynn Summers, a 48-year-old white male, was executed by lethal injection at the Texas State Penitentiary in Huntsville, Texas on October 25, 2006. Summers was found guilty of initiating the 1990 murder of Mandell Eugene Summers, a 64-year-old white male, Helen Summers, a 64-year-old white female, and Billy Mack Summers, a 60-year-old white male. Summers, who was 32-years old when he committed the capital crime, was sentenced to death on August 23, 1991.

Summers was adopted by Mandell Summers and Helen Summers when he was three years old. After Summers reached adulthood his parents and Mandell's brother, Billy Summers, lived together in Abilene, Texas. On June 11, 1990, the three family members were fatally stabbed in their home and left to burn after the house was set afire. Mandell was stabbed nine times, Helen was stabbed eight times, and Billy Mack was stabbed seven times.

Upon publication of news reports on the crime Summers became a suspect when Keenan Wilcox informed police that Summers had previously offered to pay him to murder his relatives and burn their house. On August 16 a Taylor County grand jury indicted Summers for the capital murder of his relatives and although Summers denied any involvement in the murders he was well-known to have money troubles.

Because of the publicity Summers was tried in nearby Denton County after a change of venue. The prosecution relied on the testimony of approximately 70 witnesses including family members and two ex-wives who testified fearing Summers. The infamous Dr. James Grigson also testified that Summers posed a future danger.

Evidence at trial revealed that Summers had hired Andrew Flores Cantu-Tzin, a 22-year-old Hispanic male, to murder Summers' relatives for $10,000.[90] Two accomplices, 19-year-old Raymond Gonzales, and Paul Flores, testified as part of a plea agreement that they accompanied Cantu to the murder scene and that Cantu alone committed the acts. Max Aguirre also testified that Cantu had solicited his help but that he had declined to join the conspiracy. Cantu's payment was to be from money found in the house but no money was found. The prosecution alleged that Summers stood to collect $24,000 in insurance benefits from the death of his parents.

While in custody Summers befriended William Spaulding, another inmate. Spaulding assisted Summers with legal work and prepared documents for him but when Spaulding realized that Summers was using documents prepared by him as false evidence, Spaulding contacted prison officials and told them of his encounter with Summers. During their interactions in prison Summers told Spaulding of his part in the murders and Spaulding testified as to those events at the trial (*Cantu v. State* (1996) 939

---

[90] Cantu and Summers never met. Summers admitted only knowing Cantu's brother and Cantu denied that he was involved in the murders. On January 16, 1991, Cantu was indicted for the Summers murder-for-hire. Tried the same year, on May 29 he was found guilty, and two days later he was sentenced to death. On February 16, 1999, the State of Texas executed Cantu by lethal injection.

S.W. 2d 627; *Summers v. Dretke* (2004) 380 F.3d 844; *Summers v. State* (1996) 941 S.W.2d 922).

———

Larry Eugene Hutcherson, a 37-year-old white male, was executed by lethal injection at the Holman Prison in Atmore, Alabama on October 25, 2006. Hutcherson was found guilty of 1992 murder of Irma Thelma Gray, an 89-year-old white female. Hutcherson, who was 22-years-old when he committed the capital crime, was sentenced to death on February 18, 1993, and again on June 19, 1999.

On June 26, 1992, Irma Gray's body was discovered in her home on Moffat Road in Mobile, Alabama. Gray's throat had been cut so severely that she was almost decapitated. Dr. Leroy Riddick, a forensic medical examiner, testified that the cut on her throat was ten inches long beginning at her left earlobe and progressing to within one and one-half inch of her right earlobe. The cut severed her windpipe and her carotid artery and went all the way to her spine. Gray had many other injuries that Riddick testified occurred before her throat was cut. These injuries, consistent with a beating, included numerous other cuts, bruises, and multiple fractured ribs. There was also evidence that Gray had been sodomized.

Lieutenant Frank Woodward of the Mobile Police Department testified that when he arrived at the house to investigate Gray's death, the door to the screened porch was punched inward and a window had been broken with pieces of broken glass and blood on the windowsill. The inside of the house was in total disarray. The antenna for the television was on the floor and a bracket in a windowsill, where an air conditioner would have been, was empty. Woodward found Gray's body lying face down on the kitchen floor. Blood covered the floor near her head and there was talcum powder on her lower body. There was also blood and a bloody footprint on the floor of the bathroom.

Woodward also stated that the door to the garage was partially open and that one of the windowpanes in the door was broken and there was a trail of blood leading from the window to the driver's side of the automobile that was in the garage. Officer Lamar Whitten of the Mobile Police Department stated that he searched the house and found Hutcherson's driver's license in front of a closet in one of the bedrooms and near the driver's license was a bloody knife.

A fingerprint was also discovered on the washing machine. The print matched the print of Hutcherson's right thumb. Sarah Scott of the State's forensic department testified that a rag found in the garage was covered in blood consistent with Hutcherson's blood type, as was blood on the garage windowsill and bloodstains lifted from the front porch. She also testified that bloodstains on a pair of jeans that Hutcherson was wearing when he was arrested were consistent with Gray's blood type.

Hutcherson's mother, Deborah Hutcherson, testified that around 6:00 a.m. on a morning during the last week of June 1992 she received a telephone call from her son asking her to pick him up on Moffat Road. She found her son at the Overlook Shopping Center, not far from Gray's house, whereupon Hutcherson told her that he had been in a fight and that his arm had been cut. She said that the cut on his arm was bad and that it looked like he needed stitches. She also stated that her son did not appear to be drunk but that he looked "real tired."

Sergeant Lester Clark testified that on June 27 he took Hutcherson into custody on a traffic violation out of Prichard. He said that he found Hutcherson asleep in his car outside the Tarpon Lounge about one-half mile from Gray's house. Clark took Hutcherson to the police station where he read him his *Miranda* rights. Hutcherson initially stated he did not wish to make a statement but about 45 minutes later he asked to speak with Clark who transcribed the following statement: "I want to tell you about the murder." I again advised him that he did not have to say anything, but he stated that he had to tell someone and he wanted it to be me.

The suspect continued to talk stating that, "I killed her." He stated, "I went to the house on Wednesday night, or it could have been early Thursday morning. Might have been after twelve o'clock. I had just left the Tarpon and was looking for a house to break in as I walked west on Moffat Road. I picked that house because there were no cars in the driveway and it was dark. I went in the bathroom window." And he said, "That is not-" he hesitated and he said, "That is not too clear because I had taken five Valiums and drank a lot of whiskey. I knew that I knocked out-I knew that I knocked the pane out of the window to get in. I remember I cut my arm when I broke out the garage window. I had been in the house for a while before I saw the old lady, who just showed up in the kitchen. I asked her where her money was and the jewelry. She wouldn't tell me and I began-she began to try to get out of the back door. I kept pulling her back, and I cut her throat. I took off her panties and poured powder over her, which I found in the bathroom.

"I tried to get the car started, but it wouldn't. I left and called my mamma to pick me up. She picked me up on Moffat. I went back into the house Thursday night. I had passed several times during the day and saw that no one had found her. I went through parts of the house that I did not go through Wednesday night. This is when I took out the air conditioner and the rest of the stuff, and put it next to the fence.

"I got Hardy to stop after leaving the Tarpon Friday morning and pick up the stuff. Most of the stuff might have been-might have left town by now. I sold some and I just almost gave some away to people I owed. The air conditioner I know is still here. I know where it is. It is at my stepfather's house, Jackie Lang. The microwave, I know where it is, but she is related to my wife, and I wouldn't want to get her involved, but I know it is there. Now, I feel better. I've told you."

Three witnesses later testified that Hutcherson sold them a microwave, a television, and a radio in the last week of June 1992, all of which were identified by Gray's son-in-law as having belonged to Gray. Hardy Avera testified that on Wednesday in the last week of June 1992 Hutcherson came to his house wearing jeans and black tennis shoes saying that "he thought he had killed someone."

The next day Avera saw Hutcherson at the Tarpon Lounge and he took him to Gray's house where he said that Hutcherson went inside and came back with an air conditioner and some other items. Hutcherson's stepsister was present when her father, Jackie Lang, received a telephone call from Hutcherson. Lang said that during the conversation her father wrote down on a piece of paper that Hutcherson had killed an old lady adding that Hutcherson had told her that "he would rather die in the electric chair than live with what he had done to the victim."

Hutcherson was convicted of capital murder and sentenced to death by electrocution by a jury vote of 11-1. On appeal the Court of Criminal Appeals affirmed, but the Alabama Supreme Court reversed, and the Court of Criminal Appeals remanded to trial court for further proceedings. On remand Hutcherson entered plea of guilty, and upon recommendation of a jury, he was again sentenced to death. On July 1, 2002, Alabama began administering death by lethal injection absent a request for electrocution. Before his execution Hutcherson "didn't want to beg" Governor Bob Riley for clemency (*Hutcherson v. State* (1994) 677 So.2d 1174; *Hutcherson v. State* (1997) 727 So.2d 846).

————

Donell Okeith Jackson, a 33-year-old black male, was executed by lethal injection at the Texas State Penitentiary in Huntsville, Texas on November 1, 2006. Jackson was found guilty of the 1993 murder of Mario Stubblefield, a 17-year-old black male. Jackson, who was 20-years-old when he committed the capital crime, was sentenced to death on August 13, 1996.

On August 31, 1993, Mario Stubblefield was shot once in the head as he stood outside his father's home in Houston, Texas. Stubblefield, who had previously testified before a grand jury in its investigation of a drive-by shooting involving Jackson's friend David Smith, died from the gunshot.

Eddie Clark, a neighbor who witnessed the Stubblefield murder, testified that he had seen Smith sitting in a car in front of Stubblefield's house moments before the shooting. Clark said Smith was talking with Stubblefield and another man who stood outside the car. Police later discovered the car belonged to Smith's girlfriend, Sheila Tolston. When questioned by police Tolston implicated Jackson in the murder. With this information police assembled a photograph lineup from which Clark positively identified Jackson as the man standing next to the car just before Stubblefield was shot.

During a police interview in jail Smith gave a taped statement claiming Jackson committed the murder. Police arrested Jackson and confronted him with Smith's statement. On the tape Smith claimed he did not know Jackson was going to shoot Stubblefield. When Jackson heard this statement he replied, "Man, he paid me to do it." He then gave a taped confession in which he claimed that Smith paid him $200 to kill Stubblefield.

On January 18, 1996, a Harris County grand jury indicted Jackson for the capital murder of Stubblefield. At the 1996 trial Jackson testified on his own behalf. He denied any payment or discussion of payment with Smith and claimed he had intended only to scare Stubblefield out of testifying against Smith at trial. On August 7 the jury found Jackson guilty.

During the punishment phase the State introduced evidence that Jackson had been found delinquent as a juvenile for the offense of indecency with a child, had been expelled from school for excessive absences after various other disciplinary problems, and had shot a former high school classmate in the face. Jackson presented evidence of a favorable home life and church membership, and two experts testified that he suffered from a learning disability. The trial court sentenced Jackson, who had no prior convictions, to death. On April 28, 1999, the Texas Court of Criminal Appeals affirmed the conviction and sentence (*Jackson v. State* (1999) 992 S.W.2d 469).

––––

Willie Marcel Shannon, a 33-year-old black male, was executed by lethal injection at the Texas State Penitentiary in Huntsville, Texas on November 8, 2006. Shannon was found guilty of the 1992 murder of Benjamin Garza, a 38-year-old Hispanic male. Shannon, who was 19-years old when he committed the murder, was sentenced to death on November 8, 1993.

On July 19, 1992, Benjamin Garza took his wife, Solia, and their three teenage children to a shopping center in southwest Houston, Texas. While his family went inside to shop for shoes, Garza waited outside in their 15-year-old Ford station wagon. As he leaned back in the seat and closed his eyes, Shannon entered the car from the passenger side and according to an 11-year-old witness, ordered Garza out of the car, but instead Garza fought back.[91]

––––

[91] Unknown to Shannon, Garza had been in the federal Witness Protection Program for a decade living under a new identity and probably believing that Shannon intended to kill him and not just rob his car, Garza instinctively fought back when assaulted.

343

Shannon pulled out a gun, shot Garza in the head, and kicked him out of the car. Shannon then drove off running over Garza's hand and shooting him two more times. Solia and the children rushed outside to find Garza dying on the pavement.

A few hours after the shooting Shannon wrecked the car in Chambers County, about 50 miles east of Houston. When a sheriff's deputy approached him to ask about the accident Shannon escaped into the woods on foot. About five hours after the shooting a security guard at a truck stop in Beaumont notified police that he spotted a man with a pistol in his pants looking for rides. Shannon was captured after a brief chase.

On October 23, 1992, a Harris County grand jury indicted Shannon for capital murder. During the punishment phase of the 1993 trial the State introduced evidence that Shannon had raped a hotel maid 10 minutes before killing Garza claiming that Shannon committed the carjacking because he needed a vehicle to flee in. Shannon was never charged in the rape case and he denied any involvement in it. On December 11, 1996, the Texas Court of Criminal Appeals affirmed Shannon's conviction and sentence.

"I did not intentionally shoot this man," Shannon said in an interview from death row the week before his execution. He said that he thought Garza wouldn't likely fight him over the car. On the contrary, Garza became angry and shouted, "You young punk, you just want my car?" Shannon said they struggled, and the gun went off. "I never saw him hit the ground. I didn't even know where he was hit," Shannon said. "I'm no killer. I made a mistake" (*Shannon v. State* (2003) 116 S.W.3d 52).

––––

John Yancey Schmitt, a 33-year-old white male, was executed by lethal injection at the Greensville Correctional Facility in Jarratt, Virginia on November 9, 2006. Schmitt was found guilty of 1999 murder of Earl Shelton Dunning, a 39-year-old black male. Schmitt, who was 25-years old when he committed the capital crime, was sentenced to death on February 18, 2000.

Shortly after 1:00 p.m. on February 17, 1999, Schmitt entered the NationsBank in Bon Air, Virginia wearing dark sunglasses and a bulky jacket. Schmitt kept his head lowered and appeared to scan the interior of the bank. Bank manager Sara Parker-Orr testified that she was "nervous" about Schmitt because he was wearing sunglasses inside the bank on a "really cloudy day."

After Schmitt went inside the bank, Earl Dunning, the bank's new security guard[92] entered the bank and walked across the lobby to stand at the end of the "teller line" in which customers were waiting. Schmitt then stood in the teller line behind several customers. Parker-Orr watched him leave his place in line and walk toward Dunning. When Schmitt was within "a foot or so" of Dunning, Parker-Orr heard two gunshots and then heard someone scream, "Get down, get down."

Schmitt next approached Parker-Orr's teller window and banged on the counter yelling, "Money, give me money," and "If I don't get money, I'm going to kill everybody." Parker-Orr opened her cash drawer and threw money into a black plastic bag that Schmitt was holding. Schmitt continued to bang on the counter demanding "more money." He said that he would give the tellers "ten seconds" to give him more money, and began counting backward from the number "ten."

By the time Schmitt reached "nine," teller Marlene Austin was "throwing money in the bag." Parker-Orr also gave Schmitt money from a third teller's drawer. When she

---

[92] Dunning had been on the job for less than a month having just retired from the U.S. Army after over 20 years of military service.

told Schmitt that she had no more money to give him, he left the bank.

None of the witnesses who testified at trial actually saw who shot Dunning and the shooting was not recorded by the bank's security camera system. The bank's security camera system, however, did record photographs of Schmitt approaching the end of the teller counter and standing at a teller window holding a bag and pointing a gun. Parker-Orr, Austin, and another teller, Kelli Konstaitis, all identified a photograph of Schmitt recorded by the bank's security camera system as depicting the man who robbed the bank that day.

After Schmitt left the bank witnesses telephoned the 9-1-1 emergency response number and attended to Dunning who was lying on the floor. By the time emergency medical personnel arrived Dunning was dead. An autopsy revealed that Dunning was killed as a result of a .45-caliber bullet entering the right side of his chest causing significant injuries to the aorta and exiting from the right side of his back. Witnesses in the bank testified that they did not touch or see anyone else touch Dunning's gun or its holster; the gun was found in its holster, closed and snapped.

After the murder and robbery Schmitt registered at a Williamsburg hotel the same day under the name "R. Napier" paying cash for a three-day stay at the hotel. The hotel desk clerk testified that Schmitt asked for directions to the local shopping areas, and that when Schmitt later returned to the hotel, his hair was a different color.

Captain Karl S. Leonard of the Chesterfield County Police Department identified Schmitt after reviewing the photographs taken by the bank's security camera system. On February 19 Leonard learned where Schmitt was staying in Williamsburg. The James City County Tactical Team surrounded Schmitt's hotel room, and a crisis negotiator, Lieutenant Diane M. Clarcq of the James City County Police Department attempted to persuade Schmitt to surrender. About 10:30 a.m. the following morning Schmitt surrendered and was taken into police custody.

Leonard obtained a search warrant for Schmitt's hotel room where a satchel, a .45-caliber handgun,[93] a box of shotgun shells, a black leather jacket, and a variety of newly purchased clothing items were seized. Inside the satchel was $27,091 in cash, most of which still bore "bank bands" identifying the money as coming from the Bon Air branch of NationsBank.

Schmitt was tried in Chesterfield County. During the penalty phase of the trial the jury learned that Schmitt, armed with a sawed off shotgun and accompanied by another man had robbed $65,000 from the very same bank[94] a month before Schmitt had murdered Dunning.

---

[93] John H. Willmer, a firearms and tool mark examiner employed by the Virginia Division of Forensic Science, testified that he examined the handgun found in Schmitt's hotel room and the cartridge casings and bullets found in the bank. Wilmer testified that the cartridge casings and bullets had been fired from the handgun, and concluded that the pattern of gunpowder residue found on Dunning's clothing indicated that when he was shot the distance between him and the firearm muzzle was between 12 and 36 inches.

[94] Clifford Sauer was a roofer who had previously employed Schmitt. After the January 19, 1990 robbery, Schmitt contacted Sauer for his assistance in purchasing a car. Sauer brokered the deal for the car and received a fee from Schmitt for his assistance. Sauer did not then know that Schmitt had robbed a bank but he was suspicious of Schmitt's spending habits and after some prodding Schmitt told Sauer that he had robbed a bank. Schmitt then tried to purchase a gun from Sauer and Sauer refused. He asked Sauer if he wanted to drive for another bank robbery and Sauer declined. Schmitt then told Sauer that if, "you breathe one word of this to anyone *** I'm going to have to kill you or my friends will have to kill you."

On January 30 Schmitt was arrested for obstruction of
(*continued*)

(*continued*)

justice related to a hotel disturbance in which he was involved. Schmitt told police that his name was James Comer. A few hours later Sauer received a telephone call from an employee of the Henrico County Jail asking whether he knew James Comer. Sauer responded in the affirmative. The next voice Sauer heard was that of Schmitt who told Sauer to contact Kenny Lockner, collect some money, and take it to the Henrico County Jail to bail out James Comer. After the bail was provided Schmitt was released from custody. Sauer did not realize that he was actually posting bail for Schmitt instead of Comer until he saw Schmitt walk out of the jail after the bail had been paid.

On February 5 Detective William George and other officers arrived at Sauer's residence in the City of Richmond. George told Sauer that they were looking for Schmitt in connection with a bank robbery. Sauer gave the officers permission to search his home and answered their questions. The search lasted only about 15 minutes but before leaving, George left Sauer with his card and requested permission to interview Sauer at a later date.

On February 7 George and Detective Easton conducted a one-hour long interview with Sauer in his home, a large portion of which was taped and transcribed. Sauer volunteered information regarding: Schmitt's purchase of the car; his efforts to recruit Sauer as a driver; his attempt to purchase Sauer's gun; his plans to kill Joanna Murphy, one of Schmitt's friends; and individuals who might lead police to Schmitt.

Shortly after Dunning's murder Sauer told George he had seen news of the murder and believed that Schmitt was the perpetrator. George went to Sauer's house whereupon Sauer provided him with information that led to Schmitt's girlfriend and eventually led to locating Schmitt in Williamsburg.

Sometime shortly before March 12 Sauer told George that Schmitt had been calling him from jail. George asked Sauer to tape any future telephone calls from Schmitt and Sauer agreed.

George then talked with Chief Deputy Commonwealth Attorney, Warren Von Schuch, who told George that Sauer could record calls but could not ask questions. Von Schuch instructed George to provide Sauer with a tape recorder for Sauer's phone. Later that day George delivered the recording device to Sauer

Ironically, Dunning's employment at the bank was a direct result of Schmitt's January robbery. After deliberating for nine hours the jury found the presence of the future dangerousness aggravator, and the court sentenced Schmitt to death. Governor Timothy M. Kaine rejected Schmitt's request for clemency (*Schmitt v. Commonwealth* (2001) 547 S.E.2d 186).

———

Angel Nieves Diaz, a 55-year-old Hispanic (Puerto Rican) male, was executed by lethal injection at the Florida State Prison in Starke, Florida on December 13, 2006. Diaz was found guilty of the 1979 murder of Joseph Nagy, a 49-year-old white male. Diaz, who was 26–years old when he committed the capital crime, was sentenced to death on January 24, 1986.

---

telling him the only question left unanswered was the origin of the handgun used in the second robbery. On March 12 Schmitt called Sauer from jail. During their conversation Sauer elicited from Schmitt information about the gun, the robbery, and the murder.

Between Christmas and New Years, Von Schuch provided Schmitt's counsel with a transcript of the March 12 Schmitt/Sauer tape-recorded conversation. Therein Schmitt admitted robbing the bank and shooting Dunning insisting that his gun discharged accidentally during the course of a struggle. Schmitt also chuckled under his breath when he explained how Dunning's "eyes got real big" when he pointed the gun at him.

At trial the prosecution introduced the Schmitt/Sauer tape during the sentencing phase, and while counsel objected that it constituted a violation of Schmitt's Fifth and Sixth Amendment rights because, "Sauer is clearly acting at the behest of *** and as an agent of the police," the trial court overruled Schmitt's motion without explaining the basis for its ruling and allowed the tape to be played to the jury and Sauer to testify on behalf of the prosecution.

On December 29, 1979, Diaz, Angel "Sammy" Toro, a 26-year-old white male, and an unidentified third man named "Willie" robbed the Velvet Swing Lounge, a topless-club in Miami, Florida. During the robbery Joseph Nagy, the manager, was shot and killed. No one actually witnessed the murder because "the majority of the patrons and employees had been forcibly confined to a restroom" and those that had not been moved into the restroom hid underneath the bar for fear that they too would be killed.

In 1983 Diaz and Toro were arrested for the Velvet Swing Lounge murder after Diaz's former girlfriend, Candice Braun, had told police about a night in December 1979 when Diaz returned to their apartment at around 1 a.m. and said that Toro had shot a man during robbery because Toro thought the man was reaching for a gun. Braun also recalled hearing Spanish words for "shoot," "man," and "panic," and that Diaz was very upset yelling at Toro that "it wasn't necessary."

Diaz and Toro were both charged in Dade County with capital murder. Toro was tried first and offered a second-degree murder plea for which he was sentenced to life imprisonment. Diaz was shackled during his own trial and represented by counsel until the moment before opening arguments began, when he suddenly decided to conduct his own defense against the advice of both his lawyer and the trial judge. As Diaz, a Puerto Rican native, was unable to speak English, it was necessary to have an interpreter at every stage of the proceeding. In spite of the limitation the trial judge was "amazed" by Diaz's ability to self-represent, and specifically praised Diaz's 90-minute cross-examination of a witness for the State. That witness, Ralph Gajus, a jailhouse informant who understood no Spanish, testified that Diaz had inferred to him that Diaz had shot Nagy.

The Dade County jury convicted Diaz of first-degree murder, four counts of kidnapping, two counts of armed robbery, one count of attempted robbery, and one count of possessing a firearm during the commission of a felony. The trial court sentenced Diaz to a total of 834 years' imprisonment and imposed the 8-4 jury's recommended death sentence based upon the following aggravators: Diaz was under sentence of imprisonment at the time of the crime, was previously convicted of a felony involving the use or threat of violence, committed the murder during a kidnapping, and committed the murder for pecuniary gain. On November 28, 2006, Governor Jeb Bush denied a request for clemency from the Governor of Puerto Rico. Diaz's last words (translated): "The State of Florida is killing an innocent person. The State of Florida is committing a crime, because I am innocent. The death penalty is not only a form of vengeance, but also a cowardly act by humans. I'm sorry for what is happening to me and my family, who have been put through this" (*Diaz v. Sec'y for the Dep't of Corr.* (2005) 402 F.3d 1136; *Diaz v. State* (1987) 513 So. 2d 1045; *Nieves-Diaz v. Singletary* (1987) No. 74,927).

General References

Attorney General of Texas Greg Abbott. 30 March 2007. <http://www.oag.state.tx.us/index.shtml>.

Capital Punishment Statistics. Revised 11 January 2007. <http://www.ojp.usdoj.gov/bjs/cp.htm#top>.

Carson, D. Copyright 2002-2007. Texas Execution Information. <http://www.txexecutions.org/>.

Clark County Prosecuting Attorney's Office. <http://www.clarkprosecutor.org/> accessed 1 May 2007.

Death Penalty Information Center. Copyright 2007. <http://www.deathpenaltyinfo.org/>.

Death Penalty News Bulletin – Amnesty International. 11 April 2006. <http://web.amnesty.org/pages/deathpenalty-developments-eng>.

Death Row U.S.A. Winter 2007. A quarterly report by the Criminal Justice Project of the NAACP Legal Defense and Educational Fund, Inc. <http://www.naacpldf.org/content/pdf/pubs/drusa/DRUSA_Winter_2007.pdf>.

Elliott, Martha, J.H., Connecticut Law Tribune, Michael Ross: Why a Killer Offers to Die, 29 April 1996.

Halperin, R. Death Penalty News & Updates. Updated on 23 May 2007. <http://people.smu.edu/rhalperi/>.

North Carolina Department of Correction. <http://www.doc.state.nc.us/> accessed 26 May 2007.

Ohio Department of Correction and Rehabilitation. 17 April 2006. <http://www.drc.state.oh.us/Public/Joseph%20Clark.pdf>.

The Oklahoma State Courts Network. <http://www.oscn.net/applications/oscn/start.asp?viewType=> accessed 23 May 2007.

Pro-death Penalty.com. Copyright 2007. <http://www.prodeathpenalty.com/>.

Texas Department of Criminal Justice. <http://www.tdcj.state.tx.us/stat/deathrow.htm> accessed 23 May 2007.

VINELink. <http://www.vinelink.com/stateMap.jsp>.

Virginia Department of Corrections. Copyright 1997-2006. <http://www.vadoc.state.va.us/>.

Index

aggravated rape, *definition*, 4

aggravating circumstance, *definition*, 6; 4, 8-9, 10

aggravators: arson, 100, 170, 247; avoiding arrest, 29, 87, 218, 219, 315, 321; battery, 294, 295, 336; burglary, 100, 160, 170, 226, 336; depravity of mind, 112, 134, 294; future dangerousness, 89, 120, 129, 167, 227, 294, 297, 321; heinous, atrocious or cruel, 66, 112, 134, 277, 294, 297, 315, 327; kidnapping, 64, 70, 160, 247, 277, 288, 305, 311, 332, 351; multiple murder, 29, 219; murder committed while on parole, 315; murder for hire, 103, 157; murder for pecuniary gain, 327, 351; murder of a child, 241, 298; murder of a peace officer, 79-80, 121-122, 155, 321-322; possession of a dangerous weapon, 38, 56, 64, 77, 134, 177, 196, 249, 287; premeditation, 66, 117, 247, 250, 277, 287, 305, 321, 327; prior felony conviction, 66, 83, 87, 219, 287, 315, 321, 351; rape, 42, 188, 277; robbery, 38, 42, 56, 64, 66, 70, 77, 82, 103, 164-165, 189, 192, 196, 216-217, 222, 234, 249, 257, 291, 293, 305, 321, 326, 327; sexual conduct with a minor, 288; sexual intercourse, 170; sexual penetration, 170, 250; while under imprisonment, 351

Aguilar, Jesus L., 263-265

Alabama, death penalty, 8, 12, 14, 15, 80, 103; executed by, 78, 101, 120, 137, 338; Supreme Court, 341; *see also* Riley

Alaska, death penalty, 2, 7

alcohol, influence of, 30, 31-32, 65, 97-99, 166, 177, 225, 262, 292-294

Allen, Clarence R., 203-219

Alley, Sedley, 274-277

American Samoa, death penalty, 2

Anderson, Robert J., 291-292

appellate process, 1, 9, 10-12; *see also* Supreme Court of the United States, U.S. Circuit Court of Appeals

Arkansas, death penalty, 12, 14; executed by, 186; *see also* Huckabee

Arizona, death penalty, 12, 15

Asatru, 295-296

Ashworth, Herman D., 148-153

Atkins v. Virginia, 536 U.S. 304 (2002), 9

autopsy, *see* victim autopsy

Bagwell, Dennis W., 33-37

Baird II, Arthur P., 12

Baker, Wesley E., 193-197

Barbour, Gov. Haley, 202, 329

Barton, Rocky, 283-288

Beardslee, Donald J., 24-29

Benefiel, Bill J., 73-76

Benner II, Glenn L., 227-231

Bieghler, Marvin, 224-226

Blunt, Gov. Matt, 64, 77, 94, 134, 165